EARLY NOTIONS OF GLOBAL GOVERNANCE

EARLY NOTIONS OF GLOBAL GOVERNANCE

Selected Eighteenth-Century Proposals for 'Perpetual Peace'

– with Rousseau, Bentham and Kant unabridged –

Edited and introduced by

Eşref Aksu

UNIVERSITY OF WALES PRESS
CARDIFF
2008

© Eşref Aksu, 2008

British Library Cataloguing-in-Publication Data
A catalogue record for this book is available from the British Library.

ISBN 978-0-7083-2136-2 (hardback)
ISBN 978-0-7083-2135-5 (paperback)

Typeset by Columns Design Ltd, Reading RG4 7DH
Printed in Great Britain by Antony Rowe Ltd, Chippenham, Wiltshire

This book is dedicated to Paul Feyerabend – simply for his courage to speak 'against method'.

Contents

CONTENTS

Chapter 1
Early Notions of Global Governance: Introduction

Over the past three decades, Immanuel Kant's classic essay on 'perpetual peace' has inspired several International Relations (IR) scholars in their attempt to theorize liberal internationalism and modern cosmopolitanism. Inescapably, the burgeoning global governance literature in the last decade, too, has benefited from Kant's ideas. It is important to realize, however, that Kant's essay flourished in a wider intellectual environment. This volume is the first and only contemporary compilation of classic perpetual peace proposals of the eighteenth century. The selected texts here help us trace the roots of the contemporary notions of global governance to the Age of Enlightenment.

A number of proposals have been devised in search of a continuous peace throughout the ages. Even when the Ancient World and the non-Christian or non-Western societies are excluded, we can still trace such proposals at least as far back as the beginning of the fourteenth century, when Pierre du Bois drafted his *De Recuperatione Terrae Sanctae*.[1] This 'tradition', to use the label a bit loosely but not entirely inaccurately, has undergone an evolution right through to the end of the twentieth century.[2] In this long succession of peace proposals,

---

[1] For a concise overview, see F. H. Hinsley, *Power and the Pursuit of Peace: Theory and Practice in the History of Relations between States* (Cambridge: Cambridge University Press, 1963), pp. 13–32. For another pertinent overview, which includes but is not limited to peace plans, see Derek Heater, *World Citizenship and Government: Cosmopolitan Ideas in the History of Western Political Thought* (Houndmills: Macmillan, 1996), especially ch. 3.

[2] Cavallar, for instance, relates Kant to a 'tradition' of perpetual peace proposals; see Georg Cavallar, *Pax Kantiana: Systematisch-historische Untersuchung des Entwurfs 'Zum Ewigen Frieden' (1795) von Immanuel Kant* (Wien: Böhlau,

however, the eighteenth century clearly occupies the centre stage. One reason, no doubt, is the multitude of peace and stability plans to have emerged during the Enlightenment. An equally important reason is precisely the efforts of three undeniably great philosophers to devise proposals for the permanent improvement of the international political order: Jean-Jacques Rousseau, Jeremy Bentham and Immanuel Kant.

Today, the specific notion of perpetual peace reminds us of no names other than those above – especially Kant.[3] Yet, quite understandably, these theorists' views on perpetual peace have been considered, on balance, to be relatively secondary to their monumental works in other subject areas. There is, of course, no need to elaborate on the significance of these three names for the history of political thought. As expected, there is no shortage of primary or secondary sources on any of these philosophers. In terms of primary material, the works of each of these theorists are available in several edited collections. As for secondary sources, there are numerous studies on each one, ranging from holistic in-depth analyses to focused examinations of specific aspects of their thought. There are also quite a few important comparative studies about Rousseau, Bentham and Kant.[4] Interestingly, though, none of these numerous works places the idea of perpetual peace at its centre, which is precisely what the present volume does.

This book puts the emphasis squarely on *full* (unabridged) texts by Rousseau, Bentham and Kant – with good reason. Rousseau's and Bentham's texts, especially the full versions, are still not as easily accessible as they should be, and Kant's text is frequently presented in shortened formats (for instance, with Kant's own footnotes left out).[5] The point is frequently missed

---

1992), pp. 33–8. See also the 'fourth tradition' mentioned in Sissela Bok, 'Early advocates of lasting world peace: Utopians or realists?', *Ethics and International Affairs*, 4 (1990), 147–9.

[3] We might also add Saint-Pierre to this list, but arguably his major importance has been limited to his influence on Rousseau.

[4] But one old example, which covers all three philosophers, would perhaps suffice here: Alfred Tuttle Williams, *The Concept of Equality in the Writings of Rousseau, Bentham and Kant* (New York: Teachers College, Columbia University, 1907).

[5] One would have thought that in this age of the Internet several versions of almost all classic texts could be easily located and accessed. As of September 2006, translations of Kant's *Perpetual Peace* available on the Internet included

that *any* extract or abridgement is, by definition, a reflection of the editors' views as to which parts of the original text are important and why. What we find in circulation nowadays is mostly not the original texts per se, but particular representations of those texts in the form of selections from them that *the editors think* are more appropriate for the reader to know or examine. Our main contention here is that, when it comes to such great names as Rousseau, Bentham and Kant and, in particular, when it comes to specific subjects on which all of them had something quite specific to say, we deserve the opportunity to examine and decide for ourselves how these thinkers and their texts possibly relate to each other. The editor's function here should be to present each work as completely and originally as possible, without intervening in the thought patterns of either the author or the reader. Needless to mention, though, editors' own interpretations inescapably creep into the editing process, at least to a certain extent, and can manifest themselves even in decisions as to where a comma should be placed in order to convey the 'intended' message of an original sentence. Similarly, potential loss of meaning arising from translations is a challenge we constantly face.

This volume also puts the emphasis on the three full texts *next to each other*, because students as well as researchers should be given the opportunity to examine them in juxtaposition, and analyse their differences, similarities, and wider implications. It is crucial to underline here, once again, that the authors in question are no mediocre names. They are Rousseau, Bentham and Kant. Parallel examination of their respective texts may well lead to several far-reaching studies in the future. If nothing else, the following few facts alone make it interesting for us to know how these three giant contemporaries approached the question of perpetual peace.

the versions in Immanuel Kant, *Kant's Political Writings*, ed. Hans Siegbert Reiss, tr. H. B. Nisbet, (Cambridge: Cambridge University Press, 1970); and Immanuel Kant, *Kant's Principles of Politics, including his Essay on Perpetual Peace: A Contribution to Political Science*, (ed. and tr.) William Hastie (Edinburgh: T & T Clark, 1891). However, most websites either did not present the text in full, or they did not cite the source of the translation. Access to Rousseau and Bentham, on the other hand, depended largely on the researcher's ability to locate the few relevant websites or databases.

First, Rousseau, Bentham and Kant represent the French, British and German intellectual traditions, respectively. Secondly, Rousseau and Bentham are both frequently associated with Hobbesian philosophy – though in different ways and with different conclusions. Thirdly, Rousseau was a notable early communitarian, whereas Kant was a pioneering cosmopolitan. Fourthly, Rousseau's constructive yet provocative influence on Kant is well known. And finally, Bentham and Kant are leading intellectual forefathers of diametrically opposed positions in normative philosophy, namely, of utilitarian versus deontological ethics.

Rousseau's, Bentham's and Kant's pieces were drafted in 1756, 1789, and 1795, respectively, and all three philosophers elevated the status of 'perpetual peace' as a normative ideal as well as a quasi-analytical concept by making firm reference to it. In the process of building and improving on the ideas of earlier perpetual peace proposals, they also started to do something more than pre-theorizing international relations – or such is this volume's hypothesis: they started to foreshadow the notion of global governance.

'Global governance' is not easy to define and conceptualize.[6] Overall, the notion has affinity to the ideas of international organization and globalization,[7] but it cannot be equated with either of them.[8] Both terms in the phrase, namely, 'global' and

---

[6] Johns makes this complexity amply clear in her contribution to an edited volume: 'The "global governance" of this chapter differs from that of other chapters. I examine global governance here not as a concept, a regime, an institutional practice, a coherent normative program, or a documented phenomenon. Rather, this chapter approaches global governance as a field of prevailing narratives about or experiences of the world: narratives characterized by an orientation toward convergence, regularity, and interpenetration, frequently cast as a reaction to something called "globalization" (cf. Bourdieu 1984, 466).'; see Fleur E. Johns, 'The globe and the ghetto', in Markus Lederer and Philipp S. Müller (eds), *Criticizing Global Governance* (New York, NY: Palgrave Macmillan, 2005), p. 70.

[7] As far as Hewson and Sinclair are concerned, for example, the 'change' aspect inherent in the notion of globalisation seems to be the defining element of the notion of global governance as well; see Martin Hewson and Timothy J. Sinclair (eds), *Approaches to Global Governance Theory* (Albany, NY: State University of New York Press, 1999), ch. 1.

[8] See Rorden Wilkinson (ed.), *The Global Governance Reader* (London: Routledge, 2005), pp. 4–7.

'governance', deserve attention, and both allow for several interpretations:

> While the attribute global can at least refer to two different spheres – the top-level scale of human activity or the sum of all scales of activity – the term governance . . . [may well] refer to all coexisting forms of collective regulation of social affairs, including the self-regulation of civil society, the coregulation of public and private actors, and authoritative regulation through government.[9]

Three preoccupations seem to be integral to almost all conceptualizations of global governance: the idea of *multi-level* activity (i.e. local, national, regional and global),[10] the *modes* of activity (e.g. cooperation, coordination, supervision, regulation or control),[11] and the *(re)institutionalization* of activity, which problematizes, above all, the place of 'government' alongside alternative political agents.[12] Whilst this book's hypothesis pertains to all three central preoccupations, the volume is more an *invitation* to conceptual linkage between 'perpetual peace' and 'global governance' – an initial exploration of promising avenues between the two notions – than a thorough conceptual analysis in itself.[13] If the material

---

[9] Klaus Dingwerth and Philipp Pattberg, 'Global governance as a perspective on world politics', *Global Governance*, 12 (2006), 188.

[10] See Elke Krahmann, 'National, regional, and global governance: one phenomenon or many?', *Global Governance*, 9 (2003), 323–46.

[11] The debate about 'good governance' at the global level seems to revolve, at its heart, precisely around this issue. For an example of this literature, see Thomas G. Weiss, 'Governance, good governance and global governance: conceptual and actual challenges', *Third World Quarterly*, 21 (2000), 795–814. See also Thomas Risse, 'Global governance and communicative action', in David Held and Mathias Koenig-Archibugi (eds), *Global Governance and Public Accountability* (Malden, MA: Blackwell, 2005), pp. 164–89.

[12] See James N. Rosenau and Ernst-Otto Czempiel (eds), *Governance without Government: Order and Change in World Politics* (Cambridge: Cambridge University Press, 1992).

[13] For instance, Djelic and Andersson certainly make an interesting point when they refuse to employ the term 'global governance' in their study: 'The label "transnational" suggests entanglement and blurred boundaries to a degree that the term "global" could not'; see Marie-Laure Djelic and Kerstin Sahlin-Andersson, 'Introduction: A world of governance: The rise of transnational regulation', in Djelic and Sahlin-Andersson (eds), *Transnational Governance: Institutional Dynamics of Regulation* (Cambridge: Cambridge University

presented here manages to provoke thought as to why and how historically the perpetual peace tradition may have provided a basis for the idea of global governance, this book will have accomplished its task.

The perpetual peace tradition seems to point to 'early' notions of global governance in three different senses of the word. First of all, in the simple chronological sense, perpetual peace and global governance, taken as central concepts, are separated by two to three centuries. The former, like the latter, seems to have entered the intellectual lexicon as a unifying concept in its heyday, carrying an explicitly normative intellectual agenda, yet at the same time paving the way for a quasi-analytical research orientation.[14] Secondly, 'early' is employed in the sense of *embryonic*, in that the perpetual peace tradition contains the seeds of both 'global' and 'governance'. Although there was, in relation to neither of these terms, a fully fledged, mature understanding of global governance in the eighteenth century, significant conceptual moves towards the idea can be detected in some texts of the period. And thirdly, 'early' is used in the sense of *premature*, in that the intellectual moves made by eighteenth-century thinkers towards the idea of 'governance *without* (or alongside, or beyond) government' seem to have been a bit out of place, and indeed in contradiction to the concrete political trends of the time. This last point needs some clarification.

In the eighteenth century, Europe was, on the one hand, coming to terms with the Treaty of Westphalia (1648) and, on the other, gathering momentum towards the French Revolution (1789).[15] The traditional modes of the act of governing had

---

Press, 2006), p. 4. If we assume, for a moment, that this is indeed a valid distinction, can 'perpetual peace' be considered a precursor to the idea of 'transnational' (and *not* global) governance as well?

14   Johnson, for example, argues that 'pacifism is a multifaceted phenomenon', differentiates the perpetual peace 'ideal' from other pacifist approaches, and suggests that this ideal exemplifies a 'unique way of looking at war, its roots, and its results': see James Turner Johnson, *The Quest for Peace: Three Moral Traditions in Western Cultural History* (Princeton, NJ: Princeton University Press, 1987), especially pp. 175, 184–5.

15   In his thought-provoking analysis, Walter Mignolo, too, assigns a special role to these two 'historical' (as opposed to 'structural') issues in explaining the 1 eighteenth-century cosmopolitanism; see Walter D. Mignolo, 'The many faces

been quite diverse up until Westphalia, involving a complex mixture of religious authority, linguistic-tribal allegiances, feudal structures, and overarching imperial rules. These modes would be subjected to at least two major changes within one-and-a-half centuries: the imposition, first, of a relatively new system of 'states' (with Westphalia), and then, of an even newer system of 'nation-states' (with the French Revolution). From this point of view, the eighteenth-century international processes were almost the opposite of early twenty-first-century processes. Govern*ance* was transforming into govern*ment* in the eighteenth century. Considered against this backdrop, the multi-level confederative arrangements proposed by perpetual peace thinkers as well as their sporadic thoughts about such issues as the criteria of inclusion/exclusion, the nature of the society/community to be governed, and the similarity of interests/principles of the subjects of governance were not, and arguably could not have been, clearly detached from the idea of govern*ment*.[16]

The perpetual peace proposals were heavily influenced by the idea of government, but even those that called for a *European state* were actually more about workable and down-to-earth 'institutional arrangements' than the state per se. In fact, a crucial connection point between perpetual peace and global governance seems to be their shared focus on desired alternative institutionalization (not necessarily centralization) of political authority.[17] Closer inspection of the perpetual

---

of cosmo-polis: Border thinking and critical cosmopolitanism', in Carol A. Breckenridge et al. (eds), *Cosmopolitanism* (Durham, NC: Duke University Press, 2002), pp. 168–9.

[16] Though we must also consider that these proposals used the word 'government' not only in relation to the institutionalized entity, but also to denote the act of governing, approximating the contemporary usage of 'governance'. See, for instance, Saint-Pierre's reference to the maintenance of 'the present government to avoid war' (Chapter 5), and Kant's reference to the 'government of men' in his Appendix 1 (Chapter 15). On the other hand, some contemporary writers, too, prefer to use 'government' in place of 'governance': see, for example, Robyn Lui, 'The international government of refugees', in Wendy Larner and William Walters (eds), *Global Governmentality: Governing International Spaces* (London: Routledge, 2004), pp. 116–35.

[17] For an explicitly institutional as well as institutional*ist* account of global governance, see, for example, Matthias Finger, 'Global governance through the institutional lens', in Lederer and Müller, *Criticizing Global Governance*, pp. 145–59.

peace thinkers reveals that their actual emphasis was not merely on peace as an end. Several of them did allow, quite realistically, for the possibility of future crises, violations and wars. Rather, they sought mechanisms of reliable, organized, multi-level political interaction, i.e. institutional arrangements and commonly accepted first principles of co-existence, which would both strengthen and constrain governments at once. Perpetual peace, as a tradition, was therefore not as utopian as has been frequently assumed.[18]

The perpetual peace proposals devised, refined and advocated increasingly more sophisticated and multi-faceted reform agendas. In this regard, too, they resemble contemporary global governance reform proposals. Some authors (e.g. John Bellers) explicitly addressed the relevant policy-making authorities of the day in order to be able to influence the direction of policy. Indeed, some eighteenth-century proposals may be likened almost to contemporary 'white papers' or 'position papers' in terms of their content, style, brevity, and target audience.[19]

A more thorough understanding of global governance requires the exploration of the conceptual ground covered by considerations of perpetual peace, which cannot be boiled down to Kant's *Perpetual Peace*, even if that essay is indeed the most sophisticated ring in the chain. Rousseau and Bentham are certainly of special interest in this regard, but they, too, need to be contextualized within the wider perpetual peace tradition. Consequently, Part I of the present volume presents, in chronological order, selections from representative perpetual peace proposals of the eighteenth century.[20] The selected texts belong to William Penn (1693),

---

[18] See Bok, 'Early advocates of lasting world peace'.

[19] Even Kant, an academically superior exponent of the perpetual peace tradition, makes a case in his 'secret article' as to why states should take into account philosophers' opinions; see Kant's Second Supplement in Chapter 15.

[20] Whether these selections are sufficiently 'representative' is, of course, another conceptual challenge that we face, but our evaluation of some pertinent sources seems to confirm that these selections indeed provide a reasonable framework within which Rousseau, Bentham and Kant can be contextualised. Studies that give us a taste of the pertinent eighteenth-century intellectual landscape include: Elizabeth York, *Leagues of Nations: Ancient, Mediaeval, and Modern* (London: The Swarthmore Press, 1919); Elizabeth V. Souleyman, *The Vision of*

John Bellers (1710), Abbé de Saint-Pierre (1713), James Francis Edward Stuart (called by himself and Jacobites 'King James III') (1722), Cardinal Alberoni (1736), Pierre André Gargaz (1779), and Charles Alexandre de Calonne (1796), respectively. These selections are briefly introduced in Chapter 2 in order to place the subsequent chapters in context. Against this backdrop, Part II presents and reproduces the full texts of Rousseau's, Bentham's and Kant's perpetual peace projects.

Those readers who expect handy summaries or in-depth analyses of these texts will not find them here. They should be reminded, however, that the motivation behind this volume is precisely the availability of numerous summaries and analyses of varying qualities (especially through the medium of the Internet), accompanied by a frustrating difficulty in accessing reliable original material on the basis of which those summaries and analyses must have taken shape. Any determined reader, of course, can find the original texts reproduced here. However, in an intellectual environment, where Kant's essay has become a frequent point of reference; where the texts of at least two philosophers of similar calibre – namely, Rousseau and Bentham – have been almost completely neglected; and where the wider tradition of perpetual peace thinking is conveniently overlooked, this volume serves merely as a reminder that our contemporary notions might be better grounded by turning to the primary material in the history of international political thought.

A number of editorial decisions needed to be made in preparing this volume for publication. The main aim throughout was to strike a balance between authenticity and readability. For the sake of authenticity, the authors' or translators' original expressions have been retained. Unless a typological error was suspected, weak or grammatically unsound expressions have not been replaced or modified. Some of these expressions, of course, are weak or incorrect

World Peace in Seventeenth and Eighteenth-Century France (Port Washington, NY: Kennikat Press, 1941), especially chs. 5 and 7; Peter Brock, *Pacifism in Europe to 1914* (Princeton, NJ: Princeton University Press, 1972), especially chs. 7 and 8.

only by contemporary standards, whereas they used to be correct during the transition from Early Modern to Modern English, and are still clearly understandable today.[21] Occasionally, some words have been deleted to ensure a smoother flow, without upsetting the original sentence structure; or, alternatively, minor insertions have been made into the texts in square brackets, instead of modifying or re-writing the originals (which would have implied the editor's intervention in the author's or informed translator's thought patterns). Insertions, in any case, have been kept to an absolute minimum; and they have been made only when the author's original sentence structure allowed it.

As a practical means of enhancing readability, and in order to bring a degree of standardization to the various texts at hand, spelling and punctuation have been altered as necessary. Numerous old spellings have been updated, and some apparent typographical errors corrected. Wherever the original expression enabled it, long sentences have been broken down into shorter pieces simply by playing with punctuation. In those cases where this method would not work, yet the meaning was clear, the original sentence structure has been retained. The original paragraph structure, too, has been retained as a general rule – even in Bentham's case, where the stylistic presentation of his various enumerations had to be modified to ensure readability. The exceptions to this rule are Bellers's and Alberoni's texts, where we have chosen to put together several very short (e.g. single-sentence) paragraphs.

The authors' original words (especially nouns) – even if no longer in use, or a bit awkward, or inconsistent with other authors' usage – have been retained for the sake of authenticity, provided that they are still understandable today; for instance, *Swisse* and *Swisses* (both of which are used as plural in several texts to denote contemporary 'Swiss'), *Mahometans* (Muslims), *Pensilvania* (Pennsylvania), and *powerfullest* (most powerful). On the other hand, those old words which frequently recur in the texts, e.g. such verbs as *shew* (show), have been modernized. The eighteenth-century convention of starting nouns with

---

[21] For instance, the original translation of Saint-Pierre's project refers to 'four and twenty senators'; see Saint-Pierre's Article 9 in Chapter 5.

capital letters (similar to the ongoing practice in German) has been adapted to contemporary usage. Several italicized words in certain texts, including but not limited to country and continent names, have been normalized, with the exception of non-English (e.g. Latin or French) phrases and some authors' quotations. In some texts, where either too many words were emphasized (e.g. Bellers) or obvious points were repeatedly highlighted (e.g. Saint-Pierre's frequent references to 'without war' or 'sufficient security'), these emphases – originally in capital letters or italics – have been removed, unless their context made them especially worth keeping. Outdated passives have been converted to their proper contemporary forms; for example, *obtain'd* and *possest* became, respectively, *obtained* and *possessed*. Such shortened forms in the originals as 'it's', 'don't' and 'till' have been retained due to their acceptability in contemporary vernacular usage, while other old short forms have been updated, e.g. *tho'*, *whil'st*, *'tis*, and *t'other* have become *though*, *whilst*, *it's*, and *the other*, respectively.

The authors' original notes to their texts have been reproduced here as endnotes, primarily because Kant's notes, in particular, are at times excessively long. Presenting them in footnotes would have upset the entire text flow. All footnotes in this volume, on the other hand, contain editorial comments or references.

Part I

Selections from Representative Eighteenth-Century Perpetual Peace Projects

Chapter 2
Eighteenth-Century Perpetual Peace Proposals: an Overview

The eighteenth century stands out in the evolution of the notion of perpetual peace. Arguably, the notion reached its peak with Kant's well-known and widely cited essay written at the end of the century. However, we need to explore the wider spectrum of perpetual peace conceptualizations, not only because such exploration would enable us to better place Kant's essay in its intellectual milieu, but, equally importantly, because the diversity within eighteenth-century perpetual peace thinking may have implications for the diversity in our contemporary notions of global governance. Part II of this volume will focus closely on the projects of three particularly important philosophers: Rousseau, Bentham and, of course, Kant. Before proceeding to these names, the present chapter provides brief background information for the other seven perpetual peace proposals specified in Chapter 1, contextualizes the original selections in the rest of this Part (Chapters 3–9) and begins to link them with Rousseau's, Bentham's and Kant's texts (Chapters 11, 13, and 15) in a preliminary fashion.

It is possible to detect differing approaches to, and interpretations of, the perpetual peace idea at every stage in the eighteenth century. Nevertheless it is also possible, in at least one crucial aspect, to detect an overall evolution within the tradition, which is not to say that this evolution was straightforward or linear: the proposals of the early eighteenth century were more clearly aimed at European unity than those devised towards the end of the century. The locus of the desired perpetual peace gradually shifted from

15

Europe towards the globe.[1] This is corroborated even by a cursory look at the titles of the essays presented in this volume. The idea of a *perpetual* peace was retained throughout the century, but the desired *universality* of that peace was not declared – not systematically anyway – until the last quarter of the eighteenth century, when such thinkers as Gargaz, Bentham and Kant made explicit reference to a perpetual *and* universal peace.

In this context, *An Essay towards the Present and Future Peace of Europe* by William Penn (1644–1718) deserves special mention as an early universalist project (Chapter 3). Son of an esteemed British admiral, Penn became a Quaker in his twenties, and was persecuted for his beliefs. In 1683 he founded Pennsylvania, which would become one of the original thirteen colonies of the United States of America a century later. While Penn tried to ensure a far-away safe haven for those who escaped religious intolerance, he remained, suffered hardship, and eventually died in England.

Written in 1693 against the backdrop of a deeply divided Europe of alliances, religious rivalries, widespread intolerance, and absolute monarchs (admittedly with the exceptions of England and Poland),[2] Penn's essay tried to make the case for a European entity (*Imperial States*) where the sovereign princes would meet face to face at least once every three years.[3] This entity would have the authority to compel any renegade states to comply with its decisions. Substantial delays in compliance with collective resolutions would be punishable.

Penn makes reference to a general notion of 'man', and his descriptions of man are almost as universalist as Kant's 'individual'. The role of Europeanness and Christianity are significantly demoted in his account.[4] Perhaps more significantly, Penn's plan is quite inclusive in the sense that the advocated European unity does not preclude the possibility

---

[1] For a relevant overview of how the 'European political space' was conceived in the eighteenth century, see H. E. Bodeker, '"Europe" in the discourse of the sciences of state in 18th century Germany', *Cromohs*, 8 (2003), 1–14.

[2] Elizabeth York, *Leagues of Nations*, p. 126.

[3] In fact, Penn uses a number of different names for his proposed political entity. However, it is the *Imperial States* that recurs in his section titles.

[4] See, for instance, Penn, Section III in Chapter 3.

of an even more widespread peoples' union. While the basis of peace in Europe would be the capacity to use force, Penn's demonstration of this principle is noteworthy. He discusses three examples of conquest, implicitly placing them all under the same category: the Spaniards in Flanders; the French in Burgundy; and the Turks in Christendom. The use of the word 'Christendom' – an expression of the eighteenth-century European view of unity – points to the fact that Penn does not unequivocally consider the Turks as part of Europe. But the same formulation has another, perhaps more significant, implication. In this conception, conflicts motivated by religious differences, and undermining the desired European unity, are not deemed qualitatively different from other kinds of conquest. In this sense at least, while the Turks are clearly designated as different (i.e. not part of Christendom, not part of Europe), they are not *excluded* from the notion of perpetual peace. They are considered equally responsible for the existing lack of peace, not more so. Hence, they are equally part of the peace plan.

The composition of Penn's *Imperial States* provides further support for this interpretation, especially when we examine the question of representation. This entity would be representative in three different respects. First, it would represent all sovereign entities in Europe. Secondly, all sovereignties would be represented according to their relative strengths and positions in Europe. And finally, the smaller European sovereignties in particular would have the option to be represented by greater powers of their own choosing. As to who normally would need to be represented, interestingly, neither the Turks (at the time considered to be the most dangerous 'infidels' to threaten 'Christendom') nor the Russians (perceived to be semi-barbarian outsiders, practising a dubious kind of Christianity) are excluded from this design. What is more, both are given prominent seats, with voting powers equal to those of France and Spain, and second only to the Holy Roman Empire.

Penn is convinced of Europe's superiority. This conviction, however, is not unqualified. He is acutely aware of a major contradiction: the Europe that he considers to be the seat of 'civility and arts' is also the place where 'the reputation of Christianity [would need to be] recovered in the sight of infidels, which, by the many bloody and unjust wars of Christians, not only with them, but with one another, has been greatly impaired'. He notes that Christians have not always been in the right, and observes that they have often fought against other Christians – the same sort of Christians at that. It is this bitter observation that leads him to talk about a Holy War, not against the Turks or any other 'infidels' (as would be normally expected), but against the evil of the phenomenon of war itself. For Penn, the recovery of Christian Europe's prestige in the eyes of non-Christians is far from being irrelevant; it is in fact an important aim in itself. By implication, the interaction between Europe and the rest of the known world is certainly relevant to the kind of peace he has in mind.

It would be a mistake to interpret Penn's proposal purely in terms of a normative conviction, however. Part of his reasons for including the Turks, it appears, is in fact strategic. The *Imperial States*, he thinks, will provide greater security for Christians 'against the inroads of the Turks'. Alluding to the occasional French cooperation with the Ottoman Empire, he seems to hope that Turkish participation in the proposed European entity would automatically prevent the development of any special ties between the Turks and some Christian princes. Whatever his reasons, in the final analysis Penn does propose an unexpectedly inclusive European peace proposal right at the dawn of the eighteenth century, in which there are embryonic moves towards a notion of 'global' peace through alternative institutional arrangements.[5]

A similar tendency is detectable in the project of John Bellers (1654–1725). Bellers, a friend of Penn and his fellow Quaker, produced several reform proposals on numerous subjects.[6] The following account by Eduard Bernstein – the founding father of modern social democracy – of Bellers's *Some Reasons for An European State* (1710) is worth quoting at length, not only because it neatly summarizes Bellers's project (Chapter 4), but also because the commentator's

---

[5] See, for example, his idea of 'three degrees of sovereignty' in Chapter 3, p. 36.
[6] Saint-Pierre in his own generation and Bentham in the next had the same quality.

18

identity points to Bellers's potential influence on significant theorists of subsequent generations:[7]

This pamphlet is by no means an abstract essay, but is closely related to contemporary occurrences, from which he endeavours to show the expediency of his proposals. The War of the Spanish Succession . . . still seemed to be no nearer its end; it was from this that Bellers derived an argument in favour of his proposal of an international confederation. In a dedication addressed to Queen Anne he points to the sacrifices incurred and the alliance concluded . . . and how little guarantee after all this alliance afforded . . . In an address to the Powers he further calculates the expenditure in men, money, and economical welfare, incurred through war, directly or indirectly, by European nations since 1688 alone. The method of calculation in this case also is one which is thoroughly original for that period. Finally, he unfolds his proposal. Europe is to be divided into a number of districts (say one hundred) of equal size (cantons or provinces), and each State is to send one member per canton to the Parliament of States, that is to say, each State shall be represented therein in proportion to its size and population . . . [A]ccording to the obligations undertaken in this respect by the various States, the number of their votes in the joint Parliament will be proportioned, so that, in addition to their geographical extent, their capabilities will be taken into account. Parliament will then arrange as to the reduction of standing armies and the number of men per canton to be kept under arms in peace-time. In other respects, too, Bellers shows himself in this essay far ahead of his age . . . [H]e reproduces in it a similar project of Henry IV of France. In his comments thereon he remarks that Henry had excluded the 'Muscovites' (Russia) and Turkey from his scheme, which, in his opinion, was done only in deference to the Roman See. But, says he, 'The Muscovites are Christians, and the Mahometans men, and have the same faculties and reason as other men, they only want the same opportunities and applications of their understandings to be the same men . . .; the farther this civil Union is possible to be extended, the greater will be the Peace on earth, and good will among men.'

---

[7] See Eduard Bernstein, *Cromwell and Communism* [1895], (tr.) H. J. Stenning, (London: George Allen & Unwin, 1930 and 1963); ch. 17 'John Bellers, champion of the poor and advocate of a league of nations'.

The conceptual moves we observe in Penn and Bellers, however, do not signify the beginning of a continuous trend. Abbé Charles-Irénée Castel de Saint-Pierre (1658–1743), whose perpetual peace plan (Chapter 5) is arguably as famous as those of Rousseau and Bentham, develops a consciously and unapologetically Euro-centric project in *A Project for Settling An Everlasting Peace in Europe* (1713).[8] However, the Abbé's project contains early elements of the global governance thinking in another respect. We find here a conceptual deepening of the vertical links between the constituent units of the envisaged Union of Europe. What is on offer in the Abbé's plan is an early version of supra-nationalism, a notion of a merged European political space. For instance, Saint-Pierre's obsessive reference to 'sufficient security' encompasses domestic as well as international governance. The balance of power between France and Austria, according to Saint-Pierre, 'cannot procure any sufficient security either against foreign wars or against civil wars, and consequently cannot procure any sufficient security either for the preservation of territory or for the preservation of commerce'. On the other hand, Saint-Pierre advances such ideas as perpetual arbitration, perpetual congress, and a general diet of Europe, and highlights a vision of European political society.[9]

Saint-Pierre's influence on Rousseau is well known; and he seems to have had at least some influence on Bentham as well.[10] For a long time, though, the question of whether Saint-Pierre himself was influenced by Penn and Bellers remained unanswered,[11] until Peter van den Dungen addressed this specific question, and provided an answer in the affirmative.[12]

---

[8] See his Preface in Chapter 5.

[9] See, for instance, his reference to 'a permanent society of all the sovereignties of Germany' in Chapter 5.

[10] See Collinet's 'Introduction' in Charles Irénéé Castel de Saint-Pierre, *Selections from the Second Edition of the Abrégé du Projet de Paix Perpétuelle*, (tr.) H. Hale Bellot (London: Sweet & Maxwell Limited, 1927), p. 8.

[11] Hinsley, for example, is remarkably silent on this point in his jaxtaposition of the three thinkers: see Hinsley, *Power and the Pursuit of Peace*, ch. 2.

[12] Peter van den Dungen, 'The Abbé de Saint-Pierre and the English "Irenists" of the 18th century (Penn, Bellers, and Bentham)', *International Journal on World Peace*, 17:2 (June 2000), 5–31.

Saint-Pierre, it seems, might even be considered a bridging point between Penn and Kant.

Not all perpetual peace proposals, however, were developed in close interaction with preceding and succeeding plans within the tradition, in just the same way as we find today several works on global governance that do not necessarily and comfortably fit in with systematic global governance scholarship. The Declaration of King James III (1688–1766), for instance, is a good example of how a proposal for perpetual peace was used in the policy domain, with a clear-cut political agenda in mind (Chapter 6). This declaration by the 'Old Pretender' (as he is more commonly known) was published (1722) in anticipation of the Congress of Cambrai. While the document was addressed, on the surface, at the self-styled King's supposed subjects, the intended audience was the European princes.

The plan of Cardinal Giulio Alberoni (1664–1752), on the other hand, is even more interesting from a global governance perspective (Chapter 7). As far as the proposed institutional mechanisms are concerned, Alberoni's plan seems to be quite consistent, if not altogether in line, with Penn's, Bellers's and Saint-Pierre's projects. However, writing four decades after Penn, Alberoni exhibits an entirely different attitude towards non-Europeans. His *Scheme of A 'Perpetual Diet' for Establishing the Public Tranquillity* (1736) is, in fact, the fourth part of a comprehensive plan to conquer and partition the Ottoman Empire. Such a project, of course, points to outright hostility against the Turks, and by implication against non-Europeans.[13] The plan we find here aims explicitly at Christian unity against Muslims, reflecting the crusader mentality. While the Turks are the primary target, Iranians and North Africans, too, are excluded from this notion of perpetual peace. Turks are despised as 'the most finished bigots, and slaves to superstition'. As for the Iranians and North Africans, Alberoni's main concern is to demonstrate that these nations normally would not be willing to help the

---

13 For an uncritical counter-argument that 'Alberoni was always at heart a convinced pacifist'; see Mil. R. Vesnitch, 'Cardinal Alberoni: An Italian precursor of pacifism and international arbitration', *The American Journal of International Law*, 7:1 (1913), esp. p. 66.

Turks and, even if they were willing, why and how Europe would be quite capable of countering this combined threat. Alberoni's *Perpetual Diet* consists of deputies of all sovereign princes and states of 'Christendom'. In essence, it is designed to replicate the processes of the German Diet. All controversies between the princes would be settled within one year by majority voting according to the Constitution of the Empire. Alberoni does not elaborate on the question of representation, but puts the emphasis squarely on the question of reparations and on the possibility of military execution against those who disturb public tranquillity.

From a globalist normative perspective, Alberoni's perpetual peace plan is a considerable step backward from those of Penn, Bellers and Saint-Pierre. What is proposed here is, first and foremost, a European unity, a European peace. There is neither any concern nor any conceptual move towards global peace – or, for that matter, towards a more transcendental 'universal/eternal' peace informed by theology – in Alberoni's account. The vague prescriptions as to the proposed *Perpetual Diet* are exclusively European as well. Nevertheless, Alberoni's approach to perpetual peace bears a striking resemblance to those notions of global governance which are informed by a vulgar interpretation of Samuel Huntington's highly popularized 'clash of civilizations' thesis.[14]

In Pierre André Gargaz's essay (Chapter 8), we find the intellectual reflections of a layman, of a 'nobody' so to speak. Most of what we know about this author comes from the few notes his publisher – Benjamin Franklin, the famous intellectual – has left behind.[15] Gargaz's *A Project of Universal and Perpetual Peace* (1779) is much more insightful and sophisticated than the projects by James or Alberoni, and conforms to the institutionalist thinking in Penn and others.

---

[14] See Samuel P. Huntington, *The Clash of Civilizations and the Remaking of World Order* (New York: Simon and Schuster, 1996).

[15] 'An honest peasant . . . brought me the other day a manuscript . . . which he could not procure permission to print. It appeared to me to have much good sense in it . . . This man aims at no profit from his pamphlet or his project, asks for nothing, expects nothing, and does not even desire to be known . . . I honour much the character of this véritable philosophe.'; see George Simpson Eddy, 'Introduction', in Pierre-André Gargaż, *A Project of Universal and Perpetual Peace*, (ed. & tr.) George Simpson Eddy (New York: 1922), pp. 3–4.

The author (who appears to have been a galley slave at some stage in his life) puts special effort into devising an especially practicable proposal to ensure perpetual peace. Throughout the essay, he appeals to the interests of sovereigns and of nobility – largely so that he can convince them to serve the interests of other segments of society, e.g. soldiers and sailors.[16] At the same time, though, Gargaz advocates highly unconventional ideas, such as the election by a perpetual congress of sovereign successors.[17]

Appeal to the interests of sovereigns and of nobility is much more central to the conceptualization, if not the wording, of Charles Alexandre de Calonne's (1734–1802) project. Ironically, Calonne (the General Controller of Finances in France immediately prior to the Revolution) had tried to reduce the privileges of the nobility, and was, consequently, dismissed and exiled by Louis XVI in 1787. Nevertheless, his hatred of the French Revolution led to a pragmatic project, whose realization would, in practice, imply the strengthening of royalism in Europe and elsewhere.

Written only seven years after Bentham's and just one year after Kant's piece, Calonne's *Considerations on the Most Effectual Means of Procuring A Solid and Permanent Peace* (1796) is primarily a long polemic against revolutionary France, but it also includes reflections on the possibilities of a perpetual peace (Chapter 9). Similar to Bentham, Calonne wrestles with the existing power structure in the Europe of the late eighteenth century. Although much less systematically than Bentham, Calonne highlights the principles of what he believes would count as 'good government'.[18] Consequently, the principles and institutions he envisages have universal applicability. However, Calonne's normative target is unambiguously *European* peace – nothing more. His overall argument is that no peace is possible in France until the revolutionary principles are abandoned, and no peace is possible in Europe unless there is peace in France. In

---

[16] See Gargaz's Seventh Means in Chapter 8.

[17] For a concise account of Gargaz's plan, see Souleyman, *The Vision of World Peace*, pp. 176–81.

[18] For a brief account of the centrality of 'good government' to Bentham's as well as Saint-Pierre's thought, see John Morrow, *The History of Political Thought: A Thematic Introduction* (Houndmills: Macmillan, 1998), pp. 270–3.

this project, juxtaposed with Bentham and Kant, we find once again a policy-driven understanding of perpetual peace. Despite its analytical and normative weaknesses, however, Calonne's essay does connect with the idea of global governance in a significant way: It places utmost emphasis on the relationship between domestic and international levels of governance, and highlights the impact of the former on the latter rather than vice versa. In this respect, at least, Calonne's plan provides a useful point of comparison with Kant's First Definitive Article (see Chapter 15).

Chapters 3–9 provide selections from the works mentioned above. The texts are borrowed, respectively, from the following sources: William Penn, *A Collection of the Works of William Penn*, vol. 2 (London: printed for J. Sowle, 1726); John Bellers, *Some Reasons for an European State, Proposed to the Powers of Europe by An Universal Guarantee and An Annual Congress, Senate, Diet, or Parliament, to Settle Any Disputes about the Bounds and Rights of Princes and States Hereafter* (London: 1710); Charles Irénée Castel de Saint-Pierre, *A Project for Settling An Everlasting Peace in Europe, First Proposed by Henry IV of France, and Approved of by Queen Elizabeth and Most of the Then Princes of Europe, and Now Discussed at Large and Made Practicable by the Abbot St Pierre of the French Academy* (London: printed for J. Watts, 1714); James, Prince of Wales, *Declaration of James the Third, King of England, Scotland and Ireland etc. to All His Subjects to Serve as a Foundation for a Lasting Peace* (1722); Giulio Alberoni, *Cardinal Alberoni's Scheme for Reducing the Turkish Empire to the Obedience of Christian Princes: And for A Partition of the Conquests, Together with A Scheme of A Perpetual Diet for Establishing the Publick Tranquillity*, 2nd edn, translated by Prince de la Torella (London: printed for J. Torbuck, 1736); Pierre-André Gargaz, *A Project of Universal and Perpetual Peace*, translated and edited by George Simpson Eddy (New York: 1922); Charles Alexandre de Calonne, *The Political State of Europe at the Beginning of 1796, or Considerations on the Most Effectual Means of Procuring A Solid and Permanent Peace*, translated by D. St Quentin (Dublin: printed by P. Byrne, 1796).

Chapter 3

William Penn: *An Essay towards the Present and Future Peace of Europe by the Establishment of an European Diet, Parliament, or Estates* (1693)

. . .

Section III. Government, its rise and end under all models

Government is an expedient against confusion, a restraint upon all disorder, just weights, and an even balance that one may not injure another, nor himself, by intemperance.

This was, at first without controversy, patrimonial. [U]pon the death of the father or head of the family, the eldest son or male of kin succeeded. But time breaking in upon this way of governing as the world multiplied, it fell under other claims and forms, and is as hard to trace to its original as are the copies we have of the first writings of sacred or civil matters. It is certain [that] the most natural and human [principle of governance] is that of consent, for that binds freely (as I may say) when men hold their liberty by true obedience to rules of their own making. No man is judge in his own cause, which ends the confusion and blood of so many judges and executioners. For out of society every man is his own king, [and] does what he lists at his own peril. But when he comes to incorporate himself, he submits that royalty to the convenience of the whole, from whom he receives the returns of protection. So that he is not now his own judge nor avenger; neither is his antagonist; but the law in indifferent hands between both. And if he be servant to others that before was free, he is also served of others that formerly owed him no obligation. Thus while we are not our own, everybody is ours and we get more than we lose, the safety of the society

25

being the safety of the particulars that constitute it. So that, while we seem to submit to and hold all we have from society, it is by society that we keep what we have.

Government, then, is the prevention or cure of disorder, and the means of justice as that is of peace. For this cause they have sessions, terms, assizes and parliaments to overrule men's passions and resentments that they may not be judges of their own cause, nor punishers of their own wrongs, which as it is very incident to men in their corrupt state, so, for that reason, they would observe no measure; nor, on the other hand, would any be easily reduced to their duty. Not that men know not what is right, their excesses, and wherein they are to blame. By no means. Nothing is plainer to them. But so depraved is human nature that without compulsion, some way or another, too many would not readily be brought to do what they know is right and fit, or avoid what they are satisfied they should not do: Which brings me near to the point I have undertaken and for the better understanding of which I have thus briefly treated of peace, justice and government as a necessary introduction . . .

Section IV. Of a general peace, or the Peace of Europe, and the means of it

In my first section I showed the desirableness of peace. In my next, the truest means of it: to wit justice, not war. And in my last, that this justice was the fruit of government, as government itself was the result of society, which first came from a reasonable design in men of peace. Now if the sovereign princes of Europe, who represent that society . . . would . . . agree: to meet by their stated deputies in a general diet, estates, or parliament, and there establish rules of justice for sovereign princes to observe one to another; and thus to meet yearly, or once in two or three years at farthest, or as they shall see cause; and to be styled the *Sovereign* or *Imperial Diet, Parliament,* or *State of Europe* before which . . . should be brought all differences . . . between one sovereign and another that cannot be made up by private embassies before the session begins, and [if they would further agree] that, if any of the sovereignties that constitute these *Imperial States* shall refuse to submit their claim or pretensions to them, or to abide and perform the judgment thereof and seek their remedy by arms, or delay their compliance beyond the time prefixed in their resolutions, all the other sovereignties, united as one strength, shall compel the submission and performance of the sentence, with damages to the suffering party and charges to the sovereignties that obliged their submission, to be sure Europe would quietly obtain the so much desired and needed peace to her harassed inhabitants. No sovereignty in Europe, having the power, and therefore cannot show the will to dispute the conclusion; and, consequently, peace would be procured and continued in Europe.

Section V. Of the causes of difference and motives to violate peace

There appears to me but three things upon which peace is broken, *viz.* to keep, to recover, or to add. First, to keep what is one's right from the invasion of an enemy, in which I am purely defensive. Secondly, to recover, when I think myself strong enough, that which, by violence, I or my ancestors have lost by the arms of a stronger power, in which I am offensive. Or, lastly, to increase my dominion by the acquisition of my neighbour's countries, as I find them weak and myself strong . . . This last will find no room in the *Imperial States.* They are an unpassable limit to that ambition. But the other two may come as soon as they please, and find the justice of that sovereign court. And considering how few there are of those sons of prey, and how early they show themselves, it may be not once in an age or two, this expedition being established, the balance cannot well be broken.

Section VI. Of titles upon which those differences may arise

But I easily foresee a question that may be answered in our way, and that is this: What is right? Or else we can never know what is wrong. It is very fit that this should be established. But that is fitter for the sovereign states to resolve than me. And yet that I may lead a way to the matter, I say that title is either by a long and undoubted succession, as the crowns of Spain, France, and England; or by election, as the crown of Poland and the Empire; or by marriage, as the family of the Stewarts came by England, the elector of Brandenburg to the Duchy of Cleve, and we, in ancient times, to diverse places abroad; or by purchase, as has been frequently done in Italy and Germany; or by conquest, as the Turk in Christendom, the Spaniards in Flanders (formerly mostly in the French hands), and the French in Burgundy, Normandy, Lorraine, French-County etc. This last title is, morally speaking, only questionable. It has indeed obtained a place among the rolls of titles, but it was engrossed and recorded by the point of the sword and in bloody characters. What cannot be controlled or resisted must be submitted to, but all the world knows the date of the length of such empires, and that they expire with the power of the possessor to defend them. And yet there is a little allowed to conquest too, when it has the sanction of articles of peace to confirm it. Though that has not always extinguished the fire, but it lies, like embers and ashes, ready to kindle so soon as there is fit matter prepared for it. Nevertheless, when conquest has been confirmed by a treaty and conclusion of peace, I must confess it is an adopted title; and if not so genuine and natural, yet being engrafted, it is fed by that which is the security of better titles: consent. There is but one thing more to be mentioned in this section, and that is from what time titles shall take their beginning, or how far back we may look to confirm or dispute them. It would be very bold and inexcusable in me to determine so tender a point, but be it more or less time as to the last general peace at Nimeguen, or to the commencing of this war, or to the time of the beginning of the treaty of peace, I must submit it to the great pretenders and masters in that affair. But *something* everybody must be willing to give or quit [so] that he may keep the rest and by this establishment be forever freed of the necessity of losing more.[1]

---

[1] Emphasis added.

Section VII. Of the composition of these Imperial States

The composition and proportion of this Sovereign Part, or *Imperial State*, does, at the first look, seem to carry with it no small difficulty what votes to allow for the inequality of the princes and states. But with submission to better judgments, I cannot think it invincible, for if it be possible to have an estimate of the yearly value of the several sovereign countries, whose delegates are to make up this august assembly, the determination of the number of persons or votes in the states for every sovereignty will not be impracticable. Now that England, France, Spain, the Empire etc. may be pretty exactly estimated is so plain a case (by considering the revenue of lands, the exports and entries at the custom houses, the books of rates, and surveys that are in all governments to proportion taxes for the support of them) that the least inclination to the peace of Europe will not stand or halt at this objection. I will, with pardon on all sides, give an instance far from exact; nor do I pretend to it or offer it for an estimate, for I do it at random . . . I suppose the Empire of Germany to send twelve; France, ten; Spain, ten; Italy, which comes to France, eight; England, six; Portugal, three; Sweedland, four; Denmark, three; Poland, four; Venice, three; the Seven Provinces, four; the Thirteen Cantons and little neighbouring sovereignties, two; dukedoms of Holstein and Courland, one; and if the Turks and Muscovites are taken in, as seems but fit and just, they will make ten a piece more. The whole makes ninety – a great presence when they represent the fourth, and now the best and wealthiest, part of the known world, where religion and learning, civility and arts have their seat and empire. But it is not absolutely necessary there should be always so many persons to represent the larger sovereignties, for the votes may be given by one man of any sovereignty as well as by ten or twelve, though the fuller the assembly of states is, the more solemn, effectual, and free the debates will be, and the resolutions must needs come with greater authority. The place of their first session should be central as much as is possible; afterwards as they agree.

Section VIII. Of the regulation of the Imperial States in session

To avoid quarrel for presidency, the room may be round and have diverse doors to come in and go out at, to prevent exceptions. If the whole number be cast into tens, each choosing one, they may preside by turns, to whom all speeches should be addressed, and who should collect the sense of the debates and state the question for a vote, which, in my opinion, should be by the ballot after the prudent and commendable method of the Venetians . . .

It seems to me that nothing in this imperial parliament should pass but by three quarters of the whole; at least seven above the balance. I am sure it helps to prevent treachery, because if money could ever be a temptation in such a court, it would cost a great deal of money to weigh down the wrong scale. All complaints should be delivered in writing in the nature of memorials and journals kept by a proper person in a trunk or chest, which should have as many differing locks as there are tens in the states. And if there were a clerk for each ten, and a pew or table for those clerks in the assembly, and at the end of every session one out of each ten were appointed to examine and compare the journals of those clerks, and then lock them up as I have before expressed, it would be clear and satisfactory. And each sovereignty, if they please, as is but very fit, may have an exemplification or copy of the said memorials and the journals of proceedings upon them. The liberty and rules of speech, to be sure, they cannot fail in, who will be the wisest and noblest of each sovereignty, for its own honour and safety. If any difference can arise between those that come from the same sovereignty that then one of the major number do give the balls of that sovereignty. I should think it extremely necessary that every sovereignty should be present under great penalties, and that none leave the session without leave, till all be finished; and that neutralities in debates should by no means be endured, for any such latitude will quickly open a way to unfair proceedings and be followed by a train both of seen and unseen inconveniences. I will say little of the language in which the session of the *Sovereign Estates* should be held, but to be sure it must be in Latin or French. The first would be very well for civilians, but the last most easy for men of quality.

Section IX. Of the objections that may be advanced against the Design

. . .

The first of them is this, that the strongest and richest sovereignty will never agree to it; and if it should, there would be danger of corruption more than of force one time or other. In answer to the first part, he is not stronger than all the rest, and for that reason you should promote this and compel him into it – especially before he be so, for then it will be too late to deal with such an one. To the last part of the objection, I say the way is as open now as then; and it may be the number fewer, and as easily come at. However, if men of sense and honour and substance are chosen, they will either scorn the baseness, or have wherewith to pay for the knavery. At least they may be watched so that one may be a check upon the other, and all prudently limited by the sovereignty they represent. In all great points, especially before a final resolve, they may be obliged to transmit to their principals the merits of such important cases depending, and receive their last instructions, which may be done in four and twenty days at the most, as the place of their session may be appointed.

The second is that it will endanger an effeminacy by such a disuse of the trade of soldiery; that, if there should be any need for it upon any occasion, we should be at a loss as they were in Holland in '72.

There can be no danger of effeminacy, because each sovereignty may introduce as temperate or severe a discipline in the education of youth as they please, by low living and due labour; instruct them in mechanical knowledge and in natural philosophy by operation, which is the honour of the German nobility. This would make them men; neither women nor lions, for soldiers are the other extreme to effeminacy. But the knowledge of nature and the useful as well as agreeable operations of art give men an understanding of themselves; of the world they are born into; how to be useful

31

and serviceable both to themselves and others; and how to save and help, not injure and destroy . . .

To the other part of the objection . . .: The proposal answers for it itself. One has war no more than the other, and will be as much to seek upon occasion. Nor is it to be thought that any one will keep up such an army after such an empire is on foot, which may hazard the safety of the rest. However, if it be seen requisite, the question may be asked by order of the sovereign states, why such an one either raises or keeps up a formidable body of troops, and be obliged forthwith to reform or reduce them, lest any one, by keeping up a great body of troops, should surprise a neighbour. But a small force in every other sovereignty, as it is capable or accustomed to maintain, will certainly prevent that danger and vanquish any such fear.

The third objection is that there will be great want of employment for younger brothers of families; and that the poor must either turn soldiers or thieves: I have answered that in my return to the second objection . . .

I am come now to the last objection that sovereign princes and states will hereby become not sovereign – a thing they will never endure. But this also, under correction, is a mistake, for they remain as sovereign at home as ever they were. Neither their power over their people nor the usual revenue they pay them is diminished. It may be the war establishment may be reduced, which will indeed of course follow, or be better employed to the advantage of the public. So that the sovereignties are as they were, for none of them have now any sovereignty over one another; and if this be called a lessening of their power, it must be only because the great fish can no longer eat up the little ones, and that each sovereignty is equally defended from injuries and disabled from committing them . . .

Section X. Of the real benefits that flow from this proposal about peace

. . .

[B]esides the loss of so many lives, of importance to any government both for labour and propagation, the cries of so many widows, parents, and fatherless are prevented, that cannot be very pleasant in the ears of any government and is the natural consequence of war in all government.

There is another manifest benefit which redounds to Christendom by this peaceable expedient: the reputation of Christianity will in some degree be recovered in the sight of infidels, which, by the many bloody and unjust wars of Christians (not only with them, but one with another) has been greatly impaired. For, to the scandal of that holy profession, Christians, that glory in their Saviour's name, have long devoted the credit and dignity of it to their worldly passions as often as they have been excited by the impulses of ambition or revenge. They have not always been in the right, nor has right been the reason of war. And not only Christians against Christians, but the same sort of Christians have imbrued their hands in one another's blood, invoking and interesting all they could the good and merciful God to prosper their arms to their brethren's destruction. Yet their Saviour has told them that He came to save and not to destroy the lives of men; to give and plant peace among men. And if in any sense He may be said to send war, it is the Holy War indeed, for it is to send against the devil, and not the persons of men . . .

The third benefit is that it saves money, both to the prince and people; and thereby prevents those grudgings and misunderstandings between them that are wont to follow the devouring expenses of war; and enables both to perform public acts for learning, charity, manufactures etc. – the virtues of government and ornaments of countries. Nor is this all the advantage that follows to sovereignties, upon this head of money and good husbandry, to whose service and happiness this short discourse is dedicated, for it saves the great expense that frequent and splendid embassies require, and all their appendages of spies and intelligence, which in the most prudent governments have devoured mighty sums of money – and that not without some immoral practices also, such as corrupting of servants to betray their masters by revealing their secrets; not to be defended by Christian or old Roman virtue. But here, where there is nothing to fear, there is little to know; and therefore the purchase is either cheap or may be wholly spared. I might mention pensions to the widows and orphans of such as die in wars, and of those that have been disabled in them, which rise high in the revenue of some countries.

Our fourth advantage is that the towns, cities and countries that might be laid waste by the rage of war are thereby preserved. A blessing that would be very well understood in Flanders and Hungary, and indeed upon all the borders of sovereignties, which are almost ever the stages of spoil and misery; of which the stories of England and Scotland do sufficiently inform us without looking over the water.

The fifth benefit of this peace is the ease and security of travel and traffic – an happiness never understood since the Roman Empire has been broken into so many sovereignties. But we may easily conceive the comfort and advantage of travelling through the governments of Europe by a pass from any of the sovereignties of it, which this league and state of peace will naturally make authentic. They that have travelled Germany, where is so great a number of sovereignties, know the want and value of this privilege, by the many stops and examinations they meet with by the way; but especially such as have made the great tour of Europe. This leads to the benefit of a universal monarchy, without the inconveniences that attend it, for when the whole was one empire, though these advantages were enjoyed, yet the several provinces that now make the kingdoms and states of Europe were under some hardship from the great sums of money remitted to the imperial seat, and the ambition and avarice of their several proconsuls and governors, and the great taxes they paid to the numerous legions of soldiers that they maintained for their own subjection, who were not wont to entertain that concern for them (being uncertainly there, and having their fortunes to make) which their respective and proper sovereigns have always shown for them. So that to be ruled by native princes or states, with the advantage of that peace and security that can only render a universal monarchy desirable, is peculiar to our proposal, and for that reason it is to be preferred.

Another advantage is the great security it will be to Christians against the inroads of the Turk, in their most prosperous fortune. For it had been impossible for the Porte to have prevailed so often and so far from Christendom, but by the carelessness or wilful connivance, if not aid, of some

Christian princes. And for the same reason, why no Christian monarch will adventure to oppose or break such a union, the Grand Seignior will find himself obliged to concur, for the security of what he holds in Europe, where with all his strength he would feel it an over-match for him. The prayers, tears, treason, blood, and devastation that war has cost in Christendom, for these two last ages especially, must add to the credit of our proposal, and the blessing of the peace thereby humbly recommended.

The seventh advantage of a European *Imperial Diet*, *Parliament*, or *Estates* is that it will beget and increase personal friendship between princes and states, which tends to the rooting up of wars, and planting peace in a deep and fruitful soil . . .

Nor is this all the benefit that would come by this freedom and interview of princes, for natural affection would hereby be preserved, which we see little better than lost from the time their children or sisters are married into other courts. For the present state and insincerity of princes forbid them the enjoyment of that natural comfort which is possessed by private families insomuch that from the time a daughter or sister is married to another crown, nature is submitted to interest, and that, for the most part, grounded not upon solid or commendable foundations, but ambition or unjust avarice I say, this freedom that is the effect of our pacific proposal restores nature to her just right and dignity in the families of princes . . .

To conclude this section, there is yet another manifest privilege that follows this intercourse and good understanding, which methinks should be very moving with princes, *viz*. that hereby they may choose wives for themselves such as they love, and not by proxy, merely to gratify interest – an ignoble motive . . .

The Conclusion

I will conclude this my proposal of a *European Sovereign*, or *Imperial Diet*, *Parliament*, or *Estates* with that which I have touched upon before . . . That by the same rules of justice and prudence by which parents and masters govern their families

CARDIFF
CAERDYDD

and magistrates their cities, and estates their republics, and princes and kings their principalities and kingdoms, Europe may obtain and preserve peace among her sovereignties. For wars are the duels of princes; and as government in kingdoms and states prevents men being judges and executioners for themselves . . .; so, this being soberly weighed in the whole and parts of it, it will not be hard to conceive or frame, nor yet to execute, the design I have here proposed.

And for the better understanding and perfecting of the idea I here present to the sovereign princes and estates of Europe for the safety and tranquillity of it, I must recommend to their perusals Sir William Temple's account of the United Provinces, which is an instance and answer upon practice to all the objections that can be advanced against the practicability of my proposal; nay, it is an experiment that not only comes to our case, but exceeds the difficulties that can render its accomplishment disputable. For there we shall find three degrees of sovereignties to make up every sovereignty in the *General States*. I will reckon them backwards. First, the *States General* themselves; then the immediate sovereignties that constitute them, which are those of the provinces, answerable to the sovereignties of Europe that by their deputies are to compose the *European Diet, Parliament*, or *Estates* in our proposal; and then there are the several cities of each province that are so many independent or distinct sovereignties, which compose those of the provinces, as those of the provinces do compose the *States General* at The Hague.

But I confess I have the passion to wish heartily that the honour of proposing and effecting so great and good a design might be owing to England . . . as something of the nature of our expedient was, in design and preparation, to the wisdom, justice, and valour of Henry IV of France . . . For he was upon obliging the princes and estates of Europe to a political balance, when the Spanish faction for that reason contrived and accomplished his murder by the hands of Ravilliac. I will not then fear to be censured for proposing an expedient for the present and future peace of Europe, when it was not only the design but glory of one of the greatest princes that ever reigned in it; and is found practicable in the constitution of one of the wisest and powerfullest states of it . . .

Chapter 4

John Bellers: *Some Reasons for An European State, Proposed to the Powers of Europe by An Universal Guarantee and Annual Congress, Senate, Diet, or Parliament to Settle Any Disputes about the Bounds and Rights of Princes and States hereafter* (1710)

. . .

To Anne, Queen of Great Britain etc.

Great Princess,

Crowns have cares sufficient in the best of times, and the dangers from reconciled enemies as well as from the misunderstandings that may fall among allies is no small addition to them. Therefore what expedients that can be offered to prevent them will at this juncture be the more seasonably made, which has given occasion to this essay for a general guarantee for establishing the universal peace of Europe . . .

And as it will add greatly to the Crown's security and Nation's peace, so it will be a great acquirement to the glory of the Queen, if to the Union of Scotland (which for several ages had in vain been attempted) She will please to use Her endeavours for uniting the powers of Europe in one peaceable settlement by which the kingdoms and states thereof may among themselves raise such a legal jurisdiction as may peaceably decide all their future disputes, according to what original contract they shall make, as well as the ten Saxon, Welch, Scotch and Irish kingdoms are now happily united in one government to the saving of much human blood which was formerly frequently spilt in their disputes, as is yet too much used in several parts of Europe . . .

John Bellers

To the Lords and Commons of Great Britain in Parliament assembled

The deluge of Christian blood and the vast treasure which have been spent to procure the expected peace is a most powerful argument of the necessity, when made, that it may be perpetual if possible. Who can be more sensible of the happiness of it than yourselves, whilst you have borne so much of the burden of the war? If there should be as many sessions of Parliament spent to find out such an acceptable expedient, as would fix the peace to perpetuity, as there has been to procure it, it would be time well spent; though, I hope, much fewer will do it.

A guarantee among the present confederates, as in the address of your August Assembly to the Queen, is highly necessary. Yet a general one through all Europe will make it much more effectual. Whilst every prince and state having the benefit of it, they will all account it their interest to have it inviolably kept, with such additional articles of agreement as may make it more lasting than guarantees usually are.

Now considering the endeavour and danger there may be of weakening (by dividing) the present confederacy, which they could not otherwise subdue, especially if any future disputes should arise among the present allies about the honour of princes, the bounds of countries, or the trade of their subjects etc. For which reason I humbly propose as one expedient that, by sufficient articles of agreement among the present confederates, they provide some supreme court to decide their future disputes without blood. Such a jurisdiction seeming as needful as any barrier against the most public enemy; it being unity among themselves that will keep them strong and steady to support their outworks or barriers.

Whilst for want of some such jurisdiction to extinguish those small sparks, Holland may come to think itself under a necessity to seek the alliance and protection of France again. And the cautionary towns and barriers may change sides at once as them in Flanders did at the death of the late King of Spain, from whence may arise a fresh war more fatal than the present, which to prevent is the endeavour of this essay. And, to use the words of King Henry IV of France and his associates to the then King of Spain upon the same design: It is *holy*, *pious*, *charitable*, *glorious*, and *profitable* to all Christendom.[1]

And the Council of State in Holland . . . declare that the power of France is so formidable and that former barriers and guarantees have been so insufficient against the pretensions of that crown that the other princes and states cannot cover themselves against her invasions without a mutual league and union, which they say is to be wished and endeavoured after the peace, in imitation of the union called *Fœdus Sacrum*, forever, which is between the Emperor and the Republic of Venice against the Turks.

With submission to the powers concerned, the sooner it can possibly be set on foot the better . . . The several provinces of Holland as well as the Cantons of Switzerland were the easier and firmer settled and strengthened by being united in perilous times. If the present confederates begin among themselves and then invite into it all the neutral powers, it will draw on the peace the faster (if not made before) and the more incline France itself to come into it, by which that kingdom will reap the blessing of a lasting peace which their present King's grandfather had formerly proposed . . .

Some reasons for an European State, proposed to the Powers of Europe

You are as viceroys to the great King of Heaven and Earth, to whom you must be accountable for the well-governing of the many millions of your fellow creatures and subjects . . .

Many and great are the blessings to prince and people, where the subjects are governed in peace. But oppression and

---

1 Emphases original.

war tend to the poverty and ruin of both. If we may suppose that this war since 88 has cost the French Crown 12 millions sterling a year, in 20 years it comes to 240 millions. For which 12 millions a year, if reckoned at 6 percent, the interest comes to 200 millions, which in all make 440 millions. And besides that, they have lost 30 thousand men a year at least. That, in 20 years, comes to 600 thousand, which if valued at 200*l.* a head (which every able man and his posterity may be esteemed to add to the value of the kingdom at 10*l.* a year a head at 20 years' purchase) comes to 120 millions. Every man paying or spending yearly one with the other 10*l.* a head as by the following computation:

	l.	*s.*	*d.*	
To the Crown for custom, excise etc.	0	10	0	⎤
To rent for housing or land	2	10	0	⎪ or more
To the makers of clothing	2	10	0	⎪
To the raisers of food	4	10	0	⎦
in all	10	0	0	a year.

Which at 20 years' purchase comes to 200*l.*

But where there is no men, there can be no money, nor women, nor children, nor kingdom, but a land without inhabitants. From which may be observed that 440 millions (besides the men lost) at 20 years' purchase would buy 22 millions a year rent, which is four or five times as much as the usual revenues of the Crown of France in time of peace. Therefore if it had got by conquest the revenues of four or five such crowns, with this expense it had been no great gainer.

And the 600 thousand men may be reckoned double or treble the number France has now in arms besides the many thousands of refugees, whom severities have frighted into foreign countries. What an addition of riches, strength and honour to the Crown of France would such a body of men and extraordinary sum of money have given, if they had been employed in improving the country instead of being wasted in war. Such strength and treasure would have much enlarged the cities, towns and villages, and raised the waste lands and forests into gardens and vineyards, almost to doubling the value of the kingdom. Or what colonies, provinces and a kingdom might such a number of men etc. have planted, if they had been settled in America, where the lands want inhabitants, and the fruitful earth wants tillage, and those dark corners of the world want the light of the Gospel of Peace?

France is a large country, and in a good climate, and populous, with a people well civilized, industrous, inclined to all sorts of arts and sciences, with a prince, a great encourager of learning. How happy would that nation be in the advantages it has of some of its neighbours, and how bright would be its monarch's rays, were they not clouded with war abroad, nor severities to his dissenting subjects at home? Then the increase of learned men would sound forth his praise, and the tranquillity of his subjects greatly enlarge their number.

But on the contrary, those methods which destroy the subjects, or lessen their liberties, return hatred instead of honour, and clouds instead of brightness upon the memory of such a prince. And what has been a loss to France has been the same to the rest of the kingdoms and countries of Europe (that are under the same circumstances) in proportion to the men and money which they have so spent . . .

The Proposal

That at the next general peace, there should be settled an universal guarantee and an annual congress, senate, diet, or parliament by all the princes and states of Europe, as well enemies as neuters joined as one state, with a renouncing of all claims upon each other, with such other articles of agreement as may be needful for a standing European law; the more amicably to debate and the better to explain any obscure articles in the peace, and to prevent any disputes that might otherwise raise a new war in this age or the ages to come; by which every prince and state will have all the strength of Europe to protect them in the possession of what they shall enjoy by the next peace.

But in the meanwhile, it's the interest of the present confederates to begin it among themselves. But Europe being under several forms of government, and every country being apt to esteem their own form best, it will require time and consideration among the Powers concerned to draw such a scheme as will suit the dispositions and circumstances of them all. The several methods used by the German Diets, the Union of the Provinces of Holland, the Cantons of Switzerland, the nature of guarantees with the model of Henry IV and the *Fœdus Sacrum* between the Emperor and Venice show that sovereign princes and states may be united (to protect a general peace) yet with the preservation of their sovereign's rights at home.

All which considered, I will propose one thought towards the great design, *viz.* that Europe should be divided into 100 equal cantons or provinces, or so many that every sovereign prince and state may send one member to the Senate at least. And that each canton should be appointed to raise a thousand men, or money or ships of equal value, or charge upon any public occasion (or any other number that may be thought best). And for every thousand men etc. that each kingdom or state is to raise, such kingdom or state shall have a right to send so many members to this European Senate, whose powers and rules should be first formed by an original contract among their principals. By which means, the princes and states of Europe may settle all the disputes among themselves without blood or charge, and prevent the rash from such dismal adventures as are the consequences of war, whilst they must know that every man in the Senate has 1, 2 or 3 thousand men to back what he concludes there. Which is one reason why the members in the Senate should be in proportion to the strength of the country which they represent; that the strong may not refuse to associate with the weak to preserve the public peace. And whilst conquest usually goes with the most numerous as strongest, they cannot expect an equaller sentence by the sword than what such a senate will give, nor so just.

Because that assembly must go by arguments (and not scimitars) grounded upon reason and justice, and the major part of the Senate, not being interested in the dispute, will be the more inclined to that side which has most reason with it, whilst the greatest monarchs in time of peace own themselves subjects to the sovereignty of reason . . .

Now considering Europe as one government, every kingdom and state may be limited what troops or ships of war they may keep up, [so] that they may be disabled from invading their neighbours; for without it the peace may be little better than a truce, if [better] than a cessation of arms, for, besides the hazards of sudden surprises, the multitude of troops that every state will keep up to watch their neighbours will leave them the third year of the peace (if it last so long) under little less expense than they were at the first year of the war, considering the charges of those numerous troops added to the interest they must pay for the vast debts this war will leave them in.

As the continuance of peace is of the utmost consequence both to prince and people, nothing that is needful for such a union can be too much for a prince to give up for it. The unlimited will of monarchs to invade their neighbours is no more a privilege to them than it would be for their subjects to have liberty to destroy each other, which is to reduce the earth to a desert. But as there is a necessity for raising governments in towns and cities for preserving the rights and properties of their inhabitants by a peaceable [authority] deciding their disputes, and for the same reason (and defence against their common enemies) [there is a need] to join counties and provinces into kingdoms and states. So the advantages would be the same and greater to the kingdoms and states of Europe, if such an union can be raised by them . . .

Let any treaty be set afoot that is possible: Some prince or state will complain, whether the *Pyrennean*, *Westphalia*, or that of *Munster*, *Aix le Chapelle*, *Reswick*, or the Treaty of Partition, or any other that ever was. There can be no righting the people that have been ruined and destroyed by war, nor the princes they have belonged unto, and the longer the war continues, injuries will be the more increased, for war always ruins more people than it raises, and the rights of both princes and people are best preserved in peace. Therefore the best expedient that can be offered is such a settlement as will prevent adding more injuries by war to those irreparable ones already past, after the present disputes are settled in the best manner that time and circumstances will admit of.

. . .

To the Counsellors and Ministers of State of the Kingdoms and States of Europe

As peace gives plenty and riches to those states that enjoy it, so it gives security and honour to those princes and statesmen that govern them. But as war hazards crowns, so every difficulty they fall under shakes, if not throws down, those ministers that set at helm, for whether their management be defective or not, the people cry them up or run them down by their success, that being the standard by which they judge of statemen's abilities . . .

It may be reckoned that there has been destroyed by war, in these last twenty years in all the parts of Europe, several millions of men, and 500 millions of pounds sterling spent, besides the widows and orphans left distressed, and towns and countries ravaged . . . Several ages have not produced a more seasonable time for such an undertaking than this, because the princes of Europe have seldom been more weary of war than at present. Nor have the circumstances of the kingdoms and states more required it for the firmer establishing of their several governments.

The Empire will be the better secured against the pretensions of the French and Turks; England against the attempts of France; the French against those of their neighbours; Spain against that of France; Portugal and Holland against that of Spain; Sweedland against the claim of Denmark, and Denmark against that of Sweedland; the Cantons of Switzerland against the claim of the Emperor; the princes and states of Italy against the pretensions of their powerful neighbours; and also prevent the renewing of this destructive war among the Poles, Muscovites, and Sweeds.

. . .

To the Bishops, Confessors, Chaplains, Presbyters, Ministers, and Teachers in the Kingdoms and States of Europe

As you are accounted fathers and elders in the kingdoms and countries, where you dwell, so let your hearty endeavours for establishing the public peace of Europe add to you the honour and happiness of being esteemed in Heaven, the Children of God.

. . .

How shall the rays of Christianity influence Turks and infidels? When they shall see that, under the pretence of that religion, its professors shall have the hottest animosities and hatred, there having been far more Christian blood spilt by one another than ever was spilt by the greatest of their heathen prosecutors.

. . .

Many instances show that different sentiments in religion are not inconsistent either with good neighbourhood or good government, the present confederacy and congress against France being a full instance that Roman Catholics and Protestants can unite for their common advantage and safety, and notwithstanding their different principles and ceremonies, live in peace one with another. The several states and principalities of the Empire of diverse persuasions, and the Cantons of Switzerland, with the various opinions in Holland, show that property in stock and land may be enjoyed by such, without injury to the government they live under. Protestants and Roman Catholics hold a firm friendship in experimental philosophy. Malpighius, though an Italian, and physician to the Pope, was received as a very acceptable member of the English Royal Society; and they and the Royal Academy of Paris, though of different religions, yet lament the obstruction that is given to their desired correspondence by the war. The several religious orders of the Church of Rome, though they differ in their habits and rules, yet they are under their head, the Bishop of Rome, as one body, and usually live amicably in the same kingdoms and cities. Why may not charity, prudence, and interest as well unite all Christians under their great head, Christ Jesus (whom they all own), and make them more diligent to seek out those other things they agree in, for to live in friendship rather than let those few things they now differ in blow up contention and hatred.

. . .

Persecution to force conformity in religion, as it's useless, is also as directly against the intent of Christianity as the worst of the heathen principles and practices. Plundering men for principles of religion is but offering robbery for a sacrifice, and racking them to death no better than offering of human blood. Is any of the disputed opinions more unchristian than murders, robberies, rapes, and destroying towns and countries, profaning the name of God, and all manner of evils, which are the common effects of war, as war is usually the consequence of persecutions for religion, which often bring convulsions, if not revolutions in kingdoms and states . . . And when there is a body of malcontents formed, though they be of different religions, they will seldom want a head to command them; a Teckly, a Ragotzi or a Cavaliere will be easily found. Switzerland, Holland, Hungary, and the Cevenois, with the many French Protestants in the armies of the allies, are full instances of it. Let true love take away but irregular passions and undue interest, and mankind will as naturally agree to do good one to another, as wax heated will unite . . .

Imposing religion, without reaching the understanding, is not leading men to Heaven. Men will not be saved against their own wills. Neither can a man firmly believe what he is not convinced of. Where truths are clear and understood, artists don't differ about them. There is no need of a rack to force a mathematical demonstration, nor to make a mechanic to be a good workman. Torment may make a man say anything, though he abhor his prosecutors at the same time. But it will not open any truth unto him; passion and pain bringing clouds instead of brightness to the understanding of men. Yet do but reach a man's understanding, and he cannot disbelieve what he is convinced of.

. . .

If creeds should always be made the standard of property, Europe would be depopulated as America is, and the people as barbarous as the Indians by carrying their resentments and revenge from one generation to another. Can Christians live peaceably among Turks and Indians, and not among themselves, without destroying one another? O unhappy men! An enemy has surely sowed these tares in Christendom, not so much because of different principles as of an uncharitable unchristian temper.

Having said thus much of the mischiefs that attend religious feuds and wars, to prevent which for the future, I would propose a new sort of General Council of all the several Christian persuasions in Europe.

. . .

A proposal for a General Council of all the several Christian persuasions in Europe . . .

I. As first, they should take an account what things all the several religious persuasions in Europe agree in. And then it will appear that those two essential articles of loving God and neighbours will be two of them, which, if all persuasions would but put into practice, it would effectually put an end to all wars and bloodshed for religion. And considering that as a sincere love to God qualifies any man for Heaven; so doing good to one's neighbour gives such a man a right to a peaceable living upon the earth.

II. If they would consider that, if mankind were strictly to examine into all the different sentiments that are among the thinking part of them, with the same hatred and heat that they usually contend with their reputed adversaries, they would find matter enough among their most intimate friends to raise feuds and animosities, even to the last two men that should be living. We know of but three men in the world when Cain killed Abel for religion.

By which two articles it appears that the case lies in a little room. That as liberty of conscience to the peaceable tends to make countries flourish by peace, so severities only for different sentiments of religion strictly followed tends to misery and ruin.

III. If such an assembly would explain all the things they seem to differ in that they may all have one idea of the same words, the difference in many of those things they have disputed about would be much less than they seem to be. Therefore it may with the greater reason be hoped that such an assembly would establish a peace and friendship among themselves, though they differ in religious forms, that may be for the peace and prosperity of the princes and people of Europe where they dwell.

. . .

Not regarding the many things Christians have agreed in, but imposing those few articles which they knew they differed about, long experience shows, has been the cause, open or secret, of much bloodshed in Europe. Whilst if the various capacities and dispositions of mankind had been duly considered, and only what had been necessary for the good of human society been imposed, and what related to the way to Heaven had gone no farther than advice and information, the lives of many thousands [could have] been saved . . .

An abstract of a model for the good and perpetual repose of Christendom by that Great Prince, King Henry IV of France, as in the Memoirs of the Duke of Sully . . .

I. He believed that he ought to establish in his own kingdom an unshaken peace by reconciling all spirits, both to him and among themselves, by taking away all causes of bitterness. And that, moreover, it was necessary for him to choose people capable and faithful, who might see in what his revenue or estate might be bettered, and instruct him so well in all his affairs that he might discern himself the more feasible from impossible enterprises. He granted an edict to the Protestants that the two religions might live in peace. He made an order to pay his debts and those of the kingdom contracted by the disorder of the times and the profuseness of his predecessors.

II. That done, he continually laboured to join all Christian princes by seeking all occasions to extinguish disorders and pacify differences among them. He began to make his friends and associates the princes and states which seemed best disposed towards France, [such] as the states of Holland, the Venetians, Swisse, and Grisons.[2] And also he endeavoured to

---

[2] The Grisons (Graubünden) became a Swiss canton in 1803.

negotiate with the three puissant kingdoms of the North, [namely] England, Denmark, and Sweedland, to discuss and decide their differences. And to do the same thing among the Electors and Estates, and Cities Imperial. And he sounded the lords of Bohemia, Hungary, Transilvania, and Poland, to know if they would concur with him.

These were the dispositions of his great design, of which the platform or model follows. He desired perfectly to unite all Christendom into one body to be called *The Christian Commonwealth*. For which effect he proposed to part it into 15 dominions or estates; as the most he could do to make them of equal power and strength, and whose limits should be so well specified by the universal consent of the whole 15, that none could pass beyond them. The 15 dominions were:

1. The Pontificate, or Papacy
2. Empire of Germany
3. France
4. Spain
5. Great Britain
6. Hungary
7. Bohemia
8. Poland
9. Denmark
10. Sweedland
11. Savoy, or Kingdom of Lumbardy
12. The Signory of Venice
13. The Italian Commonwealth, or little princes and cities of Italy
14. The Belgians, or Low Countries
15. The Swisses

Now to regulate the differences, which might arise between these confederates, and to decide them, there should have been established an order and form of procedure by a general council, composed of 60 persons, 4 on part of every dominion, which should have been placed in some city in the midst of Europe, [such] as Mets, Nancy, Collen,[3] or others. There

---

[3]   Köln/Cologne (Germany).

should likewise have been established three others in three several places, every one of 20 men, which should all three make report to the Grand Council.

And by the consent of the General Council, which should be called *the Senate of the Christian Commonwealth*, there should be established an order and regulation between sovereigns and subjects to hinder, on one side, the oppression and tyranny of princes, and on the other side, the tumults and rebellion of subjects.

There should likewise be raised a stock of money and men, to which every dominion should contribute according to the assessment of the Great Council, for the assistance of the dominions bordering upon infidels from their assaults, to wit Hungary and Poland against those of the Turks, and Sweedland and Poland against the Muscovites and Tartars.

In fine, by the remonstrances of all his associates, he had let the King of Spain understand his design together with the princes of the House, and had conjured them by the blood of Jesus Christ to consent to it as being holy, pious, charitable, glorious, and profitable to all Christendom. They had withal laid before him the advantages which would have come to himself, and endeavoured to make him comprehend that he would be more rich, less disturbed, and more peaceable. That in twenty years, Spain, which was almost a desert, would be re-peopled and become the most flourishing estate of Europe.

But it's hard to persuade, where unlimited and ill-designing ambition embraces rather chimeras than solid things, chooses rather to possess vast and desert countries than a reasonable extent well cultivated and well peopled. He had laid his designs and made preparations with all diligence imaginable for eight or nine years, which platform, the historian writes, was so great that, it may be said, it was conceived by an intelligence more than human.

The Conclusion

The judicious sayings of Henry IV of France show him to be a prince of great sense, and the multitude of difficulties he surmounted of great courage, but no one thing bespeaks the excellency of his mind more than his great desire for the uniting of Christendom.

His excluding the Muscovites and Ottomans out of it, I take as a compliment to the See of Rome. For as nothing makes nations and people more barbarous than war; so peace must be the first step to fit mankind for religion. War is destruction and puts men (they think) under a necessity of doing those things, which in a time of peace they would account cruel and horrid. The Muscovites are Christians and the Mahometans men, and have the same faculties and reason as other men. They only want the same opportunities and applications of their understandings to be the same men. But to beat their brains out to put sense into them is a great mistake, and would leave Europe too much in a state of war, whereas the farther this civil union is possible to be extended, the greater will be the peace on earth and good will among men.

The Bishop writes, among other helps, this King Henry had gained all the good pens in Christendom, as choosing rather to persuade than force people. But I have seen nothing upon this subject, but what that author said and what has been written by the eminent and accomplished gentleman, William Penn, governor of Pensilvania.[1] But if any gentleman knows of any other authors on this subject, a public advertisement of them would tend the more to illustrate this great design, and stir up many worthies in the several kingdoms and states of Europe that would contribute their assistance towards such a happy day in Europe.

John Bellers
. . .

Note

[1] In a small treatise sold by J. Sowle in White-Hart-Court in Gracious-Street.

Chapter 5

Abbé de Saint-Pierre: *A Project for Settling An Everlasting Peace in Europe* (1713)

Preface

My design is to propose means for settling an everlasting peace amongst all the Christian states. Let not anybody ask me what capacity I have acquired to handle a subject of so very high a nature. It's a question I can make no answer to . . . But to judge of the value of a work, does the reader stand in need of anything besides the work itself?

About four years ago, after having finished an essay useful for the interior commerce of the kingdom, being both an eyewitness of the extreme misery to which the people were reduced by the heavy taxes, and also informed by diverse particular relations of the excessive contributions, the foragings, the destructions, the violences, the cruelties, and the murders which the unhappy inhabitants of the frontiers of Christian states daily suffer; in short, being sensibly touched with the evils which war causes to the princes of Europe and their subjects, I took a resolution to penetrate into the first sources of this evil and to find out by my own reflections, whether it was so inseparable from the nature of sovereignties and sovereigns as to be absolutely without remedy. I applied myself to examine this affair in order to discover whether it was not possible to find out some practicable means to terminate their future differences without war, and so to render the peace perpetual amongst them.

. . .

I thought it necessary to begin by making some reflections upon the happiness it would be, as well as to the sovereigns of Europe as to private men, to live in peace, united by some permanent society, and upon the necessity they are at present in to have continual wars with each other about the possession or division of some advantages, and finally upon the means which they have hitherto used, either to avoid entering upon those wars or not to sink under them, when once they have entered upon them.

I found that all those means consisted in making mutual promises, either in treaties of commerce, of truce, of peace, wherein limits of dominion and other reciprocal pretensions are regulated; or else in treaties of guarantee, or of league (offensive and defensive) to establish, to maintain or to re-establish the equilibrium of power between the principal houses – a system which hitherto seems to be the highest degree of prudence that the sovereigns of Europe or their ministers ever carried their policy to.

I soon perceived that so long as they contented themselves with such methods they would never have any sufficient security for the execution of treaties, nor sufficient means for terminating equitably, and above all without war, their future differences; and that unless they could find out some better ways, the Christian princes must never expect anything but an almost continual war, which can never be interrupted but by some treaties of peace or rather by truces, which are the necessary productions of equality of forces, and of the weariness and exhaustion of the combatants, and which in the end must be the total ruin of the vanquished.[1] It's these reflections that are the subject of the first discourse. I have reduced them all into two heads, or two propositions, which I propose to myself to demonstrate:

First, the present constitution of Europe can never produce anything else but almost continual wars, because it can never procure any sufficient security for the execution of treaties.

Secondly, the equilibrium of power between the House of France and the House of Austria cannot procure any sufficient security either against foreign wars or against civil wars, and consequently cannot procure any sufficient security either for the preservation of territory or for the preservation of commerce.

The first step necessary to the obtaining of a cure for a disease great or inveterate and for which alone nothing but ineffectual medicines have hitherto been used is to endeavour, on the one side, to find out the different causes of the disease, and, on the other, the disproportion of these medicines with the disease itself.

I afterwards considered whether sovereigns might not find some sufficient security for the execution of mutual promises by establishing a perpetual arbitration; and I find that if the eighteen principal sovereignties of Europe, in order to maintain the present government to avoid war, and to procure the advantages of an uninterrupted commerce between nation and nation, would make a treaty of union and a perpetual congress, much after the model either of the seven sovereignties of Holland, the thirteen sovereignties of the Swisses, or the sovereignties of Germany, and form an European Union, from what is best in those unions, and especially in the Germanic Union which consists of above two hundred sovereignties, I found, I say, that the weakest would have a sufficient security that the great power of the strongest could not hurt them, that everyone would exactly keep their reciprocal promises, that commerce would never be interrupted, and that all future differences would be terminated without war by means of umpires, a blessing which can never be obtained any other way.

These are the eighteen principal Christian sovereignties which should each of them have a voice in the general diet of Europe: 1. France, 2. Spain, 3. England, 4. Holland, 5. Portugal, 6. Switzerland and the associates, 7. Florence and the associates, 8. Genoa and associates, 9. The Ecclesiastic State, 10. Venice, 11. Savoy, 12. Lorrain, 13. Denmark, 14. Courland and Dantzick etc., 15. The Emperor and Empire, 16. Poland, 17. Sweden, 18. Muscovy. I set down the Empire only as one sovereignty, because it is but one body. Holland, too, is mentioned but for one sovereignty, because that republic, though it consists of seven sovereign republics, is but one body; the same of Switzerland.

In examining the government of the sovereigns of Germany, I did not find that there would be more difficulty in forming the European body now than formerly there was in forming the Germanic body in executing in great that which has been already executed in little. On the contrary, I found that there would be fewer obstacles and more facility in forming the European body; and what greatly persuaded me that this project was no chimera was the information I received from one of my friends soon after I had shown him the first sketch of this work. He told me that Henry IV had formed a project, which, in the main, was much the same; and so I found in the memoirs of the Duke of Sully, his prime minister, and in Monsieur de Perefixe's history of his reign: Nay more, I found that this project had been even agreed to by a great many princes in the beginning of the last century. This gave me occasion from thence to draw some inferences to prove that the thing was far from being impracticable.[II] And this is the subject of the second discourse.

First, the same motives and the same means that formerly sufficed to form a permanent society of all the sovereignties of Germany are within the reach and power of the present sovereigns, and may suffice to form a permanent society of all the Christian sovereignties of Europe.

Second, the approbation which most of the sovereigns of Europe gave to the project for an European society, which Henry the Great proposed to them, proves that it may be hoped such a project will be approved of by their successors.

These models of permanent societies [and] the approbation that was given an hundred years ago to the project of Henry the Great are sufficient to produce two very great pre-possessions in favour of the possibility of this. I know the weight of prepossessions, and that they make more impressions upon the generality of minds than true arguments fetched from the very bottom of the subject, and from necessary con-sequences of the first principles; but I plainly foresee they will never be sufficient entirely to determine spirits of the first order; that they will be continually finding out differences and inequalities between the European society which I propose and the societies I quote as models; that Henry IV might after all be deceived in thinking that possible which was in reality im-possible. Thus I find myself obliged to demonstrate everything strictly, and am resolved to use my utmost endeavours to trace back those very motives which induced the ancient sovereigns of Germany, and those of the last century, to desire an unalterable peace; and shall try to find out methods better than theirs to form a more important establishment.

As for sufficient motives, I believe that if anyone could propose a treaty which might render the union solid and unalterable and so give everyone a sufficient security for the perpetuity of the peace, the princes would find therein much fewer inconveniences, and those much less great, a greater number of advantages, and those much more great, than in the present system of war that a great many sovereigns, especially the least powerful, would begin by signing it, and afterwards would present it to others to sign; and that even the most powerful, if they examined it thoroughly, would soon find they could never embrace any resolution, nor sign any treaty, near so advantageous as this would be.

As for practicable and sufficient means, which consist in the articles of a treaty of union, made to be to everyone a sufficient security for the perpetuity of the peace, I have spared no pains to invent them, and I believe I have done it.

Now as, on the one side, those who have read the first sketches of the fourth discourse agree that a treaty which should be composed of such articles would form that sufficient security so sought after by politicians; and as, on the other side, the signing of those articles depends solely upon the will of the sovereigns, and all those princes would be so much the more inclined to be willing to sign them and to procure the execution of them, the more evidently they shall have seen the greatness of the advantages they may reap from them. We may conclude that on their side there will be no impossibility found in the execution of the project, and that the more they shall be convinced of this security and these advantages, the more easily they will be brought to execute it. The whole project then is contained in this single argument.

If the European Society which is proposed can procure for all the Christian princes a sufficient security for the perpetuity of the peace, both without and within their dominions, there is none of them that will not find it more advantageous to sign the treaty for the establishment of that society than not to sign it.[III]

Now, the European Society which is proposed *can* procure for all the Christian princes, a sufficient security for the perpetuity of the peace both within and without their dominions.[IV]

Therefore there will be none of them but what will find it much more advantageous to sign the treaty for the establishment of that society than not to sign it.[V]

The major, or the first, proposition contains the motives, and the proof of it may be found in the third discourse after the preliminary discourses, which I thought necessary in order to dispose the mind of the reader to conceive the force of the demonstration. The minor, or the second, proposition contains the means; the proof of it may be found in the fourth discourse. As for the last proposition, or the conclusion: that is the end that I proposed to myself in this work.

As this project may begin to be known in the courts of Europe either in the middle or towards the end of a war, or in the conferences, or after the conclusion of a peace, or even in the midst of a profound peace,[VI] it was necessary to show compendiously in the fifth discourse that, upon any of these occasions, it would produce both a great facility in concluding the peace, and a great desire to render it perpetual, if it was concluded.

Having observed that several were of opinion that even though the sovereigns of Europe should one by one have signed the treaty of union, yet there would, in all appearance, remain some difficulties, almost insurmountable, in the formation of the congress, and in the means how to begin and maintain such an establishment:[VII] I was obliged, in order to remove this doubt, to propose, in the sixth discourse, several articles to which the sovereigns may agree. Not that I thought there could be none proposed more useful for the rendering the establishment more solid in itself and more convenient for each member. All I pretend to prove is that those feigned difficulties, which men may form to themselves with respect to the execution of the establishment are very far from being insurmountable, since even the articles that I propose are sufficient for that execution, and that nothing hinders the sovereigns from agreeing to them.

Such is the analysis, such the order I have followed in this work. This is the fruit I have gathered from my meditations for above four years. This is the use I have made of the judicious criticisms of my friends. And now, if ever anybody proposed a subject worthy to be attentively examined by the most excellent wits and especially by the wisest ministers and the best princes, it may be said that this is it, since it treats of no less than of the means how to procure to all the sovereigns and nations of Europe the greatest felicity that a new establishment can possibly ever procure them.

It is easy to comprehend that the more methods this project shall carry in it for rendering the peace of Europe unalterable, the more it may contribute to facilitate the conclusion of that which is now treating at Utrecht: For the allies of the House of Austria desire peace as much as we do, but they do not care for it without sufficient security for its duration. And indeed, if we were to examine the interest of those allies in the present war, we should find that it all turns upon two principal heads. The first is a sufficient security for the preservation of their dominions against the great power of the House of France, which may in time find specious pretences and favourable opportunities to make conquests upon them and to introduce into their country a religion and government for which they have a very great aversion. The other head is a sufficient security for liberty of commerce, whether that of America or that of the Mediterranean; in these two commerces consists above half the revenue of England and Holland.

But what sufficient securities can be found for the weakest against the strongest? There are but two systems for this. The first is, if it can be done, sufficiently to weaken the strongest, which is either impossible or ruinous, though it is that which the allies follow in the present war to arrive at their chimerical equilibrium. The second is sufficiently to fortify the weaker, and to give him a force sufficiently superior, without depriving the stronger of any of his force, which is what I propose to do by a treaty of society that might give to the weaker a new augmentation of very strong allies, and who would be so much the stronger, as they would be much more closely united; not to deprive the stronger of anything he possesses, but to take from him the power of ever disturbing the others, either in their possessions at home or in their commerce abroad.

In my second draft I took in all the kingdoms of the world, but my friends observed to me that even though in following ages most of the sovereigns of Asia and Africa might desire to be received into the Union, yet this prospect would seem so remote and so full of difficulties that it would cast an air of impossibility upon the whole project, which would disgust all the readers and make some believe that, though it were even refrained only to the Christian part of Europe, the execution of it would be still impossible. Therefore I subscribed to their opinion, and that the more willingly, considering that the Union of Europe would suffice to preserve Europe always in peace, and that it would be powerful enough to maintain its frontiers and commerce in spite of those who should endeavour to disturb it. The general council it might establish in the Indies would soon become the arbiter of the sovereigns of that country, and, by its authority, hinder them from taking up arms. The credit of the Union would be much the greater amongst them, as they would be assured that it only desired securities for its commerce; that that commerce cannot but be very advantageous to them; that it does not aim at any conquests; and that it will never look upon any as enemies, but those who were enemies to peace.

If the reader is willing to form a sound judgment of the work, it is, in my opinion, necessary that he should make a stop at the end of every discourse, and ask himself what effect the proofs I bring have upon him. If he thinks them sufficient, he may go on, but if he does not think them so, that may proceed either from his still meeting with difficulties or from his not having read some passages with attention enough; and nothing is more common, even with the most thoughtful readers, than sometimes to want attention. In the first case he need only make a note of his doubts and observe whether they be not sufficiently cleared up in the following part of the work. In the second case, the only remedy is to read over again the passages he did not well understand. Otherwise he would act like a judge that should report and make a judgment after a superficial reading, and without having given sufficient attention to the principal evidences of the cause. I have endeavoured to make a concatenation between the thoughts that the mind might the more easily comprehend them. Now those who are not attentive enough to perceive this concatenation can never be sensible of the force of particular arguments, and much less of the force of a demonstration, which results from the assemblage of those arguments.

I own the title gives a prejudice to the work, but as I am persuaded that it is not impossible to find out means sufficient and practicable to settle an everlasting peace among Christians, and even believe that the means which I have thought of are of that nature, I imagined that if I myself first seemed to be uncertain as to the solidity of those means, and doubtful of the possibility of executing them, the readers, though never so well disposed in favour of the system, might really doubt of it too, and that their real doubtfulness might perhaps go further than my affected doubtfulness. It is not with things in which the design is to persuade men to action, as it is with things of pure speculation. The pilot who himself seems uncertain of the success of his voyage is not likely to persuade the passenger to embark. The undertaker who himself seems to doubt of the solidity of an important work which he proposed to undertake is not all likely to persuade others to join in the enterprise. Therefore I chose rather to venture being thought ridiculous in assuming an affirmative style, and promising in the title all that I hope to make good in the body of the work, than to run the risk by a false air of modesty and uncertainty of doing the least wrong to the public, by making men of sense look upon the project as whimsical and impossible to be put in execution, when I myself formed it in full expectation to see it one day executed.

. . .

Fundamental Articles

Article 1: The present sovereigns, by their underwritten deputies, have agreed to the following articles. There shall be from this day following a society, a permanent and perpetual union, between the sovereigns subscribed, and if possible among all the Christian sovereigns, in the design to make the peace unalterable in Europe; and in that view the Union shall make, if possible, with its neighbours – the Mahometan sovereigns – treaties of league, offensive and defensive, to keep each of them in peace within the bounds of his territory by taking of them and giving to them all possible reciprocal securities. The sovereigns shall be perpetually represented by their deputies in a perpetual congress or senate in a free city.

. . .

Article 2: The European Society shall not at all concern itself about the government of any state, unless it be to preserve the fundamental form of it, and give speedy and sufficient assistance to the princes in monarchies, and to the magistrates in republics, against any that are seditious and rebellious. Thus it will be a guarantee that the hereditary sovereignties shall remain hereditary, according to the manner and custom of each nation; that those that are elective shall remain elective in the country where election is usual; that among the nations where there are capitulations or conventions which are called *pacta conventa*, those sorts of treaties shall be exactly observed; and that those who in monarchies should have taken up arms against the prince, or in republics against some of the chief magistrates, shall be punished with death and confiscation of goods.

. . .

Article 3: The Union shall employ its whole strength and care to hinder, during the regencies, the minorities, the weak reigns of each state, any prejudice from being done to the sovereign, either in his person, or in his prerogatives, neither by his subjects, nor by strangers; and if any sedition, revolt, conspiracy, suspicion of poison, or any other violence should happen to the prince, or to the royal family, the Union, as its guardian and protectress born, shall send commissioners into that state to look into the truth of the facts, and shall at the same time send troops to punish the guilty according to the rigour of the laws.

. . .

Article 4: Each sovereign shall be contented, he and his successors, with the territory he actually possesses, or which he is to possess by the treaty hereunto joined. All the sovereignties of Europe shall always remain in the condition they are in, and shall always have the same limits that they have now. No territory shall be dismembered from any sovereignty, nor shall any be added to it by succession, agreement between different houses, election, donation, cession, sale, conquest, voluntary submission of the subjects, or otherwise. No sovereign, nor member of a sovereign family, can be sovereign of any state besides that, or those, which are actually in the possession of his family. The sovereigns who, by their deputies, are now going to sign this treaty, and those who, by their deputies, shall afterwards sign it shall be reputed and understood by this signing in consideration of the advantages they are all to reap from it mutually to have given up and renounced, both for themselves and successors, all the rights and pretensions they might have one upon the other, and particularly upon the territories of each other, under what title or of what nature soever they may be; so that they shall remain quit one with the other, and not only with the sovereigns who now sign the treaty, but also with those who shall afterwards sign it; and these latter, when they sign it, shall be reciprocally quit, both with those who have already signed it, and with those who are still to sign it. The rents which the sovereigns owe to the private persons of another state shall be paid as usual. No sovereign shall assume the title of Lord of any country, of which he is not in actual possession, or the possession of which shall not be promised him by the treaty hereunto joined. The sovereigns shall not be suffered to make an exchange of any territory, nor to sign any treaty among themselves, but with the consent and under the guarantee of the Union by the three fourths of the four and twenty voices, and the Union shall remain guarantee for the execution of reciprocal promises.

. . .

Article 5: No sovereign shall henceforth possess two sovereignties, either hereditary or elective; however, the electors of the Empire may be elected emperors so long as there shall be emperors. If by right of succession there should fall to a sovereign a state more considerable than that which he possesses, he may leave that which he possesses, and settle himself in that which is fallen to him.

. . .

Article 6: The kingdom of Spain shall not go out of the House of Bourbon, or the now House of France, so long as there shall be two males of that family, of the eldest branches or of the youngest branches, on condition that the elder shall be always preferred to the younger, and the elder branch to the younger branch.

. . .

Article 7: The deputies shall incessantly labour to digest all the articles of commerce in general, and of the different commerces between particular nations; but in such a manner as that the laws may be equal and reciprocal towards all the nations, and founded upon equity. The articles, which shall have passed by plurality of the voices of the present deputies, shall be executed provisionally according to their form and tenor till they be amended and improved by three fourths of the voices, when a greater number of members shall have signed the Union. The Union shall establish in different towns chambers for maintaining of commerce, consisting of deputies authorized to reconcile, and to judge strictly and without appeal, the disputes that shall arise either upon commerce or other matters between the subjects of different sovereigns in value above ten thousand livres. The other suits of less consequence shall be decided as usual by the judges of the place where the defendant lives. Each sovereign shall lend his hand to the execution of the judgments of the chambers of commerce, as if they were his own judgments. Each sovereign shall at his own charge exterminate his inland robbers and banditti and the pirates on his coasts, upon pain of making reparation, and if he has need of help, the Union shall assist him.

. . .

Article 8: No sovereign shall take up arms to commit any hostility, but against him who shall be declared an enemy to the European Society. But if he has any cause to complain of any of the members, or any demand to make upon them, he shall order his deputy to give a memorial to the Senate in the City of Peace, and the Senate shall take care to reconcile the differences by its mediating commissioners; or if they cannot be reconciled, the Senate shall judge them by arbitral judgment, by plurality of voices provisionally, and by the three fourths of the voices definitively. This judgment shall not be given till each senator shall have received the instructions and orders of his master upon the fact and till he shall have communicated them to the Senate. The sovereign who shall take up arms before the Union has declared war, or who shall refuse to execute a regulation of the Society, or a judgment of the Senate, shall be declared an enemy to the Society, and it shall make war upon him till he be disarmed and till the judgment and regulations be executed; and he shall even pay the charges of the war, and the country that shall be conquered from him at the time of the suspension of arms shall be forever separated from his dominions. If, after the Society is formed to the number of fourteen voices, a sovereign should refuse to enter into it, it shall declare him an enemy to the repose of Europe, and shall make war upon him till he enter into it, or till he be entirely dispossessed.

. . .

Article 9: There shall be in the Senate of Europe four and twenty senators or deputies of the united sovereigns, neither more nor less; namely, France, Spain, England, Holland, Savoy, Portugal, Bavaria and associates, Venice, Genoa and associates, Florence and associates, Switzerland and associates, Lorrain and associates, Sweden, Denmark, Poland, the Pope, Moscovy, Austria, Courland and associates, Prussia, Saxony, Palatine and associates, Hanover and associates, Ecclesiastical Electors and associates. Each deputy shall have but one vote.

. . .

Article 10: The members and associates of the Union shall contribute to the expenses of the Society and to the subsidies for its security, each in proportion to his revenues, and to the riches of his people, and everyone's quota shall at first be regulated provisionally by plurality and afterwards by the three fourths of the voices, when the commissioners of the Union shall have taken, in each state, what instructions and informations shall be necessary thereupon; and if anyone is found to have paid too much provisionally, it shall afterwards be made up to him, both in principal and interest, by those who shall have paid too little. The less powerful sovereigns and associates in forming one voice shall alternately nominate their deputy in proportion to their quotas.

. . .

Article 11: When the Senate shall deliberate upon anything pressing and provisionable for the security of the society, either to prevent or quell sedition, the question may be decided by plurality of voices provisionally; and before it is deliberated, they shall begin by deciding, by plurality, whether the matter is provisionable.

. . .

Article 12: None of the eleven fundamental articles above named shall be in any point altered without the *unanimous* consent of all the members; but as for the other articles, the Society may always, by the three fourths of the voices, add or diminish, for the common good, whatever it shall think fit.

Notes

[I]   Subject of the first discourse.
[II] Subject of the second discourse.
[III] Subject of the third discourse.
[IV] Subject of the fourth discourse.
[V]   Purpose of the work.
[VI] Subject of the fifth discourse.
[VII] Subject of the sixth discourse.

Chapter 6

James Francis Edward Stuart ('King James III'): *Declaration of James the Third, King of England, Scotland and Ireland, to all his Subjects of the three Nations and to all foreign Princes and States to serve as a foundation for a lasting peace in Europe* (1722)

The obligation which we owe to our own honour and to the safety and tranquillity of our native country, which above all ties is the dearest to us, and the tenderest; the steps which are so apparently taken to enslave our people; the late un-exampled violation of the freedom of elections by which the British Constitution is entirely subverted and a new sort of tyranny introduced unknown to any other nation; conspiracies invented on purpose to give pretence for new oppressions and to arm the nation against itself at a time when it was well known all attempts were imaginary and impracticable; the lives, liberties and fortunes of our subjects at the mercy of infamous informers, cruelly exposed everyday to subordination and perjury; and every honest well-meaning man in a state of proscription.

These and many other considerations of the highest importance to the repose and security of our people, exciting our compassion, have engaged us to enter seriously into ourself to examine and consult our heart what sacrifice to make on our part for the public peace, and to consider earnestly of some method of restoring tranquillity, especially to those kingdoms of which we are the natural and undoubted father.

To express therefore and signify in the most public manner our ardent desire to compose all present differences, and to avert all future evils, that no blame may be now or hereafter imputed to us, but that whatever calamities shall happen may be onely and solely chargeable upon the obstinacy of ambition of others, we declare that provided the Elector of Hanover will deliver quietly to us the possession of our own kingdoms, we will make no inquisition for any thing that is past. We will acknowledge him in the same dignity of king in his native dominions, inviting all other princes and states to do the same. We will live in brotherly amity with him, and contribute all our endeavours to establish him and his family in prosperity and royal grandeur, where an uncontested right will free him from the crime and reproach of tyranny and usurpation, and a quiet conscience make a crown fit easy upon his head, leaving at the same time his succession to our dominions secure, whenever in due course his natural right shall take place.

Let him compare a calm undisturbed reign over a willing and obedient people, his natural born subjects, with the restless unquiet possession of an usurper in a strange land, where authority forcing the inclinations of the people can only be supported by blood, violence, and rapine, eternally subject to fears and alarms even when no danger appears, for gilt can never rest. Let him consider a fixed and solid establishment of regal power in himself and his posterity, exposed to no chance, with the frail and uncertain settlement of an usurped title which must and shall, whilst we have breath or any descendants in being, be forever disputed. Let him reflect that the divine justice never fails sooner or later to chastise the oppressor, and to redress the innocent and injured. Instead of advising with an imperious ministry, as much his tyrants as the nations, let him consult his reason, let him ask his conscience, let him examine his interest and his glory; nay his very ambition will advise him to descend from a throne, which must be always shaking, to mount another where his seat will be firm and secure.

We conjure all Christian princes and states to be aiding and assisting to us in this our just and amicable proposal, whereby without effusion of blood, or any national or public disturbance, justice may be done to an injured prince, and an equivalent provided sufficient to content an aspiring one.

As a farther inducement to all Christian powers to enter more seriously and deliberately into this important proposition, we offer ourself to make good on our part all such alliances as have been already contracted with our kingdoms, conducive to the peace and tranquillity of Europe, and to enter into any new ones that may be judged necessary for the farther strengthening and securing thereof.

That there may likewise remain no objection from the fears and apprehensions of any one man in our own dominions, conscious of having offended against us, we promise a full, free, and universal pardon to all persons of whatever degree or condition within our realms, without any exception, who shall in any reasonable time return to their allegiance, or by any act and deed, advice or otherwise effectually contribute to such a happy accommodation as may put a period to all our private and public misfortunes: that every Englishman may hereafter live quietly under his own shade, enjoy his conscience undisturbed, and rest upon his pillow in peace.

We protest solemnly before God and man that nothing can be proposed to us to make our kingdoms happy and flourishing, and to quiet the minds of all men, but we will strive with the most zealous to promote.

Our desire is to embrace the whole body of our people without any distinction or reserve; to root up the very seeds of prejudice and division that all notes of discord, separation, or difference of parties and all reproachful denominations may be forever extinguished, and that the King and his people may have but one mind, one heart and one interest.

That humanity, that love of our country, and that good will to all men, which we make the rule of our actions, prompt and incline us in first place to the ways of mercy and peace.

It is therefore that waving all present application to foreign powers who, considering how much in reality our cause is their own, might reasonably be induced to aid us in vindicating that majesty which they behold oppressed and affronted in our person, and sacrificing all resentment, passion, or desire of revenge to public good, we now seek and condescend to shake hand even with those who have most injured us.

Given at our court at Lucca, this present tenth of September 1722, and in the twenty first year of our reign.

Postscript

Since we first proposed to publish this our declaration to the world, it is come to our knowledge that diverse of our subjects continue daily to be questioned and imprisoned upon pretence of intelligence with us; that informers, spies, and false witnesses are become so numerous, and are so openly caressed and encouraged, that no innocence is safe; that the terror of these arbitrary and violent proceedings is become dreadful to all men, nor excepting the very army, where without any regard to past services, the poor soldier is exposed to cruel and unmerciful punishments upon the testimony of secret informers without any other crime pretended but bare suspicion of affection to us and our cause.

We think it therefore a farther duty incumbent upon us, as a Christian king and the common father of our people, to interpose on behalf of the innocent and to forewarn all judges, justices, privy counsellors, or counsellors, officers and commanders in chief, magistrates of all degrees, sheriffs and persons sworn upon juries to take especial heed how they rashly involve themselves in the crime of persecuting the innocent, or dip their hands in the blood of the guiltless, for we are resolved to keep a strict and exact account of the sufferings of the very meanest of our people.

And because amongst other poor, unmanly, and ungenerous practices, nothing has been so much encouraged as slander and malicious aspersions upon our own person, we declare that we would disdain even to recover our throne by such vile arts as are practised to keep us out of it; that we are incapable of using any methods even for our restoration, but what are consistent with our honour and the dignity of our birth, despising all those unmannerly calumnies which we scorn to retort even with truths unbecoming the countenance of one prince to another.

There is one above us who can silence the father of falsehood when he pleases, and upon him we rely.

Chapter 7

Cardinal Alberoni: *Scheme of A 'Perpetual Diet' for Establishing the Public Tranquillity* (1736)

. . .

Part IV. Scheme of a Perpetual Diet

I. There shall be, for the future, a perpetual diet of the ministers or deputies of all the sovereign princes and states of Christendom, established at Ratisbon, to be under the same regulations and to have the same forms and manner of proceeding as are now in use in the German Diet held there.

II. All controversies that may arise amongst Christian princes or states on account of religion, successions, marriages, or any other cause or pretence whatever, are to be there determined by such a number of voices as are required to make a majority by the Constitution of the Empire: Such determination to be made within the space of one year, to be computed from the time any controversy shall be brought before the Diet.

III. In case any of the powers at variance shall refuse to submit to such determination within six months after the same shall be notified authentically and in form, then such power to be treated as a disturber of the public tranquillity, and the Diet is to proceed against such with military execution until he or they shall submit to their decisions, and make reparation for all wrongs, and reimburse all the expenses of the war entered into for that purpose. The quota of the forces of every prince or state to be fixed upon the foot of the matriculation now established in the Empire.

Thus I have given the outlines of the most comprehensive designs that have ever yet appeared in the world – one for subduing the haughty and vast empire of the Turks; another for a partition of the conquests, and the third for securing them by this scheme of a perpetual diet. What success my endeavours will have, must be the product of time, but the judicious will soon discern the labyrinths I must have passed though to bring such projects to any shape or consistency.

Before I conclude, it will be very proper to give some character of the Turks. Of all nations upon earth, they are the most finished bigots and slaves to superstition, as well in peace as in war; a notion prevailing amongst them that they only are *true believers*, or as it were, the *elect*.[1] It is upon that fallacious principle that they assure themselves of success in all their enterprises, but if they happen to be disappointed in the event, they conclude their prophet is angry with them for some transgressions of his law, which always discourages them from making any new attempts or even any tolerable resistance against Christian armies. This ill grounded doctrine has, however, been often advantageous to the Christians in their quarrels with the infidels, and particularly in the last Hungarian War, for after they were defeated before Belgrade, the place surrendered immediately, though it was provided with a garrison of twenty thousand men, as was observed before, with a year's provision and that it is one of the strongest fortresses in the world.

It is through the prevalence of this opinion that no people are so slow in recovering their losses or disgraces, for they think it is in vain to make any vigorous efforts until they have some visible marks of being restored to the good graces of their false prophet. It is very certain their naval power has not yet recovered the blow which they received at Lepanto near two hundred years ago, nor their land forces that at Vienna in 1683. Their empire has, indeed, been in a languishing state for more than a century, which has been, with great justice, imputed to a general corruption and venality scarcely known in the world since the time of the Romans, for everything is sold amongst these true believers. And as no nation is so slow

---

[1] Emphases original.

in recovering their misfortunes, so none supports them with less fortitude, pouring all their wrath upon the heads of their unhappy commanders, whenever victory turns against them.

There is, indeed, an important objection that lies in our way, and must be removed before we conclude, that is, that in case the Christians should make war upon the Turks, the Persians and Moors (subjects of Morocco) would run to their assistance, all professing the doctrine of Mahomet. Let us suppose for the present this to be true, it would, in my judgment, produce no other alteration in our scheme than to augment the Christian forces, which can be effected with the greatest facility, considering the formidable armies now on foot in Christendom. Should that be the case, Persia must be attacked by the troops of her Czarian Majesty, and those of Poland, Denmark, and Sweden on the side of Georgia, Gilan, and the provinces on the South of the Caspian Sea. And as to the Moors, it will be easy to give them a diversion on the side of the Atlantic and in Barbary; and nothing can furnish us with a more despicable idea of the discipline of those people than the many fruitless attempts upon so inconsiderable a place as Ceuta for so many years. Besides, it must be observed that their hatred to the Turks is implacable.

But there are the most convincing reasons to believe that neither the Moors nor Persians would take any part in the Turkish quarrels as well on account of religious differences as interest; nor have I been able to collect from any history that the Persians ever sent succours to the Turks in any of their wars with the Christians. There are no nations in the world so piqued at each other, though both derived from the same stock; and the hatred of the Persians to their brethren is so boundless that it is a saying amongst them: 'There is more merit in killing one Turk than nineteen Christians'.

To this we must add that conquest of Turkey in Europe might be well effected before either the Persians or Moors could send any succours, considering the present shattered and ruinous condition of their armies and affairs. But as all those Mahometan nations – Turks, Persians and Moors – have for several years been harassed and wasted by intestine wars and rebellions, it would seem as if the divine hand was directing the Christian sword to put a period to the dominion of the infidels, and to accomplish a prophecy which is in several copies of their Alcoran, that in the latter times the sword of the Christians will rise and drive them from their empire.

Chapter 8

Pierre André Gargaz: *A Project of Universal and Perpetual Peace* (1779)

. . .

Infallible means for establishing and maintaining perpetual peace between all the sovereigns of Europe and their neighbours

First Means

Besides the mediator, known under the name of ambassador or *chargé d'affaires*, that each sovereign is accustomed to maintain in each foreign court, there shall be established in the city of Lyons, or in such other place as shall be considered the most suitable, a perpetual Congress, composed of one mediator for each sovereign of Europe and one for each of his neighbours who shall be pleased to enter into the universal union. As soon as there shall be ten mediators at the designated place (provided that there are at least five, representing hereditary sovereigns), they shall there pass judgment, by a plurality of votes, upon all the differences of their masters.

When the votes are equal, all shall side with the decision of the President, who shall always be the mediator of the oldest hereditary sovereign (that is to say, he who is the senior in age) who shall be present at the meeting which shall be convoked by any mediator whomsoever, hereditary or elective.

REFLECTIONS:

The first sovereign who shall adopt this union will probably communicate it to all those of his *confrères* whom he shall know to be inclined toward perpetual peace, and will invite each one of them to send a mediator to the place which he shall consider the most suitable for the establishment of the said Congress.

The mediators will be chosen by the sovereigns, and will be, without doubt, the most pacific, the most enlightened, and the most upright that they are able to find among their counsellors; consequently this august assembly will be the élite of the best minds of all Europe; and all the allied sovereigns will doubtless be proud to have them for counsellors and to acquiesce in their decisions.

This worthy and judicious Congress (by its integrity, by its ability, and by the full liberty that it will have of speaking without fear of displeasing any one) will, infallibly, by its just and impartial deliberations, exercise a moderating influence upon all the councils of the courts, which are, for the most part, too much attached to the imaginary interests and honours of their own countries, to the prejudice of other nations.

Second Means

On land and on sea, all the hereditary sovereigns shall yield precedence to the eldest of their *confrères*, and the latter shall accept it with all the politeness appropriate between true friends, without any regard to their power or to the antiquity of their houses or of their sovereignties. All the elective sovereigns shall likewise yield precedence to the eldest of their *confrères*, and to all the hereditary sovereigns.

REMARKS:

It is proper for the electives always to give the precedence to the hereditaries, because, it being regulated by age, the hereditaries would almost never have it, for the reason that the electors ordinarily elect sovereigns who are very old.

According to this system, the precedence will do as much honour to him who shall give it as to him who shall receive it, because each will conform himself to the honourable order established by nature and by reason. Instead of which, under the present system, the precedence does honour neither to him who receives it, nor to him who gives it, because most often it is only a sham abasement imposed by him who receives it upon him who yields it; an abasement not always pleasing to a sovereign who sees himself the elder and who has reason to believe himself more powerful, more sagacious, and more upright than is he before whom he abases himself.

One of the most ancient, widespread, and respectable customs of today among well-educated people of the same condition is that of yielding precedence to elders. Consequently, the sovereigns being all of the same condition (lieutenants of the Supreme Being) and, like him, inclined to beneficence, I dare flatter myself that they will all make it a duty and even a pleasure to conform themselves to the same custom, because it always betokens a respect really due to seniority of age.

Third Means

Each sovereign shall content himself with the countries of which he shall be found to be in possession at the time of the first deliberation of the Congress, except those that shall be found to be the subject of some dispute, which by the said first deliberation shall be awarded and united to such sovereignties as the mediators shall judge proper. That is to say, each sovereignty shall remain within the limits which shall be assigned or confirmed to it by the said first deliberation, without being able to be enlarged or diminished for any reason whatever – not even by right of appanage, or of dot, or of dower. All those things shall be paid in money or in products, but never in lands, because that has occasioned, and would certainly occasion again, an infinity of wars. There shall be made merely all the exchanges that the Congress shall deem proper of far distant countries in order to bring them near to the centre of the sovereignties and to acquire them.

NOTE:

This article, which may be considered as the basis of all the others, will surely please every upright sovereign, because he has no unjust desires to encroach upon the estate of another; and it will really be much more glorious for each sovereign to adopt it than to seek to extend the borders of his empire into the domains of others.

Fourth Means

If any sovereign in the union dies leaving no heir presumptive or if he carries his military forces into any foreign country whatever before having obtained the permission of the Congress, the said Congress shall elect (to replace him, even by force of arms, in all the estates and honours attached to the sovereignty) one of the *princes légataires* of a sovereign house whom it shall consider the most able to render happy his own people and those of his neighbours in governing a sovereignty, without any regard for the relatives of him who shall be replaced. Each sovereign of the union shall furnish all the aid that the Congress shall deem proper to establish and maintain in his sovereignty the prince whom it shall have chosen.

For the welfare of society, it is most expedient that the Congress shall not have any regard for the relatives of him, who shall be replaced, to the end that all may be interested to preserve his life and to prevent him from making war on any foreign power for the purpose of keeping the sovereignty in their family.

Fifth Means

There shall be left to all the nations entire freedom of commerce on land and on sea. That is to say, each sovereign shall be free to cause to enter into and to go out from his states all kinds of merchandise and munitions, even of war, and to exact, throughout his possessions, all the taxes he shall wish upon the imports and exports of anything whatsoever, without any sovereign having the right to object thereto for any reason.

Sixth Means

Each sovereign shall always be free to construct and maintain, on land and on sea, all fortresses (provided that they be distant two thousand five hundred geographical paces from the borders), war vessels, and troops – all armed and disciplined as he shall deem proper – so that he may at all times be able to maintain good order in his states and always be ready to defend himself against anyone who shall dare to attack him or his neighbours.

There is nothing so justifiable as maintaining oneself in one's lawful possessions, and nothing more effective than having good fortifications and good troops to guard them well, because they so greatly disconcert invaders that they dare not even attack them.

Seventh Means

Each sovereign shall perpetually maintain an invariable number of regiments, companies, officers, and chaplains for his land and sea services. As soon as there shall be lacking a single one (whoever it may be, from the highest of the general officers down to and including the last sub-lieutenant and chaplain), he shall be replaced without any delay. In each company, there shall always be at least twenty men and as many more as the sovereign shall wish for his pleasure alone or for his needs so that the numbers of privates, of corporals, and of sergeants shall be the only ones which shall increase or diminish proportionally one with the other.

REMARKS:

By the strict observance of this seventh means, there will never be idle officers or too many novices. All those who, by reason of their birth or their personal merit, shall have the right to aspire to various grades will be able to rise in time of peace as much as in time of war; and they will never be, as they are in time of peace, interested to bring about war or even to desire it. When in time of peace one leaves the places of officers and chaplains vacant, and in time of war fills them, simple good sense suggests that that naturally excites a great number of persons of credit to desire and even to bring war about so that they may attain the said places or cause their protégés to do so.

Common sense assures, too, without any doubt, that there are many persons who make war last through the justifiable fear they have that they or their protégés may be discharged as soon as peace is made, from which one must conclude that the decreasing of the number of officers in time of peace is a very bad and very unjust policy: very bad, because it causes war to last, and very unjust, because it abandons honest people who have worked hard, and leaves them without any means of supporting themselves.

These gentlemen have no other profession than that of soldier; and having very few or no resources besides, the government ought to maintain them all honestly, according to their condition, in time of peace just as in time of war.

The policy of discharging, at the end of the war, the private soldiers and the sailors who have no means of gaining their living is no less unfair. One ought equally to maintain them in time of peace, because, society being always burdened with them, they do not cost it as much in supporting them while under discipline as in disbanding them, which often forces them to resort to robbery in order to have the wherewithal to live.

In time of peace one ought also to maintain these poor fellows and to occupy them in repairing or constructing ships, fortresses, dykes, highways, bridges, irrigation canals, roads etc. At the end of the war one ought to discharge only those who have the means to support themselves honestly by working according to their condition, without being a charge upon or doing wrong to any one.

Eighth Means

The nobility will be able, without derogation to their position, to occupy themselves in many arts and trades, principally in agriculture, in the production of silks, cottons, hemp, linens, woollens and jewellery, in printing, in commerce etc., buying and selling again at wholesale or at retail all sorts of merchandise.

This eighth means will bind the nobility to protect peace in an especial manner, in order that they may not be troubled in the commerce which will do them as much honour as war and will give them much more profit.

. . .

Chapter 9

Charles Alexandre de Calonne:
The Political State of Europe at the Beginning of 1796, OR Considerations on the Most Effectual Means of Procuring A Solid and Permanent Peace (1796)

. . .

Preface

. . .

Undoubtedly each power will be delirious of obtaining, as far as is allowed by the law of events, whatever will appear conducive to increase the prosperity of its subjects, and necessary to incapacitate France from being hurtful; and this is not from a spirit of conquest, but in order to maintain (it might be properly said: *to perfect*) the equilibrium of Europe. But I repeat again that this is not what I have engaged to consider. I refer everything to the object of a general pacification, and to my favourite argument that whatever depends solely on the fate of arms is not the most efficacious expedient to render it speedy and permanent.

It is from this intimate persuasion that I have allowed myself the liberty of observing that, whatever is entertained of the extreme debility of France, if the distance is measured between retaking by open force what has been lost and conquering what is desired, it is difficult to conceive how the one and the other of these objects can be effected in a short space of time; but that, on the contrary, by pursuing the grand plan of healing and restorative measures which had been announced at first, and to which we Frenchmen are, for the

80

satisfaction of our consciences, bound to believe that the powers still virtually adhere, every desirable object would be more easily and more speedily obtained: a permanent peace, reasonable indemnities, an effectual security better guaranteed by the well understood agreement of the reciprocal interests than it could possibly be by the acquisition of fortresses or increase of dominion.

I endeavoured to develop and to strengthen this idea by associating it with the first principles of civil order. Upon these principles I have demonstrated that the real means – I think even I said the *only* means – to secure a permanent peace in Europe and to preserve public tranquillity from a series of immeasurable calamities, troubles and commotions was to use every possible endeavour to induce France to re-enter under the general laws of nations by adopting a regular government, that is, a government founded, not on the chimerical rights of man in his ideal state, but on his essential rights in the state of society; on the inviolability of the right of property which must form its basis; on the reciprocal duties which connect man with man, and which constitute the right of nations; lastly, on the establishment of a real plan of finance which, from a regard to public faith and to the rights of the citizens, must be circumscribed within the limits of the resources of every legitimate government. Those limits, those duties, those primordial rights, those bonds of society are the only preservers of the true equilibrium between the powers, the only guarantees of the tranquillity of nations. And if the war which is now necessary is not accompanied with those political expedients which lead to this desirable end, it will always be indispensable, because its principal cause will always subsist; it will not lead to a true peace, however favourable events may be, since it will not destroy that which renders peace impossible.

. . .

Chapter III: What measures are to be pursued in order to obtain a solid and permanent peace

War ought always to be directed to the attainment of peace. It would be iniquitous and inhuman if it had any other tendency.

Whatever, therefore, is necessary to obtain peace, ought to enter into the plan of the war; and military successes that did not promote this end would be fruitless.

If this proposition be true in general, it is more so for England which, being the most commercial country in the world, is also the most interested in a general pacification.

But neither England nor Europe will obtain peace (I mean permanent peace) by force of arms alone; it is likewise essential to adopt every measure that may tend to the re-establishment of a reasonable and solid government in France – a government compatible with the repose of other nations. As long as France has nothing but a phantom of political existence; as long as it will be a prey to discord, uncertain in her views, and continually agitated by the collision of the different ruling factions; as long as it will be subject to experiments of governments, which appear and disappear like so many fugitive shadows, so long will it be vain and nugatory to treat with her. Can a solid superstructure be laid on an unstable and a moving ground? Is it not evident that, whatever was concluded with a chimerical and impracticable government could have but a transient and a momentary existence?

This palpable truth is supposed to be controverted by examples which seem to evince that the changes of constitutions in France have not occasioned the violation of its treaties. The neutrality of America, Denmark, Sweden and Switzerland is alleged as a proof. It has remained inviolate since the beginning of the revolution, in spite of the vicissitudes of factions . . .

But because France, at the same moment that she declared war against all its neighbours, excepted the Swiss Republic, from whom it had nothing to fear . . .; because, in the midst of her anarchy, France has not disturbed the neutrality of very distant countries with whom she had no particular concerns and who became useful by supplying her wants; because by consenting to a peace with Prussia and Spain, she exonerated herself from a burden without ceasing to employ her numerous armies; because these two powers, having ventured to negotiate with the most versatile government in the world, having had no cause as yet to repent of treaties scarcely ratified; does it follow that other powers in the immediate vicinity of France who have various and multiplied concerns with her . . . can expect a solid and permanent peace before a government susceptible of stability can be securely established? Can a conclusion be applied from one case to another when they are so widely different? Can a country which has no particular concern with the Republic be compared to another which affords continual subjects of uneasiness and immediate objects to gratify her rapacity? Because a nation, which had ten different enemies to contend with, has treated with two or three, is it a just inference to suppose that it will or can discontinue the war, when it is demonstrated that war forms the most essential part of its existence; that it will and can live in peace with the surrounding monarchies, while it still is in the delirium of an anti-monarchical system and of a constitution as essentially the enemy of all thrones as it is irreconcilable with peace and tranquillity?

. . .

The French Republic is, by its very constitution, an enemy to peace. It is a democracy in a great empire; and a powerful democracy has never been pacific. The annals of the world attest this, and the reason is obvious. The government of the multitude, always restless and presumptuous, rejects conciliatory measures. Impelled solely by passion, it disdains formalities, and is careless of consequences. To a republic, all means appear legal, all means possible. Incapable of repose in itself, it threatens continually the tranquillity of its neighbours. What is true of republics in general is still more so when applied to the democracy of an armed nation, which presents the image of a vast camp whose warlike youth, brought up in blood, accustomed to plunder, and breathing nothing but battles, is unfit for any other profession but that of arms. What still more increases its antipathy to peace is the state of convulsion, effervescence and disorder in which it moves, because it is formed on principles subversive of the fundamental law which unites all nations; because it has broken every tie of common interest, and overthrown all the fences of public security in neither respecting the right of property nor that of nations. Whoever does not perceive that such a government, placed in the centre of Europe, must be productive of incessant wars, prove an universal calamity and the scourge of mankind, would not be more forcibly convinced by any additional arguments we might adduce to corroborate this truth.

Perhaps we shall place it nearer the reach of common apprehension in observing that whatever owes its existence to disorder cannot preserve it but by disorder; that whatever is supported by commotion must be an enemy to repose . . . Let what we said respecting the necessity to which the Revolutionists were reduced, of having recourse to war, and of declaring it against all the powers, be called back to our recollection. The same reasons still subsist. These reasons will compel them to continue the war and to renew it after every momentary suspension of hostilities. War will be indispensable to France as long as France remains without a permanent government, without a system of finance analogous to the public interest, without a chief magistrate materially concerned in the maintenance of order and tranquillity. It is written in the sacred oracles that *righteousness and peace have kissed each other*. The opposites of righteousness and peace are likewise inseparable. Revolution and war are both very intimate. They are two allies, whom it is very difficult to separate. Who does not know that a foreign war is a certain resource against civil commotions? To conclude, as many do, that a peace with France would be the surest means to subdue it, as she would thus be left to her own rage and her intestine dissensions, is an implied concession that peace cannot be obtained at present, since it is evident that the same considerations must induce the present rulers of France to reject it; and it is not to be supposed that they will prefer a situation which, to them particularly, will be worse than war itself.

Part II

Rousseau, Bentham and Kant on Perpetual Peace

Chapter 10
Perpetual Peace through Physical Force: Rousseau's Plan

The concluding text in Part I was a direct attack on the French Revolution – a transformative event in history. Exactly four decades before Calonne's polemic, in 1756, Jean-Jacques Rousseau (1712–78) was in the process of developing highly unorthodox ideas which would contribute precisely to the emergence of that revolution. Having recently moved to l'Hermitage, a secluded cottage near Montmorency lent to him by Madame d'Épinay, Rousseau was about to engage in what would prove the most significant projects of his maturity, namely, *La Nouvelle Héloïse*, the *Social Contract* and *Émile*. Each of these projects came to fruition in the six years he spent in Montmorency, all being published between January 1761 and May 1762.[1] His Montmorency period, in other words, would establish Rousseau as one of the most influential political philosophers of all time.[2] Today few works are as much studied as the *Social Contract* in political theory, and few phrases as well known as the first sentence in its Chapter One: 'Man is born free; yet everywhere he is in chains'.[3]

Prior to his arrival in Madame d'Épinay's cottage, Rousseau had already published his *Discourses* on *the Sciences and the*

---

[1] Grace Roosevelt, *Reading Rousseau in the Nuclear Age* (Philadelphia, PA: Temple University Press, 1990), pp. 92–3.

[2] For a detailed account of this stage of Rousseau's career, see Maurice Cranston, *The Noble Savage: Jean-Jacques Rousseau, 1754–1762* (London: Allen Lane, The Penguin Press, 1991).

[3] See Jean-Jacques Rousseau, *The Social Contract and Other Later Political Writings*, ed. Victor Gourevitch (Cambridge: Cambridge University Press, 1997), p. 41.

Arts (1750), on *the Origin of Inequality* (1754), and on *Political Economy* (1755). He was already an accomplished intellectual, but not yet a path-breaking political thinker. The drafting of his two essays on perpetual peace corresponds to this transition phase in his intellectual development. Shortly after his return from Geneva in 1754, Rousseau accepted to select, edit, and organize the scattered pieces of writing by Abbé de Saint-Pierre. This project is believed to be his first in Montmorency in the lead-up to his great works. D'Argenson is quoted to have observed as early as January 1956 that 'Rousseau [was] busily engaged in the analysis of the political works of Saint-Pierre'.[4]

Rousseau seems to have accepted this task primarily because the idea was put to him by Madame Dupin, whose requests could not have been easy for him to refuse. Dupin's request, in turn, had been prompted and supported by Abbé de Mably – an old friend of Rousseau. Another, and intellectually more important, reason for Rousseau's acceptance of the project was his admiration for Saint-Pierre, whom he had met quite a few times in Dupin's salon in 1742. Rousseau was an unpublished young intellectual at the time. The Abbé, on the other hand, was an eighty-four-year-old, tired, 'simple, honest and true' man,[5] and we can reasonably speculate that a figure like him must have had a special appeal for young Rousseau.

It was probably not so much the Abbé's prolific writings on numerous topics that impressed Rousseau, but the fact that he had been almost a laughing stock in the policy circles of his time for at least three decades since the publication of his allegedly utopian perpetual peace plan (Chapter 5). Rousseau was, first and foremost, a relentless *reactionary*, in his youth as well as in his old age. The well-known inconsistencies in his writings and thought patterns are in part attributable to this quality. Rousseau was the kind of thinker who would not sacrifice the need for continuous 'reaction' to any concern over

---

[4] G. Lowes Dickinson, 'Introduction', in Jean-Jacques Rousseau, *A Project of Perpetual Peace: Rousseau's Essay*, translated and edited by Edith M. Nuttall (London: Richard Cobden-Sanderson, 1927), p. vii.

[5] Roosevelt, *Reading Rousseau in the Nuclear Age*, p. 91.

artificial 'consistency'. Throughout his life Rousseau remained a constant critic of the world, including his own person.[6] Hence, we find in Rousseau's writings more a tireless exhibition of dilemmas and injustices than any consistent attempts at solutions or remedies. A ridiculed 'utopian' like the Abbé – someone who had been in constant struggle against the established wisdom of his time, who refused to give in, who tried to make a difference, and who pursued a modest yet productive lifestyle – could only be a source of admiration for young Rousseau. Twelve years after Saint-Pierre's passing, and in the wake of his own flourishing ideas, when the opportunity presented itself to bring an order to the Abbé's disorganized pieces of writing, Rousseau did not have to think too long to accept Madame Dupin's request.

Editing and organizing Saint-Pierre's works was no easy task, however. Rousseau would soon discover the full extent of the challenge ahead, when seventeen volumes of the Abbé's writings as well as six boxes of notes and rough drafts were delivered to his door. Rousseau had to deal with 'twenty-three diffuse and muddled volumes full of boring passages, repetitions, and false or short-sighted views'.[7] Eventually he would set this project aside, but not before producing his essays on Saint-Pierre's *Polysynodie* and *Project for Perpetual Peace*. The thinker ended up writing two separate pieces on the Abbé's latter work: an 'Abstract' and a 'Judgment', both of which are reproduced in their entirety in the next chapter.[8]

The *Abstract* and *Judgment* incorporate a strange and difficult mix of Saint-Pierre's and Rousseau's views on perpetual peace. In fact, whether and to what extent these two essays embody Saint-Pierre's original project remains a moot point. To a large extent, we find Rousseau's personality and Rousseau's own approach to perpetual peace in these two

---

[6] It is no coincidence that the candour of his *Confessions* (1781) remains hardly rivalled even today. Furthermore, the 'introspective' tendencies that some observers detect in this autobiography also seem to point to Rousseau's inconsistencies: see Leo Damrosch, *Jean-Jacques Rousseau: Restless Genius* (Boston, MA: Houghton Mifflin Company, 2005), pp. 434–46.

[7] Roosevelt, *Reading Rousseau in the Nuclear Age*, p. 92.

[8] Some translators have preferred the titles 'Summary' or 'Statement' for the first essay, and 'Critique' for the second one.

essays. Both the *Abstract* and the *Judgment* inescapably draw on the Abbé's thoughts and numerous drafts on the topic. However, the necessity of boiling down this massive work to a manageable size and of ensuring an attractive and readable style, coupled with Rousseau's ever-present urge to say what *he* thinks *has to be said*, leads to an original plan that reflects more Rousseau than Saint-Pierre. It is precisely this fact that makes Rousseau's essays interesting for the present volume.

Pierre Hassner observes that the separation between Rousseau's *Abstract* and *Judgment* is less than clear-cut. 'The first already contains quite a few critical remarks', he argues, 'and the second is less categorically critical than one would think'.[9] This argument is certainly valid – but only if we subscribe to the view that Rousseau's *Judgment* (or *Critique*) was indeed meant to criticize Saint-Pierre's *Project*. The same observation may lend tacit support to the alternative view that the second essay, in particular, was in fact Rousseau's critique of the then existing socio-political order rather than the Abbé's work.[10] Grace Roosevelt usefully reminds us that, while the *Abstract* was translated into English and published in London in 1761, and may well have influenced Jeremy Bentham's essay (Chapter 13), the *Judgment*, which was more persistently directed at 'the perversely excessive selfishness of princes', could not be published, given the heavy censorship, until 1782, i.e. after Rousseau's death.[11]

It has not yet been established in literature whether and how Rousseau's approach to perpetual peace influenced Bentham's and Kant's projects. This requires systematic examination. We do know, however, that Rousseau's overall work had a deep impact on Kant – not necessarily in the sense of approval or adoption, but more in the sense of intellectual provocation. It is perhaps telling that on a rare occasion when

[9] Pierre Hassner, 'Rousseau and the theory and practice of international relations', in Clifford Orwin and Nathan Tarcov (eds), *The Legacy of Rousseau* (Chicago and London: The University of Chicago Press, 1997), p. 205.

[10] In fact, nowhere in the entire text, but in a single short paragraph, do we find Rousseau commenting specifically on Saint-Pierre's plan and nothing else; see the paragraph beginning with 'Accordingly . . .' in Chapter 11, p. 126.

[11] Roosevelt, *Reading Rousseau in the Nuclear Age*, pp. 107–9.

Kant was late for his extremely punctual daily afternoon walk (for which he had acquired a legendary reputation), he had been reading Rousseau's *Émile*.[12] Roosevelt notes that Kant always acknowledged a spiritual indebtedness to Rousseau, and argues even further that both Rousseau and Saint-Pierre are very much present in Kant's *Perpetual Peace* (Chapter 15).[13] This is certainly a reasonable hypothesis, but it is a hypothesis nonetheless, and requires in-depth analysis.[14] By juxtaposing Rousseau's and Kant's full texts in this volume, and by proposing to extend the scope of future analysis so as to include Bentham's full essay, we hope to have taken a useful step in the right direction.

Rousseau is notoriously difficult to classify along any political, ideological or theoretical spectrum. His writings contain the kernels of democratic ideals as well as totalitarianism, of individualism as well as collectivism, of liberalism as well as communism. On the other hand, no matter how he is classified, Rousseau is believed to have thought very little about international relations.[15] This background, of course, does not make it particularly easy to interpret and contextualize his approach to perpetual peace. However, on the whole, the *Abstract* and *Judgment* seem to operate against a 'realist' backdrop as is understood in today's International Relations theory.

Realism is visible in Rousseau's texts in three different ways. First of all, throughout the plan, Rousseau seems to alternate between 'what is' and 'what is doable' on the one hand, and 'what ought to be' on the other. He does not proceed from either one to the other in a linear fashion. It is as if he is trying to create a continuous dialectic between the actual and the possible, without losing sight of either of them. Perhaps in contrast to crude forms of realism, and as an extension of his

---

[12] Diané Collinson and Kathryn Plant, *Fifty Major Philosophers*, 2nd edn (London and New York: Routledge, 2006), p. 137.

[13] Roosevelt, *Reading Rousseau in the Nuclear Age*, p. 108.

[14] In any case, as Roosevelt notes, Kant may never have seen Rousseau's *Judgment*; see Roosevelt, *Reading Rousseau in the Nuclear Age*, p. 108.

[15] Hassner, 'Rousseau and the theory and practice of international relations', p. 200.

overall philosophy, he clearly does want 'to know what ought to be in order to judge soundly what is'.[16] However, after exploring the limits of the possible and desirable, he also keeps coming back to 'what is' and 'what is doable'. Secondly, Rousseau's realist depiction of human agency in his plan is worth noting.[17] The concluding paragraph of the *Abstract* is particularly striking: '[W]e have not assumed men such as they ought to be: good, generous, disinterested . . .', he notes, 'but such as they are: unjust, grasping and setting their own interest above all things'. Men, in this quasi-Hobbesian account, may well be crazy, but they have 'understanding enough to see their own interest'. Finally, we find in this plan not only prominent references to the idea of an automatic balance of power, but also an acceptance 'that the Treaty of Westphalia will perhaps forever remain the foundation of our international system'.

Within this overall realist framework, Rousseau proposes a system of collective security, and even foreshadows his famous and controversial idea of 'general will'.[18] At times, we find in his passages surprisingly hopeful statements, which almost resemble the utterly optimistic scholarly works of the immediate post-Cold War period.[19] At no stage does he advance a clear-cut proposal for an international 'government'. Not only does he use the terms 'federation' and 'confederation' interchangeably and quite loosely, he also emphasizes mutual benefits that would be derived from an almost metaphysical 'community of interests', which he believes is best approximated by Europe.

Rousseau's perpetual peace, similar to several previous plans, revolves around a re-institutionalization of Europe as a political unit. His selection of Europe as an especially meaningful site of

---

[16] Roosevelt, *Reading Rousseau in the Nuclear Age*, p. 114.

[17] For interesting observations on this point, see Grace Roosevelt, 'Rousseau versus Rawls on international relations', *European Journal of Political Theory*, 5:3 (2006), 301–20.

[18] For instance, the idea that 'private interests concerned, taken together, should not be stronger than the general interest'; see Chapter 11, p. 126; for a concise discussion of Rousseau's 'general will', see David L. Williams, 'Justice and the general will: Affirming Rousseau's ancient orientation' in *Journal of the History of Ideas*, 66 (2005), 383–411.

[19] He asserts, for example, that 'the day of those barbarian eruptions, which seemed to fall from the clouds, is gone forever'; see Chapter 11, p. 118.

collective governance is not arbitrary. In fact, the early part of the *Abstract* tries to ground this view in the natural and socio-cultural interconnectedness of the European Continent. Here one might find parallels with Rousseau's general preoccupation with the themes of civilization and society. In addition, though, Rousseau constantly revisits the question of 'force' throughout his plan: '. . . as soon as a society is founded, some coercive power must be provided to co-ordinate the actions of its members and give to their common interests and mutual obligations that firmness and consistency which they could never acquire of themselves'. Neither the idea of an evolved interconnectedness, nor the idea of necessary force is, of course, original. We have already seen different versions of these suggestions in previous chapters. However, Rousseau's particular (and admittedly uneasy) blend of these themes suggests a conceptual move towards an early 'realist' notion of global governance, in the sense that the underlying dynamics of the proposed unity are believed to be social (public and private) networks, yet these existing societal bonds are not taken to *entail* a perpetual and peaceful order. The necessity of using force, either in creating the envisaged state of peace,[20] or simply in maintaining it[21] (and the reality of power more generally), is a consideration that recurs in Rousseau's conceptualization.[22]

---

[20] See Rousseau's account of Henry IV's scheme; Chapter 11, pp. 127–31.

[21] In a statement reminiscent of his notorious 'whoever refuses to obey the general will shall be compelled to do so by the whole body; this means nothing less than that he will be forced to be free' in the *Social Contract*, Rousseau makes the following assertion in his *Judgment*: '. . . this requires the concurrence of wisdom in so many heads, a fortuitous concourse of so many interests, such as chance can hardly be expected ever to bring about. But, in default of such spontaneous agreement, the one thing left is force; and then the question is no longer to persuade but to compel, not to write books but to raise armies'; see Chapter 11, p. 126.

[22] For a realist interpretation of global governance, which argues, among others, that 'the demise of the nation-state as the dominant type of polity also spells the demise of its meta-value ensembles and of GG [global governance] as well' and that '. . . all . . . global governance systems . . . reinforce the essentiality of power and do nothing to overcome it', see Jennifer Sterling-Folker, 'Realist global governance: Revisiting *cave! hic dragones* and beyond', in Alice D. Ba and Matthew J. Hoffmann (eds), *Contending Perspectives on Global Governance: Coherence, Contestation and World Order* (London: Routledge, 2005), pp. 17–38, quotations from p. 32.

The source of Rousseau's *Abstract* and *Judgment* in the following chapter is Jean-Jacques Rousseau, *A Lasting Peace through the Federation of Europe* and *The State of War*, translated by C. E. Vaughan (London: Constable and Company Limited, 1917).

Chapter 11

Jean-Jacques Rousseau: *'Abstract'* and *'Judgment' of the Abbé de Saint-Pierre's Project for Perpetual Peace* (1756)

Abstract

Never did the mind of man conceive a scheme nobler, more beautiful, or more useful than that of a lasting peace between all the peoples of Europe. Never did a writer better deserve a respectful hearing than he who suggests means for putting that scheme into practice. What man, if he has a spark of goodness, but must feel his heart glow within him at so fair a prospect? Who would not prefer the illusions of a generous spirit, which overleaps all obstacles, to that dry, repulsive reason whose indifference to the welfare of mankind is ever the chief obstacle to all schemes for its attainment?

I doubt not that many readers will forearm themselves with scepticism as the best defence against the pleasure of yielding to conviction. I pity the melancholy mood which makes them take obstinacy for wisdom. On the other hand, I trust that every generous spirit will share the thrill of emotion with which I take up the pen on a subject which concerns mankind so closely. I see in my mind's eye all men joined in the bonds of love. I call before my thoughts a gentle and peaceful brotherhood; all living in unbroken harmony; all guided by the same principles; all finding their happiness in the happiness of all. And, as I dwell upon this touching picture, the idea of an imaginary happiness will cheat me for a few moments into the enjoyment of a real one.

In these opening words, I could not refrain from giving way to the feelings which filled my heart. Now let us do our best to reason coolly. Resolved as I am to assert nothing which I cannot prove, I have the right to ask the reader in his turn to deny nothing which he is unable to refute. It is not so much the reasoners I am afraid of as those who, without yielding to my proofs, steadily refuse to bring any arguments against them.

No man can have thought long upon the means of bringing any government to perfection without realizing a host of difficulties and obstacles which flow less from its inherent nature than from its relation to its neighbours. The result of this is that the care which ought to be given to its internal welfare has to be largely spent upon its outward security; and we are compelled to think more of providing for its defence against others than of making it as good as may be in itself. If the social order were really, as is pretended, the work not of passion but of reason, should we have been so slow in seeing that in the shaping of it either too much or too little has been done for our happiness? That – each one of us being in the civil state as regards our fellow citizens, but in the state of nature as regards the rest of the world – we have taken all kinds of precautions against private wars only to kindle national wars a thousand times more terrible? And that, in joining a particular group of men, we have really declared ourselves the enemies of the whole race?

If there is any way of reconciling these dangerous contradictions, it is to be found only in such a form of federal government as shall unite nations by bonds similar to those which already unite their individual members, and place the one no less than the other under the authority of the law. Even apart from this, such a form of government seems to carry the day over all others, because it combines the advantages of the small and the large state; because it is powerful enough to hold its neighbours in awe; because it upholds the supremacy of the law; because it is the only force capable of holding the subject, the ruler, the foreigner equally in check.

Such a form of government is to some extent a novelty and its principles have been fully understood only by the moderns. But it was not unknown among the ancients. The Greeks had their amphictyons and the Etruscans their lucumonies; the Latins had their feriæ and the Gauls their city-leagues; the Achæan League gave lustre to the death-struggles of Greece. But not one of these federations was built up with half the wisdom which has gone to the making of the Germanic Body, of the Helvetic League, or of the States General. And if these bodies are still so scarce and so far from the perfection which we feel they might attain, that is because the realization of the good invariably falls short of the ideal; because, in politics as in morals, the more we enlarge our knowledge, the more we are forced to recognize the extent of our misery.

In addition to these formal confederations, it is possible to frame others, less visible but nonetheless real, which are silently cemented by community of interests, by conformity of habits and customs, by the acceptance of common principles, by other ties which establish mutual relations between nations politically divided. Thus the powers of Europe constitute a kind of whole – united by identity of religion, of moral standard, of international law; by letters, by commerce, and finally by a species of balance which is the inevitable result of all these ties and, however little any man may strive consciously to maintain it, is not to be destroyed so easily as many men imagine.

This concert of Europe has not always existed, and the special causes which produced it are still working to preserve it. The truth is that, before the conquests of the Romans, the nations of this continent, all sunk in barbarism and each utterly unknown to the others, had nothing in common beyond the character which belonged to them as men – a character which, degraded by the practice of slavery, differed little enough in their eyes from that which constitutes the brute. Accordingly the Greeks, vain and disputatious, divided mankind, it may almost be said, into two distinct races: the one – their own, of course – made to rule; the other – the entire rest of the world – created solely to be slaves. From this principle it followed that a Gaul or a Spaniard was no more to a Greek than a Kaffir or Red Indian; and the barbarians themselves were as deeply divided from each other as the Greeks from all of them.

But when these men, born to rule, had been conquered by their slaves, the Romans, when half of the known universe had passed beneath the same yoke, a common bond of laws and government was established, and all found themselves members of the same empire. This bond was still further tightened by the recognized principle, either supremely wise or supremely foolish, imparting to the conquered all the rights of the conqueror; above all, by the famous decree of Claudius, which placed all the subjects of Rome on the roll of her citizens. Thus all members of the empire were united in one body politic. They were further united by laws and civil institutions which reinforced the political bond by defining equitably, clearly, and precisely, so far as this was possible in so vast an empire, the mutual rights and duties of the ruler and the subject, of one citizen as against another. The Code of Theodosius and the later legislation of Justinian constituted a new bond of justice and reason, which came in to replace the sovereign power at the very moment when it showed unmistakable signs of slackening. This did more than anything else to stave off the break-up of the empire and to maintain its authority even over the barbarians who ravaged it.

A third and yet stronger bond was furnished by religion; and it cannot be denied that Europe, even now, is indebted more to Christianity than to any other influence for the union, however imperfect, which survives among her members. So true is this that the one nation which has refused to accept Christianity has always remained an alien among the rest. Christianity, so despised in its infancy, ended by serving as a sanctuary to its slanderers. And the Roman Empire, which had persecuted it for centuries with fruitless cruelty, drew from it a power which she could no longer find in her own strength. The missionaries did more for her than any victory. She dispatched bishops to redeem the mistake of her generals, and triumphed by the aid of the priests when her soldiers were defeated. It is thus that the Franks, the Goths, the Burgundians, the Lombards, the Avars and many others ended by recognizing the authority of the Empire which they had mastered, by admitting, at least in appearance, not only the law of the Gospel, but also that of the prince at whose command it had been preached to them.

Such was the respect which this august body inspired even in its death-throes that, to the very end, its conquerors felt themselves honoured by the acceptance of its titles. The very generals who had humbled the Empire became its ministers and officials. The proudest kings welcomed, nay, even canvassed for, the patriciate, the prefecture, the consulate. And, like the lion who fawns upon the man he could easily devour, these terrible conquerors did homage to the imperial throne which they might at any moment have cast down.

Thus the priesthood and the Empire wove a bond between various nations which, without any real community of interests, of rights, or of mutual dependence, found a tie in common principles and beliefs, the influence of which still survives even after its foundation is withdrawn. The venerable phantom of the Roman Empire has never ceased to unite the nations which once formed part of it; and as, after the fall of the Empire, Rome still asserted her authority under another form,[1] Europe, the home of the temporal and spiritual powers, still retains a sense of fellowship far closer than is to be found elsewhere. The nations of the other continents are too scattered for mutual intercourse; and they lack any other point of union such as Europe has enjoyed.

There are other and more special causes for this difference. Europe is more evenly populated, more uniformly fertile; it is easier to pass from one part of her to another. The interests of her princes are united by ties of blood, by commerce, arts and colonies. Communication is made easy by countless rivers winding from one country to another. An inbred love of change impels her inhabitants to constant travel, which frequently leads them to foreign lands. The invention of printing and the general love of letters has given them a basis of common knowledge and common intellectual pursuits. Finally, the number and smallness of her states, the cravings of luxury and the large diversity of climates which Europe offers for their satisfaction, make them all necessary to each other. All these causes combine to make of Europe not, like Asia and Africa, a purely imaginary assemblage of peoples with nothing in common save the name, but a real community with a religion and a moral code, with customs and even laws of its own, which none of the component nations can renounce without causing a shock to the whole frame.

Now look at the other side of the picture. Observe the perpetual quarrels, the robberies, the usurpations, the revolts, the wars, the murders, which bring daily desolation to this venerable home of philosophy, this brilliant sanctuary of art and science. Consider our fair speeches and our abominable acts, the boundless humanity of our maxims and the boundless cruelty of our deeds; our religion so merciful and our intolerance so ferocious; our policy so mild in our textbooks and so harsh in our acts; our rulers so beneficent and our people so wretched; our governments so temperate and our wars so savage: and then tell me how to reconcile these glaring contradictions. Tell me if this alleged brotherhood of the nations of Europe is anything more than a bitter irony to denote their mutual hatred.

But, in truth, what else was to be expected? Every community without laws and without rulers, every union formed and maintained by nothing better than chance, must inevitably fall into quarrels and dissensions at the first change that comes about. The historic union of the nations of Europe has entangled their rights and interests in a thousand complications. They touch each other at so many points that not one of them can move without giving a jar to all the rest. Their variances are all the more deadly as their ties are more closely woven. Their frequent quarrels are almost as savage as civil wars.

Let us admit, then, that the powers of Europe stand to each other strictly in a state of war, and that all the separate treaties between them are in the nature rather of a temporary truce than a real peace, whether because such treaties are seldom guaranteed by any except the contracting parties or because the respective rights of those parties are never thoroughly determined and are therefore bound – they, or the claims which pass for rights in the eyes of powers who recognize no earthly superior – to give rise to fresh wars as soon as a change of circumstances shall have given fresh strength to the claimants.

More than this: the public law of Europe has never been passed or sanctioned by common agreement. It is not based upon any general principles. It varies incessantly from time to time and from place to place. It is therefore a mass of contradictory rules which nothing but the right of the stronger can reduce to order so that, in the absence of any sure clue to guide her, reason is bound, in every case of doubt, to obey the promptings of self-interest which in itself would make war inevitable, even if all parties desired to be just. With the best intentions in the world, all that can be done is to appeal to arms, or put the question to rest for the moment by a treaty. But the old quarrel soon comes to life again, complicated by others which have arisen in the interval. All is confusion and bewilderment. The truth is obscured so hopelessly that usurpation passes for right, and weakness for wrong. In this general welter, all bearings have been so utterly lost that, if we could get back to the solid ground of primitive right, few would be the sovereigns in Europe who would not have to surrender all that they possess.

Another source of war, less obvious but not less real, is that things often change their spirit without any corresponding change of form; that states, hereditary in fact, remain elective in appearance; that we find parliaments or states-general in monarchies, and hereditary rulers in republics; that a power, in fact dependent on another, often retains the semblance of autonomy; that all the provinces ruled by the same sovereign are not always governed by the same laws; that the laws of succession differ in different dominions of the same sovereign; finally, that the tendency of every government to degenerate is a process which no human power can possibly arrest. Such are the causes, general and special, which unite us only to work our ruin. Such are the reasons which condemn us to write our high-sounding theories of fellowship with hands ever dyed afresh in blood.

The causes of the disease, once known, suffice to indicate the remedy, if indeed there is one to be found. Everyone can see that what unites any form of society is community of interests, and what disintegrates is their conflict; that either tendency may be changed or modified by a thousand accidents; and therefore that, as soon as a society is founded, some coercive power must be provided to co-ordinate the actions of its members and give to their common interests and mutual obligations that firmness and consistency which they could never acquire of themselves.

It would, indeed, be a great mistake to suppose that the reign of violence described above could ever be remedied by the mere force of circumstances or without the aid of human wisdom. The present balance of Europe is just firm enough to remain in perpetual oscillation without losing itself altogether and, if our troubles cannot increase, still less can we put an end to them, seeing that any sweeping revolution is henceforth an impossibility.

In proof of this conclusion, let us begin by glancing at the present condition of Europe. The lie of the mountains, seas and rivers which serve as frontiers for the various nations who people it seems to have fixed forever their number and their size. We may fairly say that the political order of the continent is, in some sense, the work of nature.

In truth, we must not suppose that this much vaunted balance is the work of any man, or that any man has deliberately done anything to maintain it. It is there; and men who do not feel themselves strong enough to break it conceal the selfishness of their designs under the pretext of preserving it. But, whether we are aware of it or no[t], the balance continues to support itself without the aid of any special intervention. If it were to break for a moment on one side, it would soon restore itself on another, so that, if the princes who are accused of aiming at universal monarchy were in reality guilty of any such project, they gave more proof of ambition than of genius. How could any man look a project in the face without instantly perceiving its absurdity, without realizing that there is not a single potentate in Europe so much stronger than the others as ever to have a chance of making himself their master? No conqueror has ever changed the face of the world, unless, appearing suddenly with an army of unexpected strength or with foreign troops hardened to war in other service, he fell upon nations who were undisciplined. But where is a European prince to find an army of unexpected strength sufficient to crush all the others, when the most powerful of them has only a fraction of the strength belonging to the whole body and all the rest are watching so carefully to prevent him? Will he have a larger army than all of them put together? It is impossible; or he will only ruin himself the sooner; or his troops will be less good, just because they are more numerous. Will his troops be better trained? They will be proportionally fewer – not to mention that discipline is now everywhere the same – or will have become so before long. Will he have more money? Its sources are open to all, and no great conquest was ever made by money. Will he fall upon his enemies suddenly? Famine or fortresses will bar his way at every step. Will he strive to win his way inch by inch?

Then he will give his enemies time to unite their forces to resist him. Time, money and men will all be bound to fail him. Will he try to divide the other powers and conquer them one by one? The traditional maxims of Europe make such a policy impossible; the most stupid of princes would never fall into such a trap as that. In a word, as all the sources of power are equally open to them all, the resistance is in the long run as strong as the attack; and time soon repairs the sudden accidents of fortune, if not for each prince individually, at least for the general balance of the whole.

Now let us take the supposition that two or three potentates league themselves together to conquer all the rest. Those three potentates, take them where you please, will not together have behind them as much as half of Europe. The other half will, quite certainly, make common cause against them. They will therefore have to conquer an enemy stronger than themselves. I may add that their interests are too contradictory and their mutual jealousies too great to allow of such a project ever being formed. I may add further that, even if it were formed, even if it were put in act, even if it had some measure of success, that very success would sow the seeds of discord among our victorious allies. It is beyond the bounds of possibility that the prizes of victory should be so equally divided that each will be equally satisfied with his share. The least fortunate will soon set himself to resist the further progress of his rivals who, in their turn, for the same reason will speedily fall out with one another. I doubt whether, since the beginning of the world, there has been a single case in which three, or even two, powers have joined forces for the conquest of others, without quarrelling over their contingents or over the division of the spoil, and without, in consequence of this disagreement, promptly giving new strength to their common enemy. From all this it appears improbable that, under any supposition, either a king or a league of kings is in a position to bring about any serious or permanent change in the established order of Europe.

This does not mean that the Alps, the Rhine, the sea and the Pyrenees are in themselves a barrier which no ambition can surmount, but that these barriers are supported by others which either block the path of the enemy or serve to restore the old frontiers directly the first onslaught has spent its force.

The real strength of the existing order is, in truth, to be found partly in the play of conflicting policies which in nine cases out of ten keep each other mutually in check. But there is another bulwark more formidable yet. This is the Germanic Body which lies almost in the centre of Europe and holds all the other parts in their place, serving still more perhaps for the protection of its neighbours than for that of its own members – a body formidable to all by its size and by the number and valour of its component peoples, but of service to all by its constitution which, depriving it both of the means and the will to conquer, makes it the rock on which all schemes of conquest are doomed infallibly to break. In spite of all its defects, it is certain that, so long as that constitution endures, the balance of Europe will never be broken; that no potentate need fear to be cast from his throne by any of his rivals; and that the Treaty of Westphalia will perhaps forever remain the foundation of our international system. Accordingly, the system of public right, which the Germans study so diligently, is even more important than they suppose. It is the public right not only of Germany, but even, in many ways, of Europe as a whole.

But the established order, if indestructible, is for that very reason the more liable to constant storms. Between the powers of Europe there is a constant action and reaction which, without overthrowing them altogether, keeps them in continual agitation. Ineffectual as they are, these shocks perpetually renew themselves like the waves which forever trouble the surface of the sea without ever altering its level. The nations are incessantly ravaged, without any appreciable advantage to the sovereigns.

It would be easy for me to draw the same lesson from a study of the special interests of all the courts of Europe to show that those interests are so cunningly interwoven as to hold their respective forces mutually in check. But current theories of commerce and money have bred a political bigotry which works such rapid changes in the apparent interests of princes that it is impossible to arrive at any firm conclusion as to their real interests, seeing that everything now depends upon the economic systems, for the most part thoroughly crazy, which chance to flit through a minister's brain. For all that, commerce tends more and more to establish a balance between state and state, and by depriving certain powers of the exclusive advantages they once drew from it, deprives them at the same time of one of the chief weapons they once employed for imposing their will upon the rest.

If I have dwelt upon the equal distribution of forces which springs from the present constitution of Europe, it was in order to draw from it a conclusion of the highest importance to the project for establishing a general league among her peoples. For, if we are to form a solid and lasting confederation, we must have put all the members of it in a state of such mutual dependence that no one of them is singly in a position to overbear all the others, and that separate leagues, capable of thwarting the general league, shall meet with obstacles for-midable enough to hinder their formation. Failing this, the confederation will be nothing but an empty name; and under an appearance of subjection, every member of it will in reality be independent. But, if those obstacles are such as I have described at the present moment – a moment when all the powers are entirely free to form separate leagues and offensive alliances – judge what they would become if they were a general league, fully armed and ready at any moment to forestall those who should conceive the design of destroying or resisting it. That in itself is enough to show that such a federation, so far from ending in mere vain discussions to be set at defiance with impunity, would, on the contrary, give birth to an effective power capable of forcing any ambitious ruler to observe the terms of the general treaty which he has joined with others to set up.

From the above survey three certain conclusions may be drawn: the first that, Turkey excepted, there already exists among the nations of Europe a bond – imperfect indeed, but still closer than the loose and general ties which exist between man and man in the state of nature; the second, that the imperfections of this association make the state of those who belong to it worse than it would be if they formed no com-munity at all; the third, that these rudimentary ties which make such an association injurious make it at the same time readily capable of improvement, that all its members might easily find their happiness in what actually makes their misery, that from the state of war which now reigns among them they might perfectly well draw an abiding peace.

Let us now consider the means by which this great work, begun by chance, may be completed by wisdom. Let us ask how the free and voluntary association which now unites the states of Europe may be converted, by taking to itself the strength and firmness of a genuine body politic, into an authentic confederation. There is no doubt that such a creation, by giving to the existing bond the completeness which it now lacks, will increase all its advantages and compel all the parts to unite for the benefit of the whole body. But in order that this can be brought about this confederation must be sufficiently general that it includes all important powers. It must have a judicial body equipped to establish laws and ordinances binding upon all its members; sufficient power to oblige any state either to perform or abstain from actions commonly agreed upon. Finally, it must be solid and durable enough to prevent members from withdrawing the moment they perceive their own interests opposed to the general interest. These factors will ensure that the institution is wise, useful and indestructible. It is now a question of developing these ideas to see what consequences follow, what measures are called for in order to establish it, and what reasonable expectations one may have that it can be put into practice.

From time to time there takes place among us kinds of general diets under the name of congresses to which men come from all the states of Europe only to return to them; where men assemble in order to say nothing of importance; where public issues are treated as private matters; where there is general deliberation over whether the table is to be round or square, the room is to have this or that number of doors, a certain negotiator his face or his back towards the window, or whether another is to advance a couple of inches this way or that during his reception. These and a thousand similar topics of like importance have been uselessly argued about over the last three hundred years, and are worthy, to be sure, of detaining politicians of our own century.

It could come about that at one of these assemblies the members may be endowed with some common sense. It is not entirely impossible that they sincerely want the public good; and that, for reasons which will be worked out hereafter, one can further conceive that, having overcome many difficulties, they will be instructed by their respective sovereigns to sign the general confederation that I take in its essentials to be contained in the following five articles:

By the first the sovereigns will establish between themselves a perpetual and irrevocable alliance, and designate negotiators to convene in a specific place – a Diet or a permanent Congress – in which all the outstanding issues arising between the contracting parties are to be regulated and brought to an end by means of arbitration or decision.

By the second shall be specified the number of the sovereigns whose plenipotentiaries shall have a vote in the Diet; those who shall be invited to accede to the Treaty; the order, date and method by which the presidency shall pass, at equal intervals, from one to another; finally, the quota of their respective contributions and the method of raising them for the defrayal of the common expenses.

By the third the Confederation shall guarantee to each of its members the possession and government of all the dominions which he holds at the moment of the Treaty as well as the manner of succession to them, elective or hereditary, as established by the fundamental laws of each province. Further, with a view to suppressing at a single stroke and at the source those incessant disputes which arise between them, it shall be agreed to take as the basis of the respective rights of the contracting parties the possession of the moment as settled in each case by the last treaty concluded, with a general renunciation on all sides of every anterior claim, exception being made for all disputed successions and other claims to fall due in the future, all which shall be determined by arbitration of the Diet to the absolute exclusion of all attempts to settle the matter by force or to take arms against each other under any pretext whatsoever.

By the fourth shall be specified the conditions under which any confederate who may break this treaty shall be put to the ban of Europe and proscribed as a public enemy, namely, if he shall have made preparations for war, if he shall have made a treaty hostile to the ends of the Confederation, if he shall have taken up arms to resist it or to attack any one of the confederates.

By the same article it shall be argued that all the confederates shall arm and take the offensive, conjointly and at the common expense, against any state put to the ban of Europe, and that they shall not desist until the moment when he shall have laid down his arms, carried out the decisions and orders of the Diet, made amends for his offence, paid all the costs and atoned even for such warlike preparations as he may have made in defiance of the Treaty.

Finally, by the fifth Article the plenipotentiaries of the Confederation of Europe shall receive standing powers to frame – provisionally by a bare majority, definitively (after an interval of five years) by a majority of three-quarters – those measures which, on the instruction of their courts, they shall consider expedient with a view to the greatest possible advantage of the Commonwealth of Europe and of its members, all and single. In none of the above five articles, however, shall any change ever be made except with the unanimous consent of the confederates.

These five articles, summarized and reduced to the most general form, are, I am aware, exposed to countless petty objections, several of which would call for lengthy explanations. But petty objections are easily removed in case of need, and in an enterprise of this importance they are beside the point. When the policy of the Congress comes to be considered, a thousand obstacles will present themselves and ten thousand ways of removing them. It is *our* business to ask whether in the nature of the case the enterprise is possible or no[t]. We should lose ourselves in volumes of trifles, if we had to foresee all and find an answer to all. Confining ourselves, as we do, to incontestable principles, we have no call to satisfy every reader, nor to solve every objection, nor to say how every detail will be settled. It is enough to show that a settlement is possible.

In judging this scheme, then, what are the questions that have to be considered? Two only, for I will not insult the reader by proving to him the general proposition that the state of peace is a better thing than the state of war. The first question is whether the confederation suggested would be certain to answer its purpose and give a solid and abiding peace to Europe; the second, whether it is in the interest of the various sovereigns to establish such a confederation and to pay the price I have mentioned to obtain a lasting peace.

When we have thus proved our scheme to be for the advantage both of Europe as a whole and of all the states composing her, what obstacle is left, we ask, that can possibly prevent the execution of a design which, after all, depends solely upon the will of those concerned?

In discuss[ing] the first article, for instance, let us apply what has been said above of the general order now established in Europe and of the common resolve which confines each power practically within its traditional limits and does not allow it wholly to crush any of the others. In order to make my argument clear, I give here a list of the nineteen powers here assumed to constitute the Commonwealth of Europe, to each of which I give an equal voice, making altogether nineteen votes, in the deliberations of the Diet: the Emperor of the Romans, the Emperor of Russia, the King of France, the King of Spain, the King of England, the States General, the King of Denmark, Sweden, Poland, the King of Portugal, the Sovereign of Rome, the King of Prussia, the Elector of Bavaria and his associates, the Elector Palatine and his associates, the Swiss and their associates, the ecclesiastical Electors and their associates, the Republic of Venice and her associates, the King of Naples, the King of Sardinia.

Several minor sovereigns – for instance, the Republic of Genoa, the Dukes of Parma and Modena, and others – are omitted from the list. They will be associated with one or other of the less powerful states, with whom they will share a vote, after the fashion of the joint vote (*votum curiatum*) of the Counts of the Empire. It is useless to make the list more precise because, at any moment before the scheme is put in force, things may happen which, without affecting the principle of the measure, may call for alterations of detail.

A glance at the list will be enough to prove conclusively that it is impossible either for any single power to resist the united action of all the others, or for any partial league to be formed capable of defying the confederation as a whole.

How, indeed, could such a league be formed? Between the more powerful of the confederates? We have already proved that such a league could never last; and with the list before us it is easy enough to see that it could never be reconciled with the traditional policy of any of the great powers, or with the interests inherent in their respective positions. Between a large state and a number of small ones? Then the other large states, with the Federation behind them, will crush such a league in no time; and it is clear that the Grand Alliance, being perpetually armed and concerted for action, will find no difficulty in forestalling and crushing in advance any partial and seditious alliance, likely to trouble the peace and the public order of Europe. Look at the cohesion of the Germanic Body – and that, in spite of its defective discipline and the glaring inequality of its members. Is there a single prince, not even excepting the most powerful, who would dare to expose himself to the ban of the Empire by openly defying its laws, unless indeed he had good reason to suppose that the Empire would never have the courage to take action against the culprit in good earnest?

That is why I regard it as proved that the Diet of Europe, once established, will have no rebellion to fear and that no abuses which may creep in are ever likely to defeat the aims with which it was founded. It remains to ask whether those aims are really secured by the proposed institution.

With a view to answering this question, let us consider the motives by which princes are commonly led to take up arms. These motives are: either to make conquests, or to protect themselves from aggression, or to weaken a too-powerful neighbour, or to maintain their rights against attack, or to settle a difference which has defied friendly negotiation, or lastly, to fulfil some treaty obligation. There is no cause or pretext of war which cannot be brought under one or other of these six heads, and it is manifest that not one of the six is left standing under the new order which I propose.

As for the first, the thought of conquest will have to be given up from the absolute impossibility of making them. The aggressor is sure to find his way barred by forces stronger than his own. He is powerless to gain anything, and he risks the loss of all he has. At present, an ambitious prince who wishes to extend his dominions in Europe relies upon two weapons. He begins by securing strong allies, and then seeks to catch his enemy unawares. But, under the new conditions, no special alliance could stand for a moment before the Grand Alliance which is stronger and subsists permanently;

and, as there is no longer any pretext for arming, no prince can do so without being at once detected, stopped and punished by the Federation always under arms.

Again, the very thing which destroys all hope of conquest relieves him at the same time from all fear of being attacked. And, under the guarantee of all Europe, not only are his territories as strongly assured to him as the possessions of any citizen in a well-ordered community, but they are even more so than they were when he was their sole and only defender – in exactly the same proportion as the whole of Europe is stronger than any one of her princes taken singly.

Thirdly, having no more reason to fear his neighbour, neither has he any more reason for desiring to weaken him; and having no hope of success in such an enterprise, he is under no temptation to attempt it.

As for the maintenance of his rights, I begin by remarking that a whole host of pettifogging claims and obscure pretensions will be swept away at one stroke by the third Article of Federation, which settles forever all the conflicting rights of the allied princes on the basis of what they actually hold. By the same article, we have a clear principle for settling all claims and pretensions which may be raised in the future: each will be decided in the Diet, as it arises. It may be added that, if my rights are attacked, I am bound to defend them by the weapon used against me. They cannot be attacked by force of arms without bringing the ban of the Diet upon the assailant. It is not by arms, then, that I shall have to defend them. The same may be said of injuries, wrongs and claims for damage – in short, of all the unforeseen differences which may arise between two sovereigns. The same power which is bound to maintain their rights is bound also to redress their grievances.

As for the last head, the question settles itself. It is clear at a glance that, having no longer any assailant to fear, I have no longer any use for treaties of defence; and that, as no treaty can be so strong or so trustworthy as that guaranteed by the Grand Confederation, any other treaty would be useless, illegitimate, and consequently null and void.

For all these reasons it is impossible that the Confederation, once established, can leave any seed of war between its members; impossible that our object, an abiding peace, should not be absolutely attained by the proposed system, if it were once set on foot.

It now remains to settle the other question: that relating to the interests of the several parties concerned, for everyone knows that the general interest is powerless to silence that of the individual. To prove that peace, as a general principle, is a better thing than war is to say nothing to the man who has private reasons for preferring war to peace. To show him the means for securing a lasting peace is only to encourage him to work against them.

In truth, we shall be told: 'You are taking from sovereigns the right of doing themselves justice; that is to say, the precious right of being unjust when they please. You are taking from them the power of making themselves great at the expense of their neighbours. You are forcing them to renounce those antiquated claims whose value depends on their obscurity and which grow with every fresh growth in power; that parade of might and terror with which they love to awe the world; that pride of conquest which is the chief source of their glory. In one word, you are forcing them to be equitable and peaceful. What amends do you propose to make them for all these cruel privations?'

I do not venture to answer, with the Abbé de Saint-Pierre, that the true glory of princes lies in serving the good of the community and the happiness of their subjects; that their highest interest is to win a good name; and that such a name is awarded by the wise in exact proportion to the good which the ruler had done in the world; that the scheme of founding a lasting peace is the most lofty ever conceived and the most certain, if executed, to cover its author with undying glory; that such a scheme would not only do a greater service than any other to the people but also confer higher honour upon the sovereign; that this is the only ideal not stained with blood, rapine, curses and tears – in a word, that the surest way for a sovereign to raise himself above the common herd of kings is to labour for the good of the community. Let such language, which has covered the author and his projects with ridicule in all the council chambers of Europe, be left to irresponsible declaimers. But let us never join in the cry against the arguments it embodies; and, whatever may be the truth as to the virtues of princes, let us confine ourselves to their interests.

All the powers of Europe have rights or claims as against each other. These rights are, from the nature of the case, incapable of ever being finally adjusted, because there is no common and unvarying standard for judging of their merits and because they are often based upon facts which are either disputed or of doubtful interpretation. Nor are the quarrels which spring from them any more capable of being settled beyond appeal, whether in default of any recognized umpire, or because, when the chance offers, every prince goes back shamelessly upon the cessions which have been forcibly torn from him by a stronger power through treaties or after an unsuccessful war. It is therefore a mistake to think only of the claims we have on others and to forget those they have on us, when in reality there is no more justice on one side than on the other and both are equally capable of acquiring the means for enforcing their demands. Directly fortune is taken for arbiter, actual possession acquires a value which no wise man will stake against a possible gain in the future, even where chances are equal on both sides. And the rich man who, in the hope of doubling his fortune, ventures to risk it all upon one throw is blamed by the whole world. We have shown, however, that in schemes of self-aggrandizement the chances are never equal and that, even in the present order of things, the aggressor is always bound to find his enemy stronger than himself. The inevitable conclusion is that, the more powerful having no motive for staking his possessions and the weaker no hope of gaining on the throw, both will find their advantage in renouncing what they would like to win in order to secure what they possess.

Think of the waste of men, of money, of strength in every form; think of the exhaustion in which any state is plunged by the most successful war; compare these ravages with the profit which results: and we shall find that we commonly lose where we suppose ourselves to gain; that the conqueror, always enfeebled by the war, can only console himself with the thought that the conquered is still more enfeebled than himself. And even this advantage is more in appearance than reality, for the strength which has been gained upon our opponent has been lost against the neutrals who without changing themselves are nevertheless stronger relatively to us by all the strength that we have lost.

If all kings have not yet thrown off the folly of conquests, it would seem that the wiser of them at any rate are beginning to realize that they sometimes cost more than they are worth. Without going into a thousand distinctions which would only distract us from our purpose, we may say broadly that a prince who, in extending his frontiers, loses as many of his old subjects as he gains new ones in the process only weakens himself by his aggrandizement, because with a larger territory to defend he has no more soldiers to defend it. Everyone knows, however, that, as war is waged nowadays, the smallest part of the resultant loss of life is due to losses in the field. Certainly, that is the loss which everyone sees and feels. But all the time there is taking place through the whole kingdom a loss far more serious and more irreparable than that of those who die – a loss due to those who are not born, to the increase of taxes, to the interruption of trade, to the desertion of the fields, to the neglect of their cultivation. This evil, which no one sees at first, makes itself felt cruelly in the end. And then the king is astonished to find himself so weak as the result of making himself so strong.

There is another thing which makes conquests even less profitable than they used to be. It is that kings have at last learned the secret of doubling or trebling their power not only without enlarging their territory, but even, it may be, by contracting it after the wise example of Hadrian. The secret is that the strength of kings lies only in that of their subjects; and it follows from what I have just said that, given two states supporting an equal number of inhabitants, that which covers the smaller extent of territory is in reality the more powerful. It is then by good laws, by a wise discipline, by large views on economic policy that a sagacious sovereign is sure of increasing his power without incurring any hazard. It is in carrying out works more useful than his neighbours' that he makes conquests – the early true conquests – at their expense; and every subject born to him in excess of theirs is another enemy killed.

It may be objected that I prove too much and that, if the matter were as I put it, everyone being manifestly interested in avoiding war and the public interest combining with that of individuals for the preservation of peace, that peace ought to come of itself and of itself last forever without any need of federation. Given the present state of things, however, that would be to reason very ill. It is quite true that it would be much better for all men to remain always at peace. But so long as there is no security for this, everyone, having no guarantee that he can avoid war, is anxious to begin it at the moment which suits his own interest and so forestall a neighbour who would not fail to forestall the attack in his turn at any moment favourable to himself, so that many wars, even offensive wars, are rather in the nature of unjust precautions for the protection of the assailant's own possessions than a device for seizing those of others. However salutary it may be in theory to obey the dictates of public spirit, it is certain that politically, and even morally, those dictates are liable to prove fatal to the man who persists in observing them with all the world when no one thinks of observing them towards him.

I have nothing to say on the question of military parade, because, when supported by no solid foundation either of hope or fear, such parade is mere child's play, and kings have no business to keep dolls. I am equally silent as to the glory of conquest, because, if there really were men who would break their hearts at the thought of having no one to massacre, our duty would be not to reason with such monsters, but to deprive them of all means for putting their murderous frenzy into act. All solid grounds of war being swept away by the third article, no king can have any motive for kindling its horrors against a rival which would not furnish that rival with equally strong grounds for kindling them against him. And it is a great gain to be delivered from a danger in which each finds himself alone against the world.

As for the dependence of all upon the Tribunal of Europe, it is abundantly clear by the same article that the rights of sovereignty, so far from being weakened, will, on the contrary, be strengthened and confirmed, for that article guarantees to each sovereign not only that his dominions shall be protected against foreign invasion, but also that his authority shall be upheld against the rebellion of his subjects. The prince accordingly will be nonetheless absolute, and his crown will be more fully assured. By submitting to the decision of the Diet in all disputes with his equals, and by surrendering the perilous right of seizing other men's possessions, he is in fact doing nothing more than securing his real rights and renouncing those which are purely fictitious. Besides, there is all the difference in the world between dependence upon a rival and dependence upon a body of which he is himself a member and of which each member in turn becomes the head. In the latter case, the pledges that are given him are really the security for his freedom: it would be forfeited, if lodged with a superior; it is confirmed, when lodged with equals. In support of this, I appeal to the example of the Germanic Body. It is quite true that their position is consequently less favourable than it would be in the Confederation of Europe. But, in spite of those drawbacks, there is not one of them, however jealous he may be of his dignity, who would choose, even if he had the power, to win absolute independence at the cost of severance from the Empire.

Observe further that the head of the Germanic Body, being permanent, is bound to usurp ceaselessly upon the rights of the other members. In the Diet of Europe, where the presidency passes from one to another without any regard to disparities of power, no such danger is to be feared.

There is yet another consideration which is likely to weigh even more with men so greedy of money as princes always are. Not only will an unbroken peace give them as well as their subjects every means of amassing abundant riches, they will also be spared vast expenses by the reduction of their military budget, of those innumerable fortresses, of those enormous armies, which swallow up their revenue and become daily more and more of a burden to their subjects and themselves. I know that it will not suit all sovereigns to suppress their army bodily and leave themselves with no force in hand to crush an unexpected revolt or repel a sudden invasion. I know also that they will have their contingent to furnish to the Confederation with a view both to guarding the frontiers of Europe and to maintaining the federal arm whose duty it will be, in case of need, to carry out the decrees of the Diet. But when all these charges are met and at the same time the extraordinary expenses of war suppressed forever, there will still be a saving of more than half the ordinary military budget; and that saving can be divided between the relief of the subject and the coffers of the prince. The result will be that the people will have to pay much less; that the prince, being much better off, will be in a position to encourage commerce, agriculture and the arts and to create useful foundations which will still further increase his subjects' riches and his own; and, over and above all this, that the state will enjoy a security far greater than it now draws from all its armies and from all that warlike parade which drains its strength in the very bosom of peace.

It will be said perhaps that the frontier countries of Europe will then be relatively worse off. They will still have to face the chance of war either with the Turks, or the African Corsairs, or the Tartars.

The answer to this is (1) that those countries are under the same necessity at present, from which it follows that they will not be put to any positive disadvantage, but will only have an advantage the less; and this, in fact, is an inevitable consequence of their geographical position; (2) that, being freed from all anxiety on the side of Europe, they will be much more capable of resisting attacks from other quarters; (3) that the suppression of all fortresses in the inner parts of Europe and of all expenses needed for their maintenance would enable the Federation to build a large number on the eastern frontiers without bringing any fresh charge upon its members; (4) that these fortresses, built, maintained and garrisoned at the common charge, will mean so many fresh guarantees, and so much expense saved to the frontier powers for whose benefit they are built; (5) that the troops of the Federation, posted on the frontiers of Europe, will stand permanently ready to drive back the invader; (6) and finally, that a body so formidable as the Commonwealth of Europe will make the foreigner think twice before attacking any of its members, just as the Germanic Body, though infinitely less powerful, is still strong enough to command the respect of its neighbours and offer valuable protection to all the princes who compose it.

It may be further objected that, when the nations of Europe have ceased to war among themselves, the art of war will be gradually forgotten; that her armies will lose their courage and discipline; that there will be no more soldiers or generals; and that Europe will lie at the mercy of the first comer.

My answer is that one of two things will happen. Either the neighbours of Europe will attack her and wage war against her; or they will be afraid of the Confederation and leave her in peace.

In the former case, there will be plenty of opportunities for training military genius and talent, for practising and hardening our troops. The armies of the Confederation will, in this way, be the school of Europe. Men will go to the frontiers to learn war, while in the heart of Europe there will reign the blessings of peace. The advantages of war and peace will be combined. Does anyone believe that no nation can become warlike without perpetual civil war? And are the French the less brave because Anjou and Touraine are not constantly fighting with each other?

In the latter case, it is true that there can be no more hardening for war. But neither will there be any more greed for it. Of what use would it be to train for war, when you have no intention of ever making it? And which is the better course: to cultivate a pernicious art, or to destroy the need of it forever? If the secret of perpetual health were discovered, would there be any sense in rejecting it on the ground that doctors must not be deprived of the chance of gaining experience? And in making this parallel we have still to ask which of the two arts is the more beneficent in itself and the more deserving of encouragement.

Let no one threaten us with a sudden invasion. It is perfectly obvious that Europe has no invader to fear, and that the 'first comer' will never come. The day of those barbarian eruptions, which seemed to fall from the clouds, is gone forever. Now that the whole surface of the earth lies bare to our scrutiny, no danger can reach us which we have not foreseen for years. There is no power in the world now capable of threatening all Europe; and if one ever appears, Europe will either have time to make ready or, at the worst, will be much more capable of resisting him when she is united in one corporate body than she is now, when she would have to put a sudden end to all her quarrels and league herself in haste against the common invader.

We have thus seen that all the alleged evils of confederation, when duly weighed, come to nothing. I now ask whether anyone in the world would dare to say as much of those which flow from the recognized method of settling disputes between one prince and another: the appeal to the sword – a method inseparable from the state of anarchy and war, which necessarily springs from the absolute independence conceded to all sovereigns under the imperfect conditions now prevailing in Europe. In order to put the reader in a better position to estimate these evils, I will give a short summary of them and leave him to judge of their significance:

1. The existence of no solid right, except that of the stronger.
2. The perpetual and inevitable shifting of the balance from nation to nation, which makes it impossible for any one of them to keep in its grasp the power it holds at any moment.
3. The absence of complete security for any nation, so long as its neighbours are not subdued or annihilated.
4. The impossibility of annihilating them in view of the fact that, directly one is conquered, another springs up in its place.
5. The necessity of endless precautions and expenses to keep guard against possible enemies.
6. Weakness, and consequent exposure to attack, during minorities or revolts, for, when the state is divided, who can support one faction against the other?
7. The absence of any guarantee for international agreements.
8. The impossibility of obtaining justice from others without enormous cost and loss, which even so do not always obtain it, while the object in dispute is seldom worth the price.
9. The invariable risk of the prince's possessions, and sometimes of his life, in the quest of his rights.
10. The necessity of taking part against his will in the quarrels of his neighbours and of engaging in war at the moment when he would least have chosen it.
11. The stoppage of trade and revenue at the moment when they are most indispensable.
12. The perpetual danger threatened by a powerful neighbour, if the prince is weak, and by an armed alliance, if he is strong.

13. Finally, the uselessness of prudence, when everything is left to chance; the perpetual impoverishment of nations; the enfeeblement of the state alike in victory and defeat; and the total inability of the prince ever to establish good government, ever to count upon his own possessions, ever to secure happiness either for himself or for his subjects.

In the same way, let us sum up the advantages which the arbitration of Europe would confer upon the princes who agree to it:

1. Absolute certainty that all their disputes, present and future, will always be settled without war: a certainty incomparably more useful to princes than total immunity from lawsuits to the individual.
2. The abolition, either total or nearly so, of matters of dispute, thanks to the extinction of all existing claims – a boon which in itself will make up for all the prince renounces and secure what he possesses.
3. An absolute and indefeasible guarantee not only for the persons of the prince and his family, but also for his dominions and the law of succession recognized by the custom of each province: and this not only against the ambition of unjust and grasping claimants, but also against the rebellion of his subjects.
4. Absolute security for the execution of all engagements between princes under the guarantee of the Commonwealth of Europe.
5. Perfect freedom of trade for all time whether between state and state, or between any of them and the more distant regions of the earth.
6. The total suppression for all time of the extraordinary military expenses incurred by land and sea in time of war, and a considerable reduction of the corresponding expenses in time of peace.
7. A notable increase of population and agriculture, of the public wealth and the revenues of the prince.
8. An open door for all useful foundations, calculated to increase the power and glory of the sovereign, the public wealth and the happiness of the subject.

As I have already said, I leave it to the reader to weigh all those points and to make his own comparison between the state of peace which results from confederation and the state of war which follows from the present anarchy of Europe.

If our reasoning has been sound in the exposition of this project, it has been proved: firstly, that the establishment of a lasting peace depends solely upon the consent of the sovereigns concerned, and offers no obstacle, except what may be expected from their opposition; secondly, that the establishment of such a peace would be profitable to them in all manner of ways, and that, even from their point of view, there is no comparison between its drawbacks and advantages; thirdly, that it is reasonable to expect their decision in this matter will coincide with their plain interest; and lastly, that such a peace, once established on the proposed basis, will be solid and lasting and will completely fulfil the purpose with which it was concluded.

This is not, of course, to say that the sovereigns will adopt this project (who can answer for the reason or another?), but only that they would adopt it, if they took counsel of their true interest. It must be observed that we have not assumed men such as they ought to be: good, generous, disinterested, and devoted to the public good from motives of pure humanity; but such as they are: unjust, grasping and setting their own interest above all things. All that I do assume in them is understanding enough to see their own interest, and courage enough to act for their own happiness. If, in spite of all this, the project remains unrealized, that is not because it is utopian; it is because men are crazy, and because to be sane in a world of madmen is in itself a kind of madness.

Notes

[1] Respect for the Roman Empire has so completely survived her power that many jurists have questioned whether the Emperor of Germany is not the natural sovereign of the world; and Bartholus carried this doctrine so far as to treat anyone who dared to deny it as a heretic. The writings of the canonists are full of the corresponding doctrine of the temporal supremacy of the Roman Church.

Judgment

The scheme of a lasting peace was of all others the most worthy to fascinate a man of high principle. Of all those which engaged the Abbé de Saint-Pierre, it was therefore that over which he brooded the longest and followed up with the greatest obstinacy. It is indeed hard to give any other name to the missionary zeal which never failed him in this enterprise: and that, in spite of the manifest impossibility of success, the ridicule which he brought upon himself day by day, and the rebuffs which he had continually to endure. It would seem that this well-balanced spirit, intent solely on the public good, led him to measure his devotion to a cause purely by its utility, never letting himself be daunted by difficulties, never thinking of his own personal interest.

If ever moral truth were demonstrated, I should say it is the utility, national no less than international, of this project. The advantages which its realization would bring to each prince, to each nation, to the whole of Europe, are immense, manifest, incontestable. And nothing could be more solid or more precise than the arguments which the author employs to prove them. Realize his Commonwealth of Europe for a single day, and you may be sure it will last forever; so fully would experience convince men that their own gain is to be found in the good of all. For all that, the very princes who would defend it with all their might, if it once existed, would resist with all their might any proposal for its creation. They will as infallibly throw obstacles in the way of its establishment as they would in the way of its abolition. Accordingly, Saint-Pierre's book on *A Lasting Peace* seems to be ineffectual for founding it, and unnecessary for maintaining it. 'It is then an empty dream' will be the verdict of the impatient reader. No, it is a work of solid judgment, and it is of great importance for us to possess it.

Let us begin by examining the criticisms of those who judge of reasons not by reason, but by the event, and who have no objection to bring against the scheme, except that it has never been put in practice. Well, such men will doubtless say: 'If its advantages are so certain, why is it that the sovereigns of Europe have never adopted it? Why do they ignore their own interest, if that interest is demonstrated so clearly? Do we see them reject any other means of increasing their revenue and their power? And, if this means were as efficacious as you pretend, is it conceivable that they should be less eager to try it than any of the schemes they have pursued for all these centuries; that they should prefer a thousand delusive expedients to so evident an advantage?'

Yes, without doubt, that is conceivable, unless it be assumed that their wisdom is equal to their ambition, and that the more keenly they desire their own interest the more clearly do they see it. The truth is that the severest penalty of excessive self-love is that it always defeats itself; that the keener the passion the more certain it is to be cheated of its goal. Let us distinguish then, in politics as in morals, between real and apparent interest. The former will be secured by an abiding peace; that is demonstrated in the *Project*. The latter is to be found in the state of absolute independence which frees sovereigns from the reign of law only to put them under that of chance. They are, in fact, like a madcap pilot who, to show off his idle skill and his power over his sailors, would rather toss to and fro among the rocks in a storm than moor his vessel in safety.

The whole life of kings, or of those on whom they shuffle off their duties, is devoted solely to two objects: to extend their rule beyond their frontiers, and to make it more absolute within them. Any other purpose they may have is either subservient to one of these aims, or merely a pretext for attaining them. Such pretexts are 'the good of the community', 'the happiness of their subjects', or 'the glory of the nation' – phrases forever banished from the council chamber and employed so clumsily in proclamations that they are always taken as warnings of coming misery and that the people groans with apprehension when its masters speak to it of their 'fatherly solicitude'.

From these two fundamental maxims we can easily judge of the spirit in which princes are likely to receive a proposal which runs directly counter to the one and is hardly more favourable to the other. Anyone can see that the establishment of the Diet of Europe will fix the constitution of each state as inexorably as its frontiers; that it is impossible to guarantee the prince against the rebellion of his subjects without at the same time securing the subjects against the tyranny of the prince; and that, without this, the federation could not possibly endure. And I ask whether there is in the whole world a single sovereign who, finding himself thus bridled forever in his most cherished designs, would endure without indignation the very thought of seeing himself forced to be just not only with the foreigner, but even with his own subjects?

Again, anyone can understand that war and conquest without, and the encroachments of despotism within, give each other mutual support; that money and men are habitually taken at pleasure from a people of slaves to bring others beneath the same yoke; and that, conversely, war furnishes a pretext for exactions of money, and another (no less plausible) for keeping large armies constantly on foot, to hold the people in awe. In a word, anyone can see that aggressive princes wage war at least as much on their subjects as on their enemies, and that the conquering nation is left no better off than the conquered. 'I have beaten the Romans,' so Hannibal used to write to Carthage, 'send me more troops. I have exacted an indemnity from Italy, send me more money.' That is the real meaning of the *Te Deum*s, the bonfires and rejoicings with which the people hail the triumphs of their masters.

As for disputes between prince and prince, is it reasonable to hope that we can force before a higher tribunal men who boast that they hold their power only by the sword, and who bring in the name of God solely because He 'is in Heaven'? Will sovereigns ever submit their quarrels to legal arbitration, when all the rigour of the laws has never succeeded in forcing private individuals to admit the principle in theirs? A private gentleman with a grievance is too proud to carry his case before the Court of the Marshals of France; and you expect a king to carry his claims before the Diet of Europe? Not to mention that the former offends against the laws, so risking his life twice over, while the latter seldom risks anything but the life of his subjects; and that, in taking up arms, he avails himself of a right recognized by all the world – a right for the use of which he claims to be accountable to God alone.

A prince who stakes his cause on the hazards of war knows well enough that he is running risks. But he is less struck with the risks than with the gains on which he reckons, because he is much less afraid of fortune than he is confident in his own wisdom. If he is strong, he counts upon his armies; if weak, upon his allies. Sometimes he finds it useful to purge ill humours, to weaken restive subjects, even to sustain reverses; and the wily statesman knows how to draw profit even from his own defeats. I trust it will be remembered that it is not I who reason in this fashion, but the court sophist, who would rather have a large territory with few subjects, poor and submissive, than that unshaken rule over the hearts of a happy and prosperous people, which is the reward of a prince who observes justice and obeys the laws.

It is on the same principle that he meets in his own mind the argument drawn from the interruption of commerce, from the loss of life, from the financial confusion and the real loss which result from an unprofitable conquest. It is a great miscalculation always to estimate the losses and gains of princes in terms of money; the degree of power they aim at is not to be reckoned by the millions in their coffers. The prince always makes his schemes rotate; he seeks to command in order to enrich himself, and to enrich himself in order to command. He is ready by turns to sacrifice the one aim to the other, with a view to obtaining whichever of the two is most wanting at the moment. But it is only in the hope of winning them both in the long run that he pursues each of them apart. If he is to be master of both men and things, he must have empire and money at the same time.

Let us add finally that, though the advantages resulting to commerce from a general and lasting peace are in themselves certain and indisputable, still, being common to all states, they will be appreciated by none, for such advantages make themselves felt only by contrast, and he who wishes to increase his relative power is bound to seek only such gains as are exclusive.

So it is that, ceaselessly deluded by appearances, princes would have nothing to do with peace on these terms, even if they calculated their interests for themselves. How will it be when the calculation is made for them by their ministers whose interests are always opposed to those of the people and almost always to the princes'? Ministers are in perpetual need of war as a means of making themselves indispensable to their master, of throwing him into difficulties from which he cannot escape without their aid, of ruining the state if things come to the worst as the price of keeping their own office. They are in need of it as a means of oppressing the people on the plea of national necessity, of finding places for their creatures, of rigging the market and setting up a thousand odious monopolies. They are in need of it as a means of gratifying their passions and driving their rivals out of favour. They are in need of it as a means of controlling the prince and withdrawing him from court whenever a dangerous plot is formed against their power. With a lasting peace, all these resources would be gone. And the world still persists in asking why, if such a scheme is practicable, these men have not adopted it. Is it not obvious that there is nothing impracticable about it, except its adoption by these men? What then will they do to oppose it? What they have always done: they will turn it into ridicule.

Again, even given the goodwill that we shall never find either in princes or their ministers, we are not to assume, with the Abbé de Saint-Pierre, that it would be easy to find the right moment for putting the project into act. For this, it would be essential that all the private interests concerned, taken together, should not be stronger than the general interest, and that everyone should believe himself to see in the good of all the highest good to which he can aspire for himself. But this requires the concurrence of wisdom in so many heads, a fortuitous concourse of so many interests, such as chance can hardly be expected ever to bring about. But, in default of such spontaneous agreement, the one thing left is force; and then the question is no longer to persuade but to compel, not to write books but to raise armies.

Accordingly, though the scheme in itself was wise enough, the means proposed for its execution betray the simplicity of the author. He fairly supposed that nothing was needed but to convoke a congress and lay the articles before it; that they would be signed directly and all be over on the spot. It must be admitted that, in all his projects, this good man saw clearly enough how things would work, when once set going, but that he judged like a child of the means for setting them in motion.

To prove that the project of the Christian Commonwealth is not utopian, I need do no more than name its original author. For no one will say that Henry IV was a madman, or Sully a dreamer. The Abbé de Saint-Pierre took refuge behind these great names, to revive their policy. But what a difference in the time, the circumstances, the scheme itself, the manner of bringing it forward and, above all, in its author!

To judge of this, let us glance at the state of Europe as it was at the moment which Henry chose for the execution of his project.

The power of Charles V, who reigned over one half of the world and struck awe into the other, had led him to aspire to universal empire, with great chances of success and great talents for making use of them. His son, more rich and less powerful, never ceased to nurse a design which he was incapable of carrying out, and throughout his reign kept Europe in a state of perpetual alarm. In truth, the House of Austria had acquired such an ascendancy over the other powers that no prince was safe upon his throne, unless he stood well with the Hapsburgs. Philip III, with even fewer talents, inherited all his father's pretensions. Europe was still held in awe by the power of Spain which continued to dominate the others rather by a long habit of commanding than from any power to make herself obeyed. In truth, the revolt of the Low Countries, the struggle against England, the long drain of the civil wars in France had exhausted the strength of Spain and the riches of the Indies. The House of Austria, now divided into two branches, has ceased to act with the same unity; and the Emperor, although he strained every nerve to maintain or recover the authority of Charles V, only succeeded in affronting the lesser princes and provoking conspiracies which speedily broke out and came near to costing him his throne. Such were the slow stages which prepared the fall of the House of Austria and the new birth of the liberties of Europe. No one, however, had the courage to be first to risk throwing off the yoke and exposing himself alone to the dangers of war; the example of Henry himself, who had come so ill out of the enterprise, damped the courage of all the rest. Moreover, if we except the Duke of Savoy, who was too weak and too much under the curb to move a step, there was not among all the sovereigns of the time a single one of ability enough to form and carry through

127

such an enterprise; each one of them waited on time and circumstances for the moment to break his chains. Such, in rough outline, was the state of things at the time when Henry formed the plan of the Christian Commonwealth and prepared to put it in act. The project was vast indeed and, in itself, quite beyond praise. I have no wish to dim its glory. But, prompted as it was by the secret hope of humbling a formidable enemy, it took from this urgent motive an impulse which could hardly have come from humanity alone.

Let us now see what were the means employed by this great man to pave the way for so lofty an undertaking. In the front rank of these I should be disposed to put that he had clearly recognized all the difficulties of the task so that, having formed the project in his youth, he brooded over it all his life and reserved its accomplishment for his old age. This proves in the first place that ardent and sustained passion by which alone great obstacles can be overcome; and secondly, that patient and considerate wisdom which smoothes the way in advance by forethought and calculation. For there is a great difference between an enforced undertaking, in which prudence itself counsels to leave something to chance, and one which is to be justified only by success; seeing that, being under no compulsion to engage in it, we ought never to have attempted it, unless that success were beyond doubt. Again, the deep secrecy which he maintained all his life, until the very moment in action, was as essential as it was difficult in so vast an enterprise, where the concurrence of so many men was a necessity and which so many men were interested in thwarting. It would seem that, though he had drawn the greater part of Europe to his side and was in league with her chief potentates, there was only one man to whom he had confided the full extent of his design; and, by a boon granted by Heaven only to the best of kings, that one man was an honest minister. But, though nothing was allowed to transpire of these high aims, everything was silently moving towards their execution. Twice over did Sully make the journey to London: James I was a party to the plan, and the King of Sweden had fallen in with it. A league was made with the Protestants of Germany; even the Princes of Italy had been secured. All were ready to join in the great purpose, though none could say what it was, just as workmen are employed in making the separate parts of a new machine, of whose shape and use they know nothing. What was it, then, that set all these springs in motion? Was it the craving for a lasting peace, which was foreseen by no one and with which few would have troubled their heads? Was it the public interest, which is never the interest of anyone? The Abbé de Saint-Pierre might have supposed so, but the truth is that each of them was working for his own private interest which Henry had been clever enough to display to all of them in the most attractive light. The King of England was glad to deliver himself from the perpetual conspiracies of his Catholic subjects, all of them fomented by Spain. He found a further advantage in the liberation of the United Provinces, in whose support he was spending large sums, while every moment he was placed on the brink of a war which he dreaded or in which he preferred to join once for all with the whole of Europe and then be quit of it forever. The King of Sweden was anxious to make sure of Pomerania and so win a footing in Germany. The Elector Palatine, at that time a Protestant and head of the Lutheran Confession, had designs on Bohemia and shared all the plans of the King of England. The Princes of Germany aimed at checking the encroachments of the House of Austria. The Duke of Savoy was to receive Milan and the crown of Lombardy which he passionately coveted. The Pope himself, weary of the Spanish tyranny, was in the league, bribed by the promise of the Kingdom of Naples. The Dutch, better paid than all the rest, gained the assurance of their freedom. In a word, quite apart from the common interest of humbling a haughty power which was striving to tyrannize over all of them, each state had a private interest all the more keenly felt because it was not countered by the fear of exchanging one tyrant for another. It was agreed that the conquests should be distributed among all the allies, to the exclusion of France and England, who were bound to keep nothing for themselves. This was enough to quiet the most suspicious as to the ambitions of Henry. But that wise prince was well aware that in keeping nothing for himself by this treaty, he gained more than all the rest. Without adding a yard to his own patrimony, it was enough to partition that of the only man who excelled him in power, and he became the most powerful himself. And it is perfectly clear that, in taking all the precautions which would assure the success of his enterprise, he in no way neglected those which were sure to give him the first place in the body he was creating.

More than that: he did not confine himself to forming formidable leagues beyond his frontiers, to making alliances with his own neighbours and the neighbours of his enemy. While engaging all these nations in the abasement of the first power in Europe, he did not forget to put himself in the way of securing the coveted position for himself. He spent fifteen years of peace in preparations worthy of the enterprise he had in mind. He filled his coffers with money, his arsenals with artillery, arms and munitions. He amassed resources of all kinds against unforeseen demands. But he did more than all, we may be very sure, by governing his people wisely, by silently removing all seeds of division, by putting his finances in such order as to meet all possible needs without any vexation of his subjects. So it was that, at peace within and formidable abroad, he saw himself in a position to arm and maintain sixty thousand men and twenty vessels of war, to quit his kingdom without leaving behind him the smallest germ of disorder and to carry on war for six years without touching his ordinary revenue or laying on a penny of new taxes.

To all these preparations must be added the assurance that the enterprise would be carried out, both by his minister and himself, with the same energy and prudence that had conceived and framed it, and finally, the knowledge that all the military operations would be directed by a captain of his skill, while the enemy had none left to put against him. From all this it may be judged if any element which could promise success was wanting to his prospects. Without having fathomed his designs, all Europe was watching his preparations with a kind of awe. The great revolution was about to be launched on a slight pretext. A war, destined to be the end of all wars, was about to usher in eternal peace, when a deed, the horror of which is only increased by its mystery, came to quench forever the last hope of the world. The blow which cut short the days of this good king also plunged Europe back into ceaseless wars, of which she can now never hope to see the end.

Such were the means prepared by Henry IV for founding the federation which the Abbé de Saint-Pierre proposed to set up by a book.

Let us not say, then, if his system has not been adopted, that is because it was not good. Let us rather say that it was too good to be adopted. Evils and abuses by which so many men profit come in of themselves; things of public utility, on the other hand, are seldom brought in but by force, for the simple reason that private interests are almost always ranged against them. Beyond doubt, a lasting peace is, under present circumstances, a project ridiculous enough. But give us back Henry IV and Sully and it will become once more a reasonable proposal. Or rather, while we admire so fair a project, let us console ourselves for its failure by the thought that it could only have been carried out by violent means from which humanity must needs shrink.

No confederation could ever be established except by a revolution. That being so, which of us would dare to say whether the league of Europe is a thing more to be desired or feared? It would perhaps do more harm in a moment than it would guard against for ages.

Chapter 12
Perpetual Peace through International Adjudication: Bentham's Plan

Jeremy Bentham (1748–1832) – another giant figure in political philosophy – was forty-one years old when he finally published his most well-known work, namely, *Introduction to the Principles of Morals and Legislation* (1789).[1] The same year, it appears, he also gave quite a bit of thought to the question of how to bring about an everlasting peace.[2] Bentham's *Plan for An Universal and Perpetual Peace* was first published in the second volume of Bentham's works edited by Sir John Bowring – a long-time friend of Bentham.[3] The Bowring edition presents this plan as the final part of a four-part essay entitled *Principles of International Law*. However, as is the case with several of Bentham's writings, there are serious doubts as to the authenticity of this text. What is in doubt is not so much the ideas as their presentation. In other words, few people doubt that it was indeed Bentham who wrote a great majority of *Bentham's works*. However, it is not entirely clear how precisely he organized his material, and in

---

[1] Bentham's writings can be usefully divided into two periods, namely, 1769–88 and 1788–1803. The value of his works in the second period, in particular, seems to be intensely debated; see David Lieberman, 'Jeremy Bentham: Biography and intellectual biography', *History of Political Thought*, 20:1 (1999), 187–204.

[2] 1789, it should be remembered, was also the year of the French Revolution.

[3] This first comprehensive collection of Bentham's work was published in eleven volumes in 1843, and appears to have been edited between 1838 and 1943; see John Bowring (ed.), *The Works of Jeremy Bentham* (Edinburgh: William Tait; London: Simpkin, Marshall & Co., 1843), and C. John Colombos, 'Introduction', in the Grotius Society, *Jeremy Bentham's Plan for An Universal and Perpetual Peace* (London: Sweet & Maxwell Ltd, 1927), p. 3.

what order he actually presented (or would have presented, had he not died) his ideas.[4] Bentham left behind eighty wooden boxes of unpublished manuscripts,[5] and the organization and editing of his work still continues today under the auspices of the University College of London's *Bentham Project*.[6] The early Bowring edition, in particular, seems to have 'reconstructed' several of Bentham's writings to be able to publish them in a more or less orderly manner. This attempt, however, is likely to have created even further confusion as to what Bentham actually wrote, when, in which manuscript, and in what order. After a careful analysis of original manuscripts, Gunhild Hoogensen has convincingly suggested that *A Plan for An Universal and Perpetual Peace* is in fact a synthesis of three separate texts put together by the Bowring editorial team: *Pacification and Emancipation*; *Colonies and Navy*; and *Cabinet No Secresy*.[7]

The questions of authenticity and reliability should always be kept in mind when reading Bentham. Nevertheless, as the next chapter will hopefully demonstrate, the *Plan* that is attributed to Bentham does indeed exhibit a considerable degree of internal consistency as far as the basic ideas are concerned. Whether these ideas are as coherently integrated and as fully developed as they should or could have been is, of course, another matter. This weakness, however, does not necessarily arise from the fact that this text is collated by others 'on behalf of' the author. Considering his crowded agenda and his scattered pieces of writing, it is quite possible that Bentham himself might have left his plan in a less than developed state, had he produced it in one organized piece.

Bentham was, first and foremost, a dedicated reformer. Throughout his life he remained deeply dissatisfied, especially, with the legal and judicial system of his time.[8] This was a

---

[4] For a detailed account, see Gunhild Hoogensen, 'Bentham's international manuscripts versus the published "Works"', *Journal of Bentham Studies*, 4 (2001).

[5] See Colombos, 'Introduction', p. 2.

[6] As of November 2006, the Project website was: *http://www.ucl.ac.uk/Bentham-Project/*.

[7] See Hoogensen, 'Bentham's international manuscripts'.

[8] For a useful summary of Bentham's reform activities, see Philip Schofield, *Utility and Democracy: The Political Thought of Jeremy Bentham* (Oxford: Oxford University Press, 2006), ch. 12.

major reason why he refused to practise law after his education at Lincoln's Inn. Instead, he chose a life of constant reflection on how to improve societal institutions, among them the political, administrative and judicial ones.[9] His famous *Panopticon* project remains one of the most innovative prison reform proposals of all time. Bentham's lifelong preoccupation with justice reform is also clearly evident in his perpetual peace plan, transposed to the international level.[10]

One revolutionary aspect of the *Plan* is its emphatic call for the establishment of an international court – a proposal that is unparalleled in other representatives of the perpetual peace tradition we have seen.[11] This emphasis on the international court fits comfortably with Bentham's well-known (and much criticized) legal positivism.[12] The creation of such a court may well be good in its own right, but Bentham seems to imply in addition that the court's actual value would lie in the consent extended by the states for its establishment. Following a careful analysis of their own interests, states would create an institutional precedent and give rise to 'existing positive law'. By implication, this law, once created, would replace the need for any abstract 'morality' in judging international behaviour, and could bring about perpetual peace. In parallel, the question of religion – a theme that occupies a central place in earlier peace plans, including that of Rousseau – is entirely left aside in Bentham's project.[13] The idea of perpetual peace we find in his text is as secular as that of Kant.

---

[9] On the utilitarian utopia that we find in his *Constitutional Code*, see Thomas P. Peardon, 'Bentham's Ideal Republic', in Bhikhu Parekh (ed.), *Jeremy Bentham: Ten Critical Essays* (London: Frank Cass, 1974), pp. 120–44. Bentham's *Constitutional Code* sparked considerable debate on the question of 'a tyranny of the majority': see James Steintrager, *Bentham* (London: George Allen & Unwin Ltd, 1977), pp. 97–116. Interestingly, Kant's remarks on 'democracy as despotism' seem to refer precisely to this notion of democracy: see Chapter 15, First Definitive Article.

[10] Bentham, it should be quickly noted, is the inventor of the term 'international law'.

[11] See Proposition XIII in Chapter 13.

[12] For a different interpretation, see M. W. Janis, 'Jeremy Bentham and the fashioning of "international law"', *The American Journal of International Law*, 78 (1984), 412–15.

[13] The secular tone of the *Plan* is consistent with Bentham's overall indifference to religious authority; see Collinson and Plant, *Fifty Major Philosophers*, p. 146.

Bentham's pragmatism and utilitarianism are even more evident in his plan than his legal positivism. All through his project, the thinker takes the existing global power configuration as *is*, and tries to make it work. Hence we find in the *Plan* a clearly defined and narrowly targeted audience, namely, Britain and France who dominate the late-eighteenth-century international system. In contrast to Kant, for example, Bentham does not advance any superior *a priori* principles. Rather, even his most far-fetched proposal – namely, the idea of decolonization – tries carefully to address the calculable interests of the parties concerned. What would be lost and what would be gained if the colonial powers gave up their colonies, and how that would increase the benefit for all is a constant theme in the *Plan*.

Bentham advances two fundamental propositions in his project, both of which are 'early' in all three senses of the word implied in this volume (see Chapter 1): disarmament[14] and decolonization.[15] Compared with earlier perpetual peace proposals, Bentham's fundamental propositions stand out. Unlike several other thinkers, he does not want to create a collective and multiplied force. On the contrary, he is at pains to make a case as to why disarmament is both feasible and beneficial. As for decolonization, here, too, we find a reversal of several earlier proposals, because the thinker suggests, in effect, the breaking up of already established territorial units. His plan does not involve the creation of an upper layer of territorial governance in the form of a federation, confederation or some other kind of union.[16] Perhaps more strikingly, Bentham takes his reasoning even further, arguing that neither of his two fundamental propositions 'would completely answer the purpose without the other'. In other words, his plan contains early versions of the kind of conceptual issue-linkages that we

---

[14] While Bentham does not use this precise concept, he clearly points to it. We use the term here in its broader sense, avoiding any technical distinctions between the contemporary ideas of 'arms control', 'arms management', 'arms limitation' and 'arms reduction'.

[15] Bentham's exact phrase is 'emancipation of distant dependencies'.

[16] For a useful overview of several different types of federative unions, see Daniel J. Elazar (ed.), *Federal Systems of the World: A Handbook of Federal, Confederal, and Autonomy Arrangements*, 2nd edn (Essex, UK: Longman, 1994).

find in such global governance projects as the famous *Our Global Neighbourhood*.[17]

Set against this backdrop, Bentham's proposal for the creation of a diet or congress acquires a different meaning from what we have seen in earlier proposals. Given the priority assigned to the twin aims of disarmament and decolonization, Bentham's international congress is neither an ultimate mechanism of collective force, nor a recipe for ever-expanding organic political unity. The philosopher places utmost emphasis on consultation, public opinion, freedom of press, and transparency. The envisaged congress, therefore, would be purely instrumental, and targeted at various domestic audiences. Its power would consist, to quote Bentham, 'in reporting its opinion; in causing that opinion to be circulated in the dominions of each state; and in putting the refractory state under the ban of Europe'. Inescapably, the 'ban of Europe' might involve the use of force. Nevertheless, compared with Rousseau, for instance, Bentham almost completely rules out physical power in the act of governing.[18] Although he admits that force might be required to enforce the decrees of the international court, he argues that 'the necessity for the employment of this resource would . . . be superseded forever by . . . guaranteeing the liberty of the press in each state, in such sort that the Diet might find no obstacle to its giving . . . to its decrees . . . the most extensive and unlimited circulation'. Indeed, the use of force is such a delicate issue from Bentham's point of view that his proposed

---

[17] Commission on Global Governance, *Our Global Neighbourhood: The Report of the Commission on Global Governance* (Oxford: Oxford University Press, 1995). The experienced practitioners and researchers participating in a more recent volume on global governance reform have argued, for instance, that 'reform within a single domain will not happen by actions taken within that domain alone because there are too many conflicting forces, contradictions, and complexities to permit decisive action': see Colin I. Bradford Jr. and Johannes F. Linn, 'Introduction and overview', in Bradford Jr. and Linn (eds), *Global Governance Reform: Breaking the Stalemate* (Washington, D.C.: Brookings Institution Press, 2007), pp. 3, 116–18.

[18] The observation that 'the reason of Bentham appears the perfect anti-thesis of the reason of Rousseau' may well shed light on this difference; see Henry Sidgwick, 'Bentham and Benthamism in politics and ethics', *The Fortnightly Review*, 21 (January–June 1877), 630.

international court is definitely 'not to be armed with any coercive powers'.[19]

Bentham's plan takes considerable steps, albeit not entirely systematically, towards a more polished notion of global governance. He does suggest a regulatory, consultative, international agency (a diet or congress); emphasizes the primacy of international law as an instrument of perpetual peace; adamantly advocates transparency in foreign affairs; shifts the discourse from 'princes/sovereigns' towards 'people/ nations'; and, last but not least, conceptually incorporates the idea of domestic constituencies into the conduct of international affairs. No doubt it is possible to argue that several of these conceptual moves derive their strength and motivation from the changing socio-political milieu of the late eighteenth century. Such argument, however, needs careful evaluation. After all, not all of Bentham's contemporaries drew similar conclusions, even though they witnessed the same changes in the global setting.[20] In any event, placed within the overall perpetual peace tradition, Bentham's work does signal a multifaceted evolution towards the idea of 'global governance' and deserves more systematic attention than it has attracted thus far.[21]

Bentham's *Plan* in the next chapter is borrowed from the original Bentham edition: Jeremy Bentham, *The Works of Jeremy Bentham*, vol. 2, edited by John Bowring (Edinburgh: William Tait; London: Simpkin, Marshall & Co., 1843).

---

[19] Precisely on this point, however, we may need to face the considerable literature elaborating on Bentham's intellectual connection with Thomas Hobbes; see James E. Crimmins, 'Bentham and Hobbes: An issue of influence', *Journal of the History of Ideas*, 63 (2002), 677–95.

[20] See Gargaz and Calonne in Chapters 8 and 9, respectively.

[21] As Hoogensen usefully reminds us, however, the difficulty of placing Bentham in 'the traditional paths assigned to his predecessors and contemporaries such as Kant, Rousseau and the Abbé St. Pierre' should be constantly kept in mind: see Gunhild Hoogensen, *International Relations, Security and Jeremy Bentham* (London: Routledge, 2005), p. 9.

Chapter 13

Jeremy Bentham: *A Plan for An Universal and Perpetual Peace* (1789)

The object of the present essay is to submit to the world a plan for an universal and perpetual peace. The globe is the field of dominion to which the author aspires; the press the engine, and the only one he employs; the cabinet of mankind the theatre of his intrigue.

The happiest of mankind are sufferers by war; and the wisest, nay, even the least wise, are wise enough to ascribe the chief of their sufferings to that cause.

The following plan has for its basis two fundamental propositions:

1. The reduction and fixation of the force of the several nations that compose the European system;
2. The emancipation of the distant dependencies of each state.[1]

Each of these propositions has its distinct advantages; but neither of them, it will appear, would completely answer the purpose without the other.

As to the utility of such an universal and lasting peace, supposing a plan for that purpose practicable, and likely to be adopted, there can be but one choice. The objection, and the only objection to it, is the apparent impracticability of it – that it is not only hopeless, but that to such a degree that any proposal to that effect deserves the name of visionary and ridiculous. This objection I shall endeavour in the first place to remove, for the removal of this prejudice may be necessary to procure for the plan a hearing.

What can be better suited to the preparing of men's minds for the reception of such a proposal than the proposal itself?

Let it not be objected that the age is not ripe for such a proposal. The more it wants of being ripe, the sooner we should begin to do what can be done to ripen it; the more we should do to ripen it. A proposal of this sort is one of those things that can never come too early nor too late.

Who that bears the name of Christian can refuse the assistance of his prayers? What pulpit can forbear to second me with its eloquence? Catholics and Protestants, Church-of-England men and Dissenters, may all agree in this, if in nothing else. I call upon them all to aid me with their countenance and their support.

The ensuing sheets are dedicated to the common welfare of all civilized nations; but more particularly of Great Britain and France.

The end in view is to recommend three grand objects: simplicity of government, national frugality, and peace.

Reflection has satisfied me of the truth of the following propositions:

I: That it is not the interest of Great Britain to have any foreign dependencies whatsoever.

II: That it is not the interest of Great Britain to have any treaty of alliance, offensive or defensive, with any other power whatever.

III: That it is not the interest of Great Britain to have any treaty with any power whatsoever, for the purpose of possessing any advantage whatsoever in point of trade, to the exclusion of any other nation whatsoever.

IV: That it is not the interest of Great Britain to keep up any naval force beyond what may be sufficient to defend its commerce against pirates.

V: That it is not the interest of Great Britain to keep on foot any regulations whatsoever of distant preparation for the augmentation or maintenance of its naval force; such as the Navigation Act, bounties on the Greenland trade, and other trades regarded as nurseries for seamen.

VI, VII, VIII, IX & X: That all these several propositions are also true of France.

As far as Great Britain is concerned, I rest the proof of these several propositions principally upon two very simple principles:

1. That the increase of growing wealth of every nation in a given period is necessarily limited by the quantity of capital it possesses at that period.
2. That Great Britain, with or without Ireland, and without any other dependency, can have no reasonable ground to apprehend injury from any one nation upon earth.

Turning to France, I substitute to the last of the two just-mentioned propositions the following:

3. That France, standing singly, has at present nothing to fear from any other nation than Great Britain: nor, if standing clear of her foreign dependencies, would she have anything to fear from Great Britain.

XI: That supposing Great Britain and France thoroughly agreed, the principal difficulties would be removed to the establishment of a plan of general and permanent pacification for all Europe.

XII: That for the maintenance of such a pacification, general and perpetual treaties might be formed, limiting the number of troops to be maintained.

XIII: That the maintenance of such a pacification might be considerably facilitated by the establishment of a Common Court of Judicature for the decision of differences between the several nations, although such court were not to be armed with any coercive powers.

XIV: That secrecy in the operations of the Foreign Department ought not to be endured in England, being altogether useless and equally repugnant to the interests of liberty and to those of peace.

140

PROPOSITION I: *That it is not the interest of Great Britain to have any foreign dependencies whatsoever.*

The truth of this proposition will appear if we consider:

first, that distant dependencies increase the chances of war

    a. by increasing the number of possible subjects of dispute.

    b. by the natural obscurity of title in case of new settlements or discoveries.

    c. by the particular obscurity of the evidence resulting from the distance.

    d. by men's caring less about wars when the scene is remote than when it is nearer home.

secondly, that colonies are seldom, if ever, sources of profit to the mother country.

Profitable industry has five branches:

(1) Production of new materials, including agricultures, mining, and fisheries; (2) manufactures; (3) home trade; (4) foreign trade; (5) carrying trade. The quantity of profitable industry that can be carried on in a country being limited by that of the capital which the country can command, it follows that no part of that quantity can be bestowed upon any one branch, but it must be withdrawn from, or withholden from, all the others. No encouragement, therefore, can be given to any one, but it must be a proportionable discouragement to all the others. Nothing can be done by Government to induce a man to begin or continue to employ his capital in any one of those branches, but it must induce him in the same degree to withdraw or withhold that capital from all the rest. Of these five branches, no one is to such a degree more beneficial to the public than the rest as that it should be worth its while to call forth the powers of law to give it an advantage. But if there were any, it would unquestionably be the improvement and cultivation of land, every fictitious encouragement to any one of these rival branches being a proportionable discouragement to agriculture. Every encouragement to any of those branches of manufacture which produce articles that are at present sold to the colonies is a proportionable discouragement to agriculture.

When colonies are to be made out to be beneficial to the mother country, and the quantum of the benefit is to be estimated, the mode in which the estimate is made is curious enough. An account is taken of what they export, which is almost the whole of their produce. All this, it is said, while you have the colonies, is yours; this is exactly what you lose if you lose your colonies. How much of all this is really yours? Not one single halfpenny. When they let you take it from them, do they give it to you for nothing? Not they, indeed; they make you pay for it just as anybody else would do. How much? Just so much as you would pay them if they belonged to themselves or to anybody else.

For maintaining colonies there are several avowed reasons, besides others which are not avowed: of the avowed reasons, by far the principal one is the benefit of trade. If your colonies were not subject to you, they would not trade with you; they would not buy any of your goods, or let you buy any of theirs; at least, you could not be sure of their doing so: if they were subject to anybody else they would not do so; for the colonies of other nations are, you see, not suffered to trade with you. Give up your colonies, you give up so much of your trade as is carried on with your colonies. No, we do not give up any such thing – we do not give up anything whatsoever. Trade with colonies cannot, any more than with anywhere else, be carried on without capital: just as much of our capital as is employed in our trade with the colonies – just so much of it is not employed elsewhere – just so much is either kept or taken from other trades.

Suppose, then, any branch of trade or manufacture to decline – even suppose it lost altogether – is this any permanent loss to the nation? Not the smallest. We know the worst that can happen from any such loss; the capital that would otherwise have been employed in the lost branch will be employed in agriculture. The loss of the colonies, if the loss of the colony trade were the consequence of the loss of the colonies, would at the worst be so much gain to agriculture.

Other reasons against distant dominion may be found in a consideration of the good of the Government. Distant mischiefs make little impression on those on whom the remedying of them depends. A single murder committed in London makes more impression than if thousands of murders and other cruelties were committed in the East Indies. The situation of Hastings, only because he was present, excited compassion in those who heard the detail of the cruelties committed by him with indifference.

The communication of grievances cannot be too quick from those who feel them to those who have the power to relieve them. The reason which in the old writs the King is made to assign for his interfering to afford relief is the real cause which originally gave birth to that interference – it is one of those few truths which have contrived to make their way through the thick cloud of lies and nonsense they contain. 'See what it is that these people want', says the sovereign to the ministers of justice, 'that I may not any more be troubled with their noise'. The motive assigned to the unjust judge in the Gospel is the motive which the Sovereign, who is styled the fountain of justice, is thus made to avow.

The following, then, are the final measures which ought to be pursued:

i. Give up all the colonies.
ii. Found no new colonies.

The following is a summary of the reasons for giving up all the colonies:

A) Interest of the mother-country.

1. Saving the expense of the establishments, civil and military.

2. Saving the danger of war (a) for enforcing their obedience; (b) on account of the jealousy produced by the apparent power they confer.

3. Saving the expense of defending them in case of war on other grounds.

4. Getting rid of the means of corruption afforded by the patronage (a) of their civil establishments; (b) of the military force employed in their defence.

5. Simplifying the whole frame of government, and thereby rendering a competent skill in the business of government more attainable (a) to the members of administration; (b) to the people.[II]

The stock of national intelligence is deteriorated by the false notions which must be kept up in order to prevent the nation from opening its eyes and insisting upon the enfranchisement of the colonies.

At the same time, bad government results to the mother-country from the complication of interests, the indistinct views, and the consumption of time, occasioned by the load of distant dependencies.

B) Interest of the colonies.

Diminishing the chance of bad government resulting from (a) opposite interest; (b) ignorance.

The real interests of the colony must be sacrificed to the imaginary interests of the mother-country. It is for the purpose of governing it badly, and for no other, that you can wish to get or to keep a colony. Govern it well, it is of no use to you. Govern it as well as the inhabitants would govern it themselves – you must choose those to govern it whom they themselves would choose. You must sacrifice none of its interests to your own – you must bestow as much time and attention to their interests as they would themselves. In a word, you must take those very measures, and none others, which they themselves would take. But would this be governing? And what would it be worth to you if it were?

After all, it would be impossible for you to govern them so well as they would govern themselves on account of the distance.[III]

The following are approximating measures:

1. Maintain no military force in any of the colonies.

2. Issue no moneys for the maintenance of any civil establishment in any of the colonies.

3. Nominate to the offices in the colonies as long as they permit you; yield as soon as they contest such nomination.

4. Give general instructions to governors to consent to all acts presented to them.

5. Issue no moneys for fortifications.

PROPOSITION II: *That it is not the interest of Great Britain to have any treaty of alliance, offensive or defensive, with any other power whatever.*

Reason: saving the danger of war arising out of them.

And more especially ought not Great Britain to guarantee foreign constitutions.

Reason: saving the danger of war resulting from the odium of so tyrannical a measure.

PROPOSITION III: *That it is not the interest of Great Britain to have any treaty with any power whatsoever, for the purpose of possessing any advantages whatsoever, in point of trade, to the exclusion of any other nation whatsoever.*

That the trade of every nation is limited by the quantity of capital is so plainly and obviously true, as to challenge a place among self-evident propositions. But self-evident propositions must not expect to be readily admitted, if admitted at all, if the consequences of them clash with prevalent passions and confirmed prejudices.

Nations are composed of individuals. The trade of a nation must be limited by the same causes that limit the trade of the individual. Each individual merchant, when he has as much trade as his whole capital, and all the credit he can get by means of his capital can suffice for carrying on, can have no more. This being true of each merchant, is not less true of the whole number of merchants put together.

Many books directly recognize the proposition that the quantity of trade a nation can carry on is limited – limited by the quantity of its capital. None dispute the proposition; but almost all, somewhere or other, proceed upon the opposite supposition; they suppose the quantity of trade to have no limitation whatsoever.

It is a folly to buy manufactured goods; wise to buy raw materials. Why? Because you sell them to yourselves, or, what is still better, to foreigners, manufactured; and the manufacturer's profit is all clear gain to you. What is here forgotten is that the manufacturer, to carry on his business, must have a capital; and that just so much capital as is employed in that way is prevented from being employed in any other.

Hence the perfect inutility and mischievousness of all laws and public measures of government whatsoever, for the pretended encouragement of trade – all bounties in every shape whatsoever – and non-importation agreements and engagements to consume home manufactures in preference to foreign – in any other view than to afford temporary relief to temporary distress.

But of the two – prohibitions and bounties, penal encouragements and remuneratory – the latter are beyond comparison the most mischievous. Prohibitions, except while they are fresh and drive men at a great expense out of the employments they are embarked in, are only nugatory. Bounties are wasteful and oppressive: they force money from one man in order to pay another man for carrying on a trade, which, if it were not a losing one, there would be no need of paying him for.

What, then, are all modes of production in industry alike? May not one be more profitable than another? Certainly. But the favourite one – is it, in fact, more profitable than any other? That is the question and the only question that ought to be put; and that is the very question which nobody ever thinks of putting.

Were it ever put and answered, and answered ever so clearly, it never could be of any use as a ground for any permanent plan of policy. Why? Because almost as soon as one branch is known to be more profitable than the rest, so soon it ceases so to be. Men flock to it from all other branches, and the old equilibrium is presently restored. Your merchants have a monopoly as against foreigners? True, but they have no monopoly as against one another. Men cannot, in every instance, quit the less productive branch their capitals are already employed in, to throw them into this more productive one? True, but there are young beginners as well as old stagers; and the first concern of a young beginner, who has a capital to employ in a branch of industry, is to look out for the most profitable.

Objection: *Oh! but it is manufacture that creates the demand for the productions of agriculture. You cannot, therefore, increase the productions of agriculture but by increasing manufactures.* No such thing. I admit the antecedent; I deny the consequence. Increase of manufactures certainly does create an increase in the demand for the productions of agriculture. Equally certain is it that the increase of manufacture is not necessary to produce an increase in that demand. Farmers can subsist without ribbons, gauzes, or fine cambrics. Weavers of ribbons, gauzes, or fine cambrics, cannot subsist without the productions of agriculture; necessary subsistence never can lose its value. Those who produce it are themselves a market for their produce. Is it possible that provisions should be too cheap? Is there any present danger of it? Suppose (in spite of the extreme absurdity of the supposition) that provisions were growing gradually too cheap, from the increase of the quantity produced, and the want of manufacturers to consume them, what would be the consequence? The increasing cheapness would increase the facility and disposition to marry: it would thence increase the population of the country; and the children thus produced, eating as they grew up, would keep down this terrible evil of a superabundance of provisions.

Provisions, the produce of agriculture, constantly and necessarily produce a market for themselves. The more provisions a man raises over and above what is necessary for his own consumption, the more he has to give to others, to induce them to provide him with whatever, besides provisions, he chooses to have. In a word, the more he has to spare, the more he has to give to manufacturers, who, by taking it from him and paying him with the produce of their labours, afford the encouragement requisite for the productions of the fruits of agriculture.

It is impossible, therefore, that you can ever have too much agriculture. It is impossible that while there is ground untilled, or ground that might be better tilled than it is, that any detriment should ensue to the community from the withholding or withdrawing capital from any other branch of industry, and employing it in agriculture. It is impossible, therefore, that the loss of any branch of trade can be productive of any detriment to the community, excepting always the temporary distress experienced by the individuals concerned in it for the time being, when the decline is a sudden one.

The following are the measures the propriety of which results from the above principles:

1. That no treaties granting commercial preferences should be made.

2. That no wars should be entered into for compelling such treaties.

3. That no alliances should be contracted for the sake of purchasing them.

4. That no encouragements should be given to particular branches of trade, by

    a. prohibition of rival manufactures.
    b. taxation of rival manufactures.
    c. bounties[IV] on the trade meant to be favoured.

5. That no treaties should be entered into insuring commercial preferences.

They are useless as they add nothing to the mass of wealth; they only influence the direction of it.

PROPOSITION IV: *That it is not the interest of Great Britain to keep up any naval force beyond what may be sufficient to defend its commerce against pirates.*

It is unnecessary, except for the defence of the colonies, or for the purposes of war, undertaken either for the compelling of trade or the formation of commercial treaties.

PROPOSITION V: *That it is not the interest of Great Britain to keep on foot any regulations whatsoever of distant preparation for the augmentation or maintenance of its naval force, such as the Navigation Act, bounties on the Greenland trade, and other trades regarded as nurseries for seamen.*

This proposition is a necessary consequence of the foregoing one.

PROPOSITIONS VI, VII, VIII, IX & X: Propositions similar to the foregoing are equally true applied to France.

PROPOSITION XI: *That, supposing Great Britain and France thoroughly agreed, the principal difficulties would be removed to the establishment of a plan of general and permanent pacification for all Europe.*

PROPOSITION XII: *That for the maintenance of such a pacification, general and perpetual treaties might be formed, limiting the number of troops to be maintained.*[V]

If the simple relation of a single nation with a single other nation be considered, perhaps the matter would not be very difficult. The misfortune is that almost everywhere compound relations are found. On the subject of troops, France says to England: *Yes, I would voluntarily make with you a treaty of disarming, if there were only you; but it is necessary for me to have troops to defend me from the Austrians.* Austria might say the same to France; but it is necessary to guard against Prussia, Russia, and the Porte. And the like allegation might be made by Prussia with regard to Russia.

Whilst as to naval forces, if it concerned Europe only, the difficulty might perhaps not be very considerable. To consider France, Spain and Holland as making together a counterpoise to the power of Britain – perhaps on account of the disadvantages which accompany the concert between three separate nations, to say nothing of the tardiness and publicity of procedures under the Dutch Constitution – perhaps England might allow to all together a united force equal to half or more than its own.

An agreement of this kind would not be dishonourable. If the covenant were on one side only, it might be so. If it regards both parties together, the reciprocity takes away the acerbity. By the treaty which put an end to the first Punic War, the number of vessels that the Carthaginians might maintain was limited. This condition, was it not humiliating? It might be: but if it were, it must have been because there was nothing correspondent to it on the side of the Romans. A treaty which placed all the security on one side – what cause could it have had for its source? It could only have had one, that is, the avowed superiority of the party the incontestably secured. Such a condition could only have been a law dictated by the conqueror to the party conquered: The law of the strongest. None but a conqueror could have dictated it; none but the conquered would have accepted it.

On the contrary, whatsoever nation should get the start of the other in making the proposal to reduce and fix the amount of its armed force would crown itself with everlasting honour. The risk would be nothing – the gain certain. This gain would be the giving an incontrovertible demonstration of its own disposition to peace, and of the opposite disposition in the other nation in case of its rejecting the proposal.

The utmost fairness should be employed. The nation addressed should be invited to consider and point out whatever further securities it deemed necessary, and whatever further concessions it deemed just.

The proposal should be made in the most public manner: it should be an address from nation to nation. This, at the same time that it conciliated the confidence of the nation addressed, would make it impracticable for the government of that nation to neglect it, or stave it off by shifts and evasions. It would sound the heart of the nation addressed. It would discover its intentions, and proclaim them to the world.

The cause of humanity has still another resource. Should Britain prove deaf and impracticable, let France, without conditions, emancipate her colonies, and break up her marine. The advantage even upon this plan would be immense, the danger none. The colonies, I have already shown, are a source of expense, not of revenue – of burden to the people, not of relief. This appears to be the case, even upon the footing of those expenses which appear upon the face of them to belong to the colonies, and are the only ones that have hitherto been set down to their account. But in fact the whole expense of the marine belongs also to that account, and no other. What other destination has it? What other can it have? None. Take away the colonies, what use would there be for a single vessel more than the few necessary in the Mediterranean to curb the pirates?

In case of a war, where at present (1789) would England make its first and only attack upon France? In the colonies.

What would she propose to herself from success in such an attack? What but the depriving France of her colonies. Were these colonies – these bones of contention – no longer hers, what then could England do? What could she wish to do?

There would remain the territory of France; with what view could Britain make any attack upon it in any way? Not with views of permanent conquest – such madness does not belong to our age. Parliament itself, one may venture to affirm, without paying it any very extraordinary compliment, would not wish it. It would not wish it, even could it be accomplished without effort on our part, without resistance on the other. It would not, even though France herself were to solicit it. No parliament would grant a penny for such a purpose. If it did, it would not be a parliament a month. No king would lend his name to such a project. He would be dethroned as surely and as deservedly as James the Second. To say 'I will be King of France' would be to say, in other words, 'I will be absolute in England'.

Well, then, no one would dream of conquest. What other purpose could an invasion have? The plunder and destruction of the country? Such baseness is totally repugnant, not only to the spirit of the nation, but to the spirit of the times. Malevolence could be the only motive – rapacity could never counsel it. Long before an army could arrive anywhere, everything capable of being plundered would be carried off. Whatever is portable, could be much sooner carried off by the owners than by any plundering army. No expedition of plunder could ever pay itself.[VI]

Such is the extreme folly, the madness of war. On no supposition can it be otherwise than mischievous, especially between nations circumstanced as France and England. Though the choice of the events were absolutely at your command, you could not make it of use to you. If unsuccessful, you may be disgraced and ruined. If successful, even to the height of your wishes, you are still but so much the worse. You would still be so much the worse, though it were to cost you nothing. For not even any colony of your own planting, still less a conquest of your own making, will so much as pay its own expenses.

The greatest acquisitions that could be conceived would not be to be wished for, could they even be attained with the greatest certainty and without the least expense. In war, we are as likely not to gain as to gain – as likely to lose as to do either. We can neither attempt the one nor defend ourselves against the other without a certain and most enormous expense.

Mark well the contrast. All trade is in its essence advantageous – even to that party to whom it is least so. All war is in its essence ruinous; and yet the great employments of government are to treasure up occasions of war and to put fetters upon trade.

Ask an Englishman what is the great obstacle to a secure and solid peace, he has his answer ready: It is the ambition (perhaps he will add: the treachery) of France. I wish the chief obstacle to a plan for this purpose were the dispositions and sentiments of France. Were that all, the plan need not long wait for adoption!

Of this visionary project, the most visionary part is without question that for the emancipation of distant dependencies. What will an Englishman say, when he sees two French ministers[VII] of the highest reputation, both at the head of their respective departments, both joining in the opinion that the accomplishment of this event, nay, the speedy accomplishment of it, is inevitable, and one of them scrupling not to pronounce it as eminently desirable.

It would only be the bringing things back on these points to the footing they were on before the discovery of America. Europe had then no colonies, no distant garrisons, no standing armies. It would have had no wars but for the feudal system, religious antipathy, the rage of conquest, and the uncertainties of succession. Of these four causes, the first is happily extinct everywhere; the second and third almost everywhere (and at any rate in France and England); the last might, if not already extinguished, be so with great ease.

The moral feelings of men in matters of national morality are still so far short of perfection that, in the scale of estimation, justice has not yet gained the ascendancy over force. Yet this prejudice may, in a certain point of view, by accident, be rather favourable to this proposal than otherwise. Truth, and the object of this essay, bid me to say to my countrymen: it is for you to begin the reformation; it is you that have been the greatest sinners. But the same considerations also lead me to say to them: you are the strongest among nations; though justice be not on your side, force is; and it is your force that has been the main cause of your injustice. If the measure of moral approbation had been brought to perfection, such positions would have been far from popular; prudence would have dictated the keeping them out of sight, and the softening them down as much as possible.

Humiliation would have been the effect produced by them on those to whom they appeared true; indignation on those to whom they appeared false. But, as I have observed, men have not yet learned to tune their feelings in unison with the voice of morality in these points. They feel more pride in being accounted strong than resentment at being called unjust; or, rather, the imputation of injustice appears flattering rather than otherwise when coupled with the consideration of its cause. I feel it in my own experience; but if *I*, listed as I am as the professed and hitherto the only advocate in my own country in the cause of justice, set a less value on justice than is its due, what can I expect from the general run of men?

PROPOSITION XIII: *That the maintenance of such a pacification might be considerably facilitated by the establishment of a Common Court of Judicature for the decision of differences between the several nations, although such court were not to be armed with any coercive powers.*

It is an observation of somebody's, that no nation ought to yield any evident point of justice to another. This must mean evident in the eyes of the nation that is to judge – evident in the eyes of the nation called upon to yield. What does this amount to? That no nation is to give up anything of what it looks upon as its rights – no nation is to make any concessions. Wherever there is any difference of opinion between the negotiators of two nations, war is to be the consequence.

While there is no common tribunal, something might be said for this. Concession to notorious injustice invites fresh injustice.

Establish a common tribunal, the necessity for war no longer follows from difference of opinion. Just or unjust, the decision of the arbiters will save the credit, the honour of the contending party.

Can the arrangement proposed be justly styled visionary, when it has been proved of it that:

    a. it is in the interest of the parties concerned.
    b. they are already sensible of that interest.
    c. the situation it would place them in is no new one, nor any other than the original situation they set out from.

Difficult and complicated conventions have been effectuated: for examples, we may mention:

    1. the armed neutrality.
    2. the American Confederation.
    3. the German Diet.
    4. the Swiss League.

Why should not the European fraternity subsist as well as the German Diet or the Swiss League? These latter have no ambitious views. Be it so; but is not this already become the case with the former?

How then shall we concentrate the approbation of the people and obviate their prejudices?

One main object of the plan is to effectuate a reduction, and that a mighty one, in the contributions of the people. The amount of the reduction for each nation should be stipulated in the treaty; and even previous to the signature of it, laws for the purpose might be prepared in each nation and presented to every other, ready to be enacted as soon as the treaty should be ratified in each state.

By these means the mass of the people – the part most exposed to be led away by prejudices – would not be sooner apprized of the measure than they would feel the relief it brought them. They would see it was for their advantage it was calculated, and that it could not be calculated for any other purpose.

The concurrence of all the maritime powers, except England, upon a former occasion, proved two points: the reasonableness of that measure itself, and the weakness of France in comparison with England. It was a measure, not of ambition, but of justice – a law made in favour of equality, a law made for the benefit of the weak. No sinister point was gained, or attempted to be gained, by it. France was satisfied with it. Why? Because she was weaker than Britain. She *could* have no other motive; on no other supposition could it have been of any advantage to her. Britain was vexed at it. Why? For the opposite reason: she could have no other.

Oh, my countrymen! Purge your eyes from the film of prejudice; extirpate from your hearts the *black specks* of excessive jealousy, false ambition, selfishness, and insolence. The operations may be painful, but the rewards are glorious indeed! As the main difficulty, so will the main honour be with you.

What though wars should hereafter arise? The intermediate savings will not the less be so much clear gain.

Though, in the generating of the disposition for war, unjust ambition has doubtless had by far too great a share, yet jealousy – sincere and honest jealousy – must be acknowledged to have had a not inconsiderable one. Vulgar prejudice, fostered by passion, assigns the heart as the seat of all the moral diseases it complains of, but the principal and more frequent seat is really the head. It is from ignorance and weakness that men deviate from the path of rectitude more frequently than from selfishness and malevolence. This is fortunate, for the power of information and reason over error and ignorance is much greater and much surer than that of exhortation and all the modes of rhetoric over selfishness and malevolence.

It is because we do not know what strong motives other nations have to be just, what strong indications they have given of the disposition to be so – how often we ourselves have deviated from the rules of justice – that we take for granted, as an indisputable truth, that the principles of injustice are in a manner interwoven into the very essence of the hearts of other men.

The diffidence which forms part of the character of the English nation may have been one cause of this jealousy. The dread of being duped by other nations – the notion that foreign heads are more able, though at the same time foreign hearts are less honest than our own – has always been one of our prevailing weaknesses. This diffidence has perhaps some connection with the *mauvaise honte* which has been remarked as commonly showing itself in our behaviour, and which makes public speaking and public exhibition in every line a task so much more formidable to us than to other people.

This diffidence may, perhaps, in part be accounted for from our living less in society and accustoming ourselves less to mixed companies than the people of other nations.

But the particular cast of diffidence in question, the apprehension of being duped by foreign powers, is to be referred in part, and perhaps principally, to another cause: the jealousy and slight opinion we entertain of our ministers and public men. We are jealous of them as our superiors, contending against us in the perpetual struggle for power. We are diffident of them as being our fellow-countrymen, and of the same mould as ourselves.

Jealousy is the vice of narrow minds; confidence the virtue of enlarged ones. To be satisfied that confidence between nations is not out of nature where they have worthy ministers, one need but read the account of the negotiation between De Wit and Temple as given by Hume. I say 'by Hume', for as it required negotiators like De Wit and Temple to carry on such a negotiation in such a manner, so it required a historian like Hume to do it justice. For the vulgar among historians know no other receipt for writing that part of history than the finding out whatever are the vilest and basest motives capable of accounting for men's conduct in the situation in question, and then ascribing it to those motives without ceremony and without proof.

Temple and De Wit, whose confidence in each other was so exemplary and so just – Temple and De Wit were two of the wisest as well as most honourable men in Europe. The age which produced such virtue was, however, the age of the pretended Popish plot, and of a thousand other enormities which cannot now be thought of without horror. Since then the world has had upwards of a century to improve itself in experience, in reflection, in virtue. In every other line its improvements have been immense and unquestioned. Is it too much to hope that France and England might produce, not a Temple and a De Wit (virtue so transcendent as theirs would not be necessary), but men who, in happier times, might achieve a work like theirs with less extent of virtue?

Such a Congress or Diet might be constituted by each power sending two deputies to the place of meeting – one of these to be the principal, the other to act as an occasional substitute.

The proceedings of such Congress or Diet should be all public.

Its power would consist:

(1) in reporting its opinion;

(2) in causing that opinion to be circulated in the dominions of each state.

Manifestoes are in common usage. A manifesto is designed to be read either by the subjects of the state complained of, or by other states, or by both. It is an appeal to them. It calls for their opinion. The difference is that in that case nothing of proof is given; no opinion regularly made known.

The example of Sweden is alone sufficient to show the influence which treaties, the acts of nations, may be expected to have over the subjects of the several nations, and how far the expedient in question deserves the character of a weak one, or the proposal for employing and trusting to it that of a visionary proposal.

The war commenced by the King of Sweden against Russia was deemed by his subjects, or at least a considerable part of them, offensive, and as such, contrary to the constitution established by him with the concurrence of the states. Hence a considerable part of the army either threw up their commissions or refused to act; and the consequence was the King was obliged to retreat from the Russian frontier and call a diet.

This was under a government commonly, though not truly, supposed to be changed from a limited monarchy, or rather aristocracy, to a despotic monarchy. There was no act of any recognized and respected tribunal to guide and fix the opinion of the people. The only document they had to judge from was a manifesto of the enemy couched in terms such as resentment would naturally dictate, and therefore none of the most conciliating – a document which had no claim to be circulated, and of which the circulation, we may be pretty well assured, was prevented as much as it was in the power of the utmost vigilance of the government to prevent it.

(3) after a certain time, in putting the refractory state under the ban of Europe.

There might, perhaps, be no harm in regulating, as a last resource, the contingent to be furnished by the several states for enforcing the decrees of the Court. But the necessity for the employment of this resource would, in all human probability, be superseded forever by having recourse to the much more simple and less burdensome expedient of introducing into the instrument by which such court was instituted a clause guaranteeing the liberty of the press in each state, in such sort that the Diet might find no obstacle to its giving, in every state, to its decrees and to every paper whatever, which it might think proper to sanction with its signature, the most extensive and unlimited circulation.

PROPOSITION XIV: *That secrecy in the operations of the Foreign Department in England ought not to be endured, being altogether useless and equally repugnant to the interests of liberty and peace.*

The existence of the rule which throws a veil of secrecy over the transactions of the Cabinet with foreign powers, I shall not take upon me to dispute. My objection is to the propriety of it.

Being asked in the House of Lords by Lord Stormont[VIII] about secret articles, the Minister for Foreign Affairs refuses to answer. I blame him not. Subsisting rules, it seems to be agreed, forbid reply. They throw a general veil of secrecy over the transactions of the Cabinet with foreign powers. I blame no man for the fault of the laws. It is these laws that I blame as repugnant to the spirit of the Constitution and incompatible with good government.

I take at once the boldest and the broadest ground. I lay down two propositions:

1. That in no negotiation, and at no period of any negotiation, ought the negotiations of the Cabinet in this country to be kept secret from the public at large; much less from Parliament and after inquiry made in Parliament.[IX]

2. That whatever may be the case with preliminary negotiations, such secrecy ought never to be maintained with regard to treaties actually concluded.

In both cases, to a country like this, such secrecy is equally mischievous and unnecessary.

It is mischievous. Over measures of which you have no knowledge, you can apply no control. Measures carried on without your knowledge: you cannot stop – how ruinous soever to you, and how strongly soever you would disapprove of them if you knew them. Of negotiations with foreign powers carried on in time of peace, the principal terminations are treaties of alliance, offensive or defensive, or treaties of commerce. But, by one accident or other, everything may lead to war.

That in new treaties of commerce as such, there can be no cause for secrecy is a proposition that will hardly be disputed. Only such negotiations, like all others, may eventually lead to war; and everything connected with war, it will be said, may come to require secrecy.

But rules which admit of a minister's plunging the nation into a war against its will are essentially mischievous and unconstitutional.

It is admitted that ministers ought not to have it in their power to impose taxes on the nation against its will. It is admitted that they ought not to have it in their power to maintain troops against its will. But by plunging it into war without its knowledge they do both.

Parliament may refuse to carry on a war after it is begun. Parliament may remove and punish the minister who has brought the nation into a war.

Sorry remedies these. Add them both together, their efficacy is not worth a straw. Arrestment of the evil and punishment of the authors are sad consolations for the mischief of a war, and of no value as remedies in comparison with prevention. Aggressive war is a matter of choice; defensive, of necessity. Refusal of the means of continuing a war is a most precarious remedy – a remedy only in name. What, when the enemy is at your doors, refuse the materials for barricading them?

Before aggression, war or no war depends upon the aggressor. Once begun, the party aggrieved acquires a vote. He has his negative upon every plan for terminating the war. What is to be done? Give yourself up without resistance to the mercy of a justly exasperated enemy? But this or the continuance of the war is all the choice that is now left. In what state of things can this remedy be made to serve? Are you unsuccessful? The remedy is inapplicable. Are you successful? Nobody will call for it.

Punishment of the authors of the war – punishment, whatever it may be, to the personal adversaries of the ministers – is no satisfaction to the nation. This is self-evident. But what is closer to the purpose, and not less true, is that, in a case like this, the fear of punishment on such an account is no check to them: of a majority in Parliament they are in possession; or they would not be ministers. That they should be abandoned by this majority is not in the catalogue of events that ought to be looked upon as possible, but between abandoning them and punishing them there is a wide difference. Lord North was abandoned in the American war. He was not punished for it. His was an honest error in judgment, unstained by any *malâ fide* practice, and countenanced by a fair majority in Parliament. And so may any other impolitic and unjust war be. This is not a punishing age. If bribe-taking, oppression, peculation, duplicity, treachery, every crime that can be committed by statesmen sinning against conscience, produce no desire to punish, what dependence can be placed on punishment in a case where the mischief may so easily happen without any ground for punishment? Mankind are not yet arrived at that stage in the track of civilization. Foreign nations are not yet considered as objects susceptible of an injury. For the citizens of other civilized nations we have not so much feeling as for our negroes. There are instances in which ministers have been punished for making peace;[X] there are none where they have been so much as questioned for bringing the nation into war; and if punishment had been ever applied on such an occasion, it would be not for the mischief done to the foreign nation, but purely for the mischief brought upon their own – not for the injustice, but purely for the imprudence.

It has never been laid down as a rule that you should pay any regard to foreign nations. It has never been laid down that you should stick at anything which would give you an advantage in your dealings with foreign nations. On what ground could a minister be punished for a war, even the most unsuccessful, brought on by any such means? 'I did my best to serve you', he would say, 'the worse the measure was for the foreign nation, the more I took upon me; the greater, therefore, the zeal I showed for your cause; the event has proved unfavourable. Are zeal and misfortune to be represented as crimes?'

A war unjust on the part of our own nation, by whose ministers it is brought on, can never be brought on but in pursuit of some advantage which, were it not for the injustice towards the foreign nation, it would be for our interests to pursue. The injustice and the danger of retaliation being on all hands looked upon as nothing, the plea of the minister would always be: 'It was *your* interest I was pursuing.' And the uninformed and unreflecting part of the nation, that is, the great body of the nation, would echo to him: 'Yes, it was our interest you were preserving.' The voice of the nation on these subjects can only be looked for in newspapers. But on these subjects the language of all newspapers is uniform: 'It is we that are always in the right, without a possibility of being otherwise. Against us other nations have no rights. If according to the rules of judging between individual and individual, we are right, we are right by the rules of justice; if not, we are right by the laws of patriotism, which is a virtue more respectable than justice.' Injustice, oppression, fraud, lying . . . whatever acts would be crimes, whatever habits would be vices if manifested in the pursuit of individual interests: when manifested in pursuit of national interests, become sublimated into virtues. Let any man declare, who has ever read or heard an English newspaper, whether this be not the constant tenor of the notions they convey. Party, on this one point, makes no difference. However hostile to one another on all other points, on this they have never but one voice; they write with the utmost harmony. Such are the opinions, and to these opinions the facts are accommodated as of course. Who would blush to misrepresent, when misrepresentation is a virtue?

But newspapers, if their voice make but a small part of the voice of the people, the instruction they give makes on these subjects the whole of the instruction which the people receive.

Such being the national propensity to error on these points, and to error on the worst side, the danger of parliamentary punishment for misconduct of this kind must appear equivalent to next to nothing, even in the eyes of an unconcerned and cool spectator. What must it appear, then, in the eyes of ministers themselves, acting under the seduction of self-partiality, and hurried on by the tide of business? No, the language which a minister on such occasions will hold to himself will be uniformly this: 'In the first place, what I do is not wrong. In the next place, if it were, nothing should I have to fear from it.'

Under the present system of secrecy, ministers have, therefore, every seduction to lead them into misconduct, while they have no check to keep them out of it. And what species of misconduct? That in comparison of which all others are but peccadilloes. Let a minister throw away £30,000 or £40,000 in pensions to his creatures. Let him embezzle a few hundred thousand for himself. What is that to fifty or a hundred millions, the ordinary burden of a war? Observe the consequence. This is the department of all others in which the strongest checks are needful. At the same time, thanks to the rules of secrecy of all the departments, this is the only one in which there are no checks at all. I say, then, the conclusion is demonstrated. The principle which throws a veil of secrecy over the proceedings of the Foreign Department of the Cabinet is pernicious in the highest degree, pregnant with mischiefs superior to everything to which the most perfect absence of all concealment could possibly give rise.

There still remains a sort of inexplicit notion which may present itself as secretly furnishing an argument on the other side: Such is the condition of the British nation; peace and war may be always looked upon as being to all human probability in good measure in her power; when the worst comes to the worst, peace may always be had by some unessential sacrifice. I admit the force of the argument; what I maintain is that it operates in my favour. Why? It depends upon two propositions: the matchless strength of this country and the uselessness of her foreign dependencies. I admit both, but both operate as arguments in my favour. Her strength places her above the danger of surprise, and above the necessity of having recourse to it to defend herself. The uselessness of her foreign dependencies proves *a fortiori* the uselessness of engaging in wars for their protection and defence. If they are not fit to keep without war, much less are they worth keeping at the price of war. The inutility of a secret cabinet is demonstrated by this short dilemma. For offensive measures, cabinet secrecy can never be necessary to this nation; for defence, it can never be necessary to any.

My persuasion is that there is no state whatever in which any inconveniences capable of arising from publicity in this department would not be greatly overbalanced by the advantages – be the state ever so great or ever so small, ever so strong or ever so weak; be its form of government pure or mixed, single or confederated, monarchical, aristocratical, or democratical. The observations already given seem in all these cases sufficient to warrant the conclusion.

But in a nation like Britain the safety of publicity, the inutility of secrecy in all such business, stands upon peculiar grounds. Stronger than any two other nations, much stronger of course than any *one*, its superiority deprives it of all pretence of necessity in carrying points by surprise. Clandestine surprise is the resource of knavery and fear, of unjust ambition combined with weakness. Her matchless power exempts her from the one; her interest, if her servants could be brought to be governed by her evident interests, would forbid the other.

Taking the interest of the first servant of the state (as distinct from and opposite to the nation), clandestinity may undoubtedly be, in certain cases, favourable to the projects of sceptred thieves and robbers. Without taking the precautions of a thief, the Great Frederic might probably enough not have succeeded in the enterprise of stealing Silesia from her lawful sovereign. Without an advantage of this sort, the triple gang might, perhaps, not have found it quite so easy to secure what they stole from Poland. Whether there can or cannot exist occasions on which it might, in this point of view, be the interest of a king of Great Britain to turn highwayman is a question I shall waive; but a proposition I shall not flinch from is, that it never can be the interest of the nation to abet him in it. When those sceptred sinners sold themselves to the service of Mammon, they did not serve him for nought: the booty was all their own. Were we (I speak as one of the body of the nation) to assist our King in committing a robbery upon France, the booty would be his. He would have the naming to the new places, which is all the value that in the hands of a British robber such booty can be to anybody. The privilege of paying for the horse and pistols is all that would be ours. The booty would be employed in corrupting our confidential servants, and this is the full and exact amount of what we should get by it.

Conquests made by New Zealanders have some sense in them. While the conquered fry, the conquerors fatten. Conquests made by the polished nations of antiquity – conquests made by Greeks and Romans – had some sense in them. Lands, movables, inhabitants: everything went into the pocket. The invasions of France in the days of the Edwards and the Henrys had a rational object. Prisoners were taken, and the country was stripped to pay their ransom. The ransom of a single prisoner, a Duke of Orleans, exceeded one-third of the national revenue of England.

Conquests made by a modern despot of the continent have still some sense in them. The new property, being contiguous, is laid on to his old property; the inhabitants, as many as he thinks fit to set his mark upon, go to increase his armies; their substance, as much as he thinks fit to squeeze from them, goes into his purse.

Conquests made by the British nation would be violations of common sense, were there no such thing as justice. They are bungling imitations of miserable originals, bating the essential circumstances. Nothing but confirmed blindness and stupidity can prompt us to go on imitating Alexander and Cæsar, and the New Zealanders, and Catherine and Frederic, without the profit.

If it be the King alone who gets the appointment to the places, it is a part of the nation, it may be said, that gets the benefit of filling them. A precious lottery! Fifty or one hundred millions: the cost of the tickets; so many years' purchase of ten or twenty thousand a year: the value of the prizes. This if the scheme succeed. What if it fail?

I do not say there are no sharers in the plunder. It is impossible for the head of a gang to put the whole of it into his own pocket. All I contend for is, that robbery by wholesale is not so profitable as by retail. If the whole gang together pick the pockets of strangers to a certain amount, the ringleaders pick the pockets of the rest to a much greater. Shall I or shall I not succeed in persuading my countrymen that it is not their interest to be thieves?

'Oh, but you mistake!' cries somebody. 'We do not now make war for conquests, but for trade.' More foolish still. This is a still worse bargain than before. Conquer the whole world, it is impossible you should increase your trade one halfpenny; it is impossible you should do otherwise than diminish it. Conquer little or much, you pay for it by taxes; but just so much as a merchant pays in taxes, just so much he is disabled from adding to the capital he employs in trade. Had you two worlds to trade with, you could only trade with them to the amount of your capital and what credit you might meet with on the strength of it. This, being true of each trader, is so of all traders. Find a fallacy in this short argument if you can. If you obtained your new right of trading given you for nothing, you would not be a halfpenny the richer. If you paid for them by war or preparations for war, by just so much as you paid for these you would be the poorer.

The good people of England, along with the right of self-government, conquered prodigious right of trade. The revolution was to produce for them not only the blessings of security and power, but immense and sudden wealth. Year has followed after year and, to their endless astonishment, the progress to wealth has gone on no faster than before. One piece of good fortune still wanting they have never thought of: that on the day their shackles were knocked off, some kind sylph should have slipped a few thousand pounds into every man's pocket. There is no law against my flying to the moon. Yet I cannot get there. Why? Because I have no wings. What wings are to flying, capital is to trade.

There are two ways of making war for trade: forcing independent nations to let you trade with them, and conquering nations (or pieces of nations) to make them trade with you. The former contrivance is to appearance the more easy, and the policy of it the more refined. The latter is more in the good old way, and the king does his own business and the nation's at the same time. He gets the naming to the places; and the nation cannot choose but join with him, being assured that it is all for the sake of getting them the trade. The places he lays hold of, good man, only out of necessity, and that they may not go a-begging. On his own account, he has no more mind for them than a new-made bishop for the mitre or a new-made speaker for the chair. To the increase of trade both these plans of war equally contribute. What you get in both cases is the pleasure of the war.

The legal right of trading to part of America was conquered by France from Britain in the last war. What have they got by it? They have got Tobago, bankruptcy, and a revolution for their fifty millions. Ministers, who to account for the bankruptcy are forced to say something about the war, call it a national one. The King has not got by it, therefore the nation has. What has it got? A fine trade, were there but capital to carry it on. With such room for trade, how comes there to be no more of it? This is what merchants and manufacturers are putting themselves to the torture to account for. The sylph so necessary elsewhere was still more necessary to France, since, over and above her other work, there was the fifty millions spent in powder and shot to replace.

The King of France, however, by getting Tobago, probably obtained two or three thousand pounds' worth of places to give away. This is what he got, and this is all that anybody got for the nation's fifty millions. Let us go on as we have begun, strike a bold stroke, take all their vessels we can lay hold of without a declaration of war, and who knows but what we may get it back again. With the advantages we now have over them, five times the success they are so pleased with would be but a moderate expectation. For every fifty millions thus laid out, our King would get in places to the amount, not of two or three thousand pounds only, but, say, of ten, fifteen, or twenty thousand pounds. All this would be prodigious glory; and fine paragraphs and speeches, thanksgivings, and birthday odes might be sung and said for it; but for economy I would much rather give the King new places to the same amount at home, if at this price his ministers would sell us peace.

The conclusion is that, as we have nothing to fear from any other nation or nations, nor want anything from other nations, we can have nothing to say to other nations, nor to hear from them, that might not be as public as any laws. What, then, is the veil of secrecy that enwraps the proceedings of the Cabinet? A mere cloak for wickedness and folly; a dispensation to ministers to save them from the trouble of thinking; a warrant for playing all manner of mad and silly pranks, unseen and uncontrolled; a licence to play at hazard with their fellows abroad, staking our lives and fortunes upon the throw.

What, then, is the true use and effect of secrecy? That the prerogatives of place may furnish an aliment to petty vanity; that the members of *the circulation* may have, as it were, a newspaper to themselves; that under favour of the monopoly, ignorance and incapacity may put on airs of wisdom; that a man, unable to write or speak what is fit to be put into a newspaper, may toss up his head and say 'I don't read newspapers', as if a parent were to say 'I don't trouble my head about schoolmasters'; and that a minister, secure from scrutiny in that quarter, may have the convenient opportunity, upon occasion, of filling the posts with obsequious cyphers instead of effective men. Anything will do to make a minister whose writing may be written for him and whose duty in speaking consists in silence.

This much must be confessed: if secrecy, as against the nation, be useless and pernicious to the nation, it is not useless and pernicious with regard to its servants. It forms part of the *douceurs* of office – a perquisite which will be valued in proportion to the insignificance of their characters and the narrowness of their views. It serves to pamper them up with notions of their own importance, and to teach the servants of the people to look down upon their masters.

Oh! But if everything that were written were liable to be made public, were published, who would treat with you abroad? Just the same persons as treat with you at present. Negotiations, for fear of misrepresentation, would perhaps be committed somewhat more to writing than at present. And where would be the harm? The king and his ministers might not have quite such copious accounts, true or false, of the tittle-tattle of each court, or they must put into different hands the tittle-tattle and the real business. And suppose your head servants were not so minutely acquainted with the mistresses and buffoons of kings and their ministers: what matters it to you as a nation, who have no intrigues to carry on, no petty points to compass?

It were an endless task to fill more pages with the shadows that might be conjured up in order to be knocked down. I leave that task to any that will undertake it. I challenge party men; I invite the impartial lovers of their country and mankind to discuss the question, to ransack the stores of history, and imagination as well as history, for cases, actual or possible, in which the want of secrecy in this line of business can be shown to be attended with any substantial prejudice.

As to the Constitution, the question of cabinet secrecy, having never been tried by the principles of the Constitution, has never received a decision. The good old Tudor and Stuart principles have been suffered to remain unquestioned here. Foreign politics are questions of state. Under Elizabeth and James, nothing was to be inquired into; nothing was to be known; everything was matter of state. On other points the veil has been torn away; but with regard to these, there has been a sort of tacit understanding between ministers and people.

Hitherto war has been the national rage. Peace has always come too soon; war too late. To tie up the ministers' hands and make them continually accountable would be depriving them of numberless occasions of seizing those happy advantages that lead to war; it would be lessening the people's chance of their favourite amusement. For these hundred years past, ministers, to do them justice, have generally been more backward than the people. The great object has rather been to force them into war, than to keep them out of it. Walpole and Newcastle were both forced into war.

It admits of no doubt, if we are really for war, and fond of it for its own sake, we can do no better than let things continue as they are. If we think peace better than war, it is equally certain that the law of secrecy cannot be too soon abolished.

Such is the general confusion of ideas, such the power of the imagination, such the force of prejudice, that I verily believe the persuasion is not an uncommon one. So clear in their notions are many worthy gentlemen that they look upon war, if successful, as a cause of opulence and prosperity. With equal justice might they look upon the loss of a leg as a cause of swiftness.

Well, but if it be not directly the cause of opulence, it is indirectly. From the successes of war come, say they, our prosperity, our greatness. Thence the respect paid to us by foreign powers; thence our security. And who does not know how necessary security is to opulence?

No, war is, in this way, just as unfavourable to opulence as in the other. In the present mode of carrying on war – a mode which it is in no man's power to depart from – security is in proportion to opulence. Just so far then as war is, by its direct effects, unfavourable to opulence, just so far is it unfavourable to security.

Respect is a term I shall beg leave to change; respect is a mixture of fear and esteem, but for constituting esteem, force is not the instrument, but justice. The sentiment really relied upon for security is fear. By respect then is meant, in plain English, fear. But in a case like this, fear is much more adverse than favourable to security. So many as fear you, join against you till they think they are too strong for you, and then they are afraid of you no longer. Meantime they all hate you, and jointly and severally they do you as much mischief as they can. You, on your part, are not behindhand with them. Conscious or not conscious of your own bad intentions, you suspect theirs to be still worse. Their notion of your intentions is the same. Measures of mere self-defence are naturally taken for projects of aggression. The same causes produce, on both sides, the same effects; each makes haste to begin for fear of being forestalled. In this state of things, if on either side there happen to be a minister, or a would-be minister, who has a fancy for war, the stroke is struck and the tinder catches fire.

At school, the strongest boy may perhaps be the safest. Two or more boys are not always in readiness to join against one. But though this notion may hold good in an English school, it will not bear transplanting upon the theatre of Europe.

Oh! But if your neighbours are really afraid of you, their fear is of use to you in another way; you get the turn of the scale in all disputes. Points that are at all doubtful, they give up to you of course. Watch the moment, and you may every now and then gain points that do not admit of doubt. This is only the former old set of fallacies exhibited in a more obscure form, and which, from their obscurity only, can show as new. The fact is, as has been already shown, there is no nation that has any points to gain to the prejudice of any other. Between the interests of nations, there is nowhere any real conflict. If they appear repugnant anywhere, it is only in proportion as they are misunderstood. What are these points? What points are these which, if you had your choice, you would wish to gain of them? Preferences in trade have been proved to be worth nothing; distant territorial acquisitions have been proved to be worth less than nothing. When these are out of the question, what other points are there worth gaining by such means?

Opulence is the word I have first mentioned, but opulence is not the word that would be first pitched upon. The repugnancy of the connection between war and opulence is too glaring. The term 'opulence' brings to view an idea too simple, too intelligible, too precise. Splendour, greatness, glory: these are terms better suited to the purpose. Prove first that war contributes to splendour and greatness, you may persuade yourself it contributes to opulence, because when you think of splendour, you think of opulence. But splendour, greatness, glory – all these fine things – may be produced by useless success, and unprofitable and enervating extent of dominion obtained at the expense of opulence; and this is the way in which you may manage so as to prove to yourself that the way to make a man run the quicker is to cut off one of his legs. And true enough it is, that a man who has had a leg cut off, and the stump healed, may hop faster than a man, who lies in bed with both legs broken, can walk. And thus you may prove that Britain is in a better case after the expenditure of a glorious war than if there had been no war, because France or some other country was put by it into a still worse condition.

In respect, therefore, of any benefit to be derived in the shape of conquest or of trade, of opulence or of respect, no advantage can be reaped by the employment of the unnecessary, the mischievous, and unconstitutional system of clandestinity and secrecy in negotiation.

Notes

[1] Two original writers have gone before me in this line, Dean Tucker and Dr Anderson. The object of the first was to persuade the world of the inutility of war, but more particularly of the war then raging when he wrote; the object of the second was to show the inutility of the colonies.

II Reasons for giving up Gibraltar:

1. The expense of the military establishment, *viz.* fortifications, garrisons, ordnance, recruiting, service, victualling.
2. The means of corruption resulting from the patronage.
3. The saving the danger of war with Spain, to which the possession of the place is a perpetual provocation.
4. The price that might be obtained from Spain for the purchase of it.
5. Saving the occasional expense of defending it and victualling it in war.
6. The possession of it is useless. It is said to be useful only on account of the Levant trade, but (a) we could carry on that trade equally well without Gibraltar; (b) if we could not, we should suffer no loss; the capital employed in that trade would be equally productive if employed in any other; (c) supposing this [Levant trade to be] the most productive of all trades, yet what we lost by losing Gibraltar would only be equal to the difference between the percentage gained in that trade and the percentage gained in the next most productive trade, for (d) we could still do as the Swedes, Danes, Dutch etc., and as we did before we had possession of Gibraltar.

Reasons for giving up the East Indies:

1. Saving the danger of war.
2. Getting rid of the means of corruption resulting from the patronage, civil and military.
3. Simplifying the government.
4. Getting rid of prosecutions that consume the time of parliament, and beget suspicion or injustice.
5. Preventing the corruption of the morals of the natives by the example of successful rapacity.

III It is in proportion as we see things – as they are brought within the reach of our attention and observation – that we care for them. A minister who would not kill one man with his own hands, does not mind causing the death of myriads by the hands of others at a distance.

IV All bounties on particular branches of trade do rather harm than good.

V Precedents: 1. Convention of disarmament between France and Britain, 1787 – this is a precedent of the measure or stipulation itself; 2. Armed neutrality code – this is a precedent of the mode of bringing about the measure, and may serve to disprove the impossibility of a general convention among nations; 3. Treaty forbidding the fortifying of Dunkirk.

VI This brings to recollection the achievements of the war from 1755 to 1763. The struggle betwixt prejudice and humanity produced in conduct a result truly ridiculous. Prejudice prescribed an attack upon the enemy in his own territory; humanity forbade the doing him any harm. Not only nothing was gained by these expeditions, but the mischief done to the country invaded was not nearly equal to the expense of the invasion. When a Japanese rips open his own belly, it is in the assurance that his enemy will follow his example. But in this instance the Englishman ripped open his own belly that the Frenchman might get a scratch. Why was this absurdity acted? Because we were at war; and when nations are at war something must be done, or at least appear to be done; and there was nothing else to be done. France was already stripped of all its distant dependencies.

VII Turgot and Vergennes.

VIII May 22, 1789.

IX It lies upon the other side, at least, to put a case in which want of secrecy may produce a specific mischief.

X The fate of Queen Anne's last ministry may be referred in some degree to this cause, and owing to the particular circumstances of their conduct they perhaps deserved it: See the Report of the Secret Committee of the House of Commons in the year 1715. The great crime of the Earl of Bute was making peace. The Earl of Shelburne was obliged to resign for having made peace. The great crime of Sir R. Walpole was keeping the peace. The nation was become tired of peace. Walpole was reproached with proposing half a million in the year for secret service money. His errors were rectified – war was made – and in one year there was laid out in war four times what he had spent in the ten years before.

Chapter 14
Perpetual Peace through Universal Hospitality: Kant's Plan

Immanuel Kant's (1724–1804) *Perpetual Peace* is by far the most well-known exponent of the perpetual peace tradition.[1] Interestingly, though, Kant was one of the least 'political' of all thinkers we have introduced in this volume. Not only did he remain politically inactive throughout his life, but also *theorizing* politics, whether domestic or international, seems to have been just a modest by-product of his groundbreaking systematic philosophy. Equally striking is the fact that Kant was also the most 'local' of all thinkers we have seen so far, yet produced the most universal(ist) of all perpetual peace proposals. From within the confines of Königsberg in East Prussia,[2] where he spent his entire life without travelling long distances, Kant formulated a distinctively cosmopolitan international theory.[3]

Rousseau's two essays on perpetual peace, as mentioned in Chapter 10, preceded his major works. Bentham put his perpetual peace ideas (see Chapter 12) on paper in more or less

---

[1] Kant's essay, *Zum Ewigen Frieden*, has been translated into English under slightly differing titles, including *Towards Perpetual Peace* and *On Perpetual Peace*. But it is most widely known simply as *Perpetual Peace*, and here, too, it will be referred to as such.

[2] Kaliningrad in today's Russian Federation.

[3] Fine and Cohen identify four major cosmopolitan 'moments' in time: those of Zeno, Kant, Arendt and Nussbaum; see Robert Fine and Robin Cohen, 'Four Cosmopolitan Moments', in Steven Vertovec and Robin Cohen (eds), *Conceiving Cosmopolitanism: Theory, Context, and Practice* (Oxford: Oxford University Press, 2002), pp. 137–62. For the 'Stoic' roots of Kant's approach, see Martha C. Nussbaum, 'Kant and Stoic cosmopolitanism', *The Journal of Political Philosophy* 5 (1997), 1–25.

the same year as his most significant work. Kant, in contrast to both, drafted his *Perpetual Peace* very late in his career. He was seventy-one years old when his plan was first published, and had already produced several monumental works of philosophy to his name:[4] *Critique of Pure Reason* (1781), *Prolegomena to Any Future Metaphysics* (1783), *Groundwork of the Metaphysic of Morals* (1785), *Critique of Practical Reason* (1788), and *Critique of Judgment* (1790). From one angle, therefore, *Perpetual Peace* may be taken merely as a modest afterthought. From the reverse angle, though, this essay can also be seen as the culmination of Kant's entire thought – a transposition of his overall philosophy onto the international realm, the immediate stimulus for which came with Europe's recognition of the French Republic at the Treaty of Basel.

A historically informed careful comparison between the overall philosophies of Kant, Rousseau and Bentham may prove necessary in order to establish convincingly the relationship, indeed potential interaction, between their approaches to perpetual peace. As clarified from the outset, such a task is clearly outside this volume's scope and intention. Very much in passing, though, we might suggest a few general points to bear in mind when reading Kant's well-known plan in juxtaposition with Rousseau's and Bentham's texts. These points arise from the pertinent literature, but they do not, of course, constitute the final word on the intellectual relationship between these influential thinkers, and on the conceptual linkages between their perpetual peace projects and our contemporary notions of global governance.

Firstly, while Kant was clearly inspired by Rousseau to a considerable extent,[5] he did not share Rousseau's rather pessimistic views of society and civilization. He did not, in particular, accept the society's allegedly corrupting effects.

---

[4] *Perpetual Peace* was first published in 1795; its second edition appeared in 1796; and the essay was translated into English and French shortly thereafter; see Eric S. Easley, *The War over* Perpetual Peace: *An Exploration into the History of a Foundational International Relations Text* (Houndmills: Palgrave Macmillan, 2004), p. 5.

[5] Elizabeth York mentions Newton, Hume and Rousseau as the successive major influences on the evolution of Kant's thought; see York, *Leagues of Nations*, p. 254.

For him, a distinction between 'natural' and 'moral' species was a more proper way of situating good and evil.[6] What this comes down to is that in Rousseau we find only *one* human nature. Kant, on the other hand, points to the possibility of co-existing human natures:[7] one natural, the other moral.[8] This fundamental difference, if thoroughly explored, might give us clues as to why and how Rousseau kept coming back to the question of force, while Kant's approach kept expanding from what might be termed *realistic* wishful thinking towards a more *idealistic* wishful thinking.[9]

Secondly, Kant's views on happiness, law, and morality differ radically from those of Bentham. Indeed, the Kantian *deontological* approach is arguably diametrically opposed to the Benthamite utilitarianism and legal positivism. As Robert Anchor puts it, 'there is little room in Kant's philosophy for the realization of happiness; at best man can only make himself "worthy of happiness"'.[10] Legality and morality, in Kant's overall conceptualization, are related to duties;[11] and duties cannot be grounded in happiness. Patrick Riley uses the following example to demonstrate Kant's point: happiness might well involve killing, whereas it simply is our duty not to kill. In Kant's view, therefore, 'happiness cannot be instrumental to morality the same way that political or public legal justice is'.[12] This contrast with Bentham's *felicific calculus* of happiness may help us contextualize the differing versions of universalism we detect in the respective perpetual peace plans

---

6   See Robert Anchor, *The Enlightenment Tradition* (Berkeley, CA: University of California Press, 1967), p. 115.
7   His Second Definitive Article, for instance, refers to man's 'higher natural moral capacity' as well as 'the evil principle in his nature, the existence of which he is unable to deny'.
8   Anchor, *The Enlightenment Tradition*, p. 116.
9   Can we detect a bit of Rousseau in Kant's remark: 'Hence, in the practical realization of that idea [of collective unity and common will], no other beginning of a law-governed society can be counted upon than one that is brought about by force'? See his Appendix 1 in Chapter 15; p. 204.
10 Anchor, *The Enlightenment Tradition*, p. 115.
11 Kant's Appendix 1 gives us important clues in this regard.
12 Patrick Riley, *Will and Political Legitimacy: A Critical Exposition of Social Contract Theory in Hobbes, Locke, Rousseau, Kant, and Hegel* (Cambridge, MA: Harvard University Press, 1982), p. 129.

of these two philosophers.[13] On the other hand, possible resemblances in their essays may prove only superficial, or may require a more nuanced interpretation,[14] if we read the texts in this wider intellectual context.[15]

Kant's plan contains much more wishful thought than even the earliest perpetual peace plans we have seen. The fact that there is today a political entity (the European Union) which, in certain respects at least, closely resembles the schemes advocated by Penn, Bellers and others is a testament to this. Their relatively unsophisticated plans did prove realistic and materialize. Kant's project, in comparison, is still so much further detached from world affairs that the adjective 'wishful' looks entirely justified. But is this the criterion by which the greatness of a perpetual peace plan should be judged? Perhaps not. Kant's overall critiques of pure as well as practical reason, of rationalism as well as empiricism, enable him to develop a political vision which can safely enjoy the luxury of being wishful. In Kant, the limits of what is possible and doable are commanded from a metaphysical level, and not, for instance, from the relative positions, strengths, or advantages of this or that state, as is the case with Bentham.[16] There is plenty of space for *a priori* assumptions in this approach,[17] and laying the philosophical groundwork for their validity took Kant an entire lifetime. The realistic possibilities of a perpetual peace, therefore, are not confined to the immediately visible political 'realities' or any clearly detectable human capacities.

Kant advances six Preliminary Articles in his plan, which seem to involve realistic wishful thinking. In fact, his Preliminary Article 5 contains the classic 'non-interference' principle; and his Preliminary Article 3 is no more unrealistic

---

[13] In this context, Kant's statement in his Second Definitive Article is interesting: 'reason, from her throne of the supreme law-giving moral power, absolutely condemns war as a morally lawful proceeding, and makes a state of peace, on the other hand, an immediate duty.'

[14] See, for instance, Kant's Sixth Preliminary Article, which may well arouse suspicions of legal positivism.

[15] See Kant's remarks on 'regular jurists' in his Appendix 1.

[16] Kant's two appendices are particularly relevant in this context.

[17] See Howard Williams, 'Kant on the Social Contract', in David Boucher and Paul Kelly (eds), *The Social Contract from Hobbes to Rawls* (London: Routledge, 1994), pp. 135–7.

than Bentham's disarmament proposal.[18] Especially once he moves to his three Definitive Articles, however, we encounter a more idealistic kind of wishful thinking, but we also find here strong indications of a notion of global governance. The first of Kant's Definitive Articles advocates a republican constitution for every state in the international system. The second envisages an international law founded on a federation of free (and, of course, republican) states. Finally, the Third Definitive Article advances Kant's most far-fetched principle, namely, that the rights of men as world citizens would be limited by the conditions of 'universal hospitality'. Even a cursory look at these three articles reveals that Kant's vision involves overlapping spheres of governance.[19]

The First Definitive Article clearly places the domain of domestic governance in the notion of perpetual peace. It elaborates in detail why all states should have a republican constitution.[20] The Second Definitive Article, conceptually, has evident linkages with several earlier plans, but the article is particularly noteworthy in demoting the emphasis on 'federation' by making a firm reference to the law of nations instead. Finally, the last Definitive Article takes a very difficult and provocative step towards contemporary cosmopolitanism. It is, of course, for readers to decide for themselves what exactly Kant's proposals entail in normative as well as analytical terms. After all, this volume is designed precisely to shift the analytical burden onto the reader by making the full texts available in a relatively easy format, thereby trying to minimize possible editorial interference in the authors' as well as readers' thought patterns. Nevertheless, it should be mentioned that Kant's text

---

18 See Chapter 12, pp. 149–53.
19 On Kant's three levels of law, including the 'law of world citizenship', see Sharon Anderson-Gold, *Cosmopolitanism and Human Rights* (Cardiff: University of Wales Press, 2001), pp. 28–43. Nuscheler usefully points to the influence of these three articles on the Commission of Global Governance: see Franz Nuscheler, 'Global governance, development, and peace', in Paul Kennedy, Dirk Messner and Franz Nuscheler (eds), *Global Trends and Global Governance* (London: Pluto Press, 2002), pp. 162–3.
20 Williams suspects that Kant's republicanism may have been influenced by James Harrington, a British utopian; see Howard Williams, *Kant's Critique of Hobbes: Sovereignty and Cosmopolitanism* (Cardiff: University of Wales Press, 2003), pp. 200–6.

has provoked much discussion and has given rise to radically divergent interpretations since its first publication. A much-needed overview of these diverse interpretations has recently become available with the publication of Eric Easley's *The War over Perpetual Peace*.

The most immediate impact of *Perpetual Peace* on global governance scholarship has been felt in two major strands of theory, both of which have by now their respective counter-literatures as well. The first strand, operating more on the level of positive theory, drew its inspiration from the idea that certain types of domestic governance (*democracies* as understood today) are more conducive to peace, internally as well as internationally.[21] This so-called *democratic peace* theory has led to a distinctive body of literature in the last two decades, and has produced a significant number of quantitative as well as qualitative studies.[22] The second strand, pioneered by such figures as David Held, has a more explicit normative orientation: the *cosmopolitan democracy* approach.[23] Here the main preoccupation is to devise and progressively refine a contemporary proposal to democratize

[21] This, of course, requires a critical examination and sophisticated interpretation of Kant's First Definitive Article; see Chapter 15. For a critique of equating Kantian republicanism with democracy, see Bruce Buchan, 'Explaining war and peace: Kant and liberal IR theory', *Alternatives*, 27 (2002), 407–28.

[22] See, for instance, Michael Doyle, 'Kant, liberal legacies, and foreign affairs', Parts 1 and 2, *Philosophy and Public Affairs*, 12 (1983), 205–35; 325–53; Georg Cavallar, 'Kantian perspectives on democratic peace: Alternatives to Doyle', *Review of International Studies*, 27 (2001), 229–48; Lars-Erik Cederman, 'Back to Kant: Reinterpreting the democratic peace as a macrohistorical learning process', *American Political Science Review 95* (2001), 15–31; Michael Williams, 'The discipline of the democratic peace: Kant, liberalism, and the social construction of security communities', *European Journal of International Relations*, 7 (2001), 525–53; Gordon P. Henderson, 'The public and peace: the consequences for citizenship of the democratic peace literature', *International Studies Review*, 8 (2006), 199–224. The counter-literature includes, for instance, Sebastian Rosato, 'The flawed logic of the democratic peace', *American Political Science Review*, 97 (2003), 585–602; and Thomas Schwartz and Kiron K. Skinner, 'The myth of the democratic peace', *Orbis*, 46 (2002), 159–72.

[23] For example, most of the works cited in the following comprehensive (but nevertheless incomplete) bibliographical essay connect with Kant one way or another: Daniele Archibugi and Mathias Koenig-Archibugi, 'Globalization, democracy and cosmopolis: A bibliographical essay', in Daniele Archibugi

global governance, with all that this implies for domestic, international, and transnational modes of interaction. Kant's project is used as a sound early model to gain insights into how the existing democratic gaps at various levels of governance might be bridged.

Kant's essay in our final chapter is reproduced from Immanuel Kant, *Perpetual Peace: A Philosophical Essay*, translated by Mary Campbell Smith (London: Swan Sonnenschein, 1903).[24] Kant's footnotes in the essay have been checked against the German originals in Immanuel Kant, *Werke in Zwölf Bänden*, Vol. XI, (Frankfurt: Suhrkamp Verlag, 1964).

(ed.), *Debating Cosmopolitics* (London: Verso, 2003), pp. 273–91. Leading examples in this strand include Daniele Archibugi and David Held (eds), *Cosmopolitan Democracy: An Agenda for a New World Order* (Cambridge: Polity, 1995); David Held, *Democracy and the Global Order: From the Modern State to Cosmopolitan Governance* (Stanford, CA: Stanford University Press, 1996); Daniele Archibugi, David Held and Martin Köhler (eds), *Re-imagining Political Community: Studies in Cosmopolitan Democracy* (London: Polity, 1998). An example for the counter-literature is Heikki Patomäki, 'Problems of democratizing global governance: time, space and the emancipatory process', *European Journal of International Relations*, 9 (2003), 347–76.

[24] This is one of the most competent translations of Kant's essay, and has been reprinted several times, e.g. by George Allen and Unwin (London, 1917) and by Garland Publishing (New York, 1972); see Stephen Palmquist's *Exhaustive Bibliography of English Translations of Kant* (1994), available online at: *http://www.hkbu.edu.hk/~ppp/fne/bibl.html* (October 2006). Smith's own footnotes in her translation are omitted here.

Chapter 15

Immanuel Kant: *Perpetual Peace: A Philosophical Essay* (1795)

We need not try to decide whether this satirical inscription (once found on a Dutch innkeeper's signboard above the picture of a churchyard) is aimed at mankind in general, or at the rulers of states in particular, unwearying in their love of war, or perhaps only at the philosophers who cherish the sweet dream of perpetual peace. The author of the present sketch would make one stipulation, however. The practical politician stands upon a definite footing with the theorist: with great self-complacency he looks down upon him as a mere pedant whose empty ideas can threaten no danger to the state (starting as it does from principles derived from experience), and who may always be permitted to knock down his eleven skittles at once without a worldly-wise statesman needing to disturb himself. Hence, in the event of a quarrel arising between the two, the practical statesman must always act consistently, and not scent danger to the state behind opinions ventured by the theoretical politician at random and publicly expressed. With which saving clause (*clausula salvatoria*) the author will herewith consider himself duly and expressly protected against all malicious misinterpretation.

First Section: Containing the preliminary articles of perpetual peace between states

(1) No treaty of peace shall be regarded as valid, if made with the secret reservation of material for a future war.

For then it would be a mere truce, a mere suspension of hostilities, not peace. A peace signifies the end of all hostilities, and to attach to it the epithet 'eternal' is not only a verbal pleonasm, but matter of suspicion. The causes of a future war existing, although perhaps not yet known to the high contracting parties themselves, are entirely annihilated by the conclusion of peace, however acutely they may be ferreted out of documents in the public archives. There may be a mental reservation of old claims to be thought out at a future time, which are, none of them, mentioned at this stage, because both parties are too much exhausted to continue the war, while the evil intention remains of using the first favourable opportunity for further hostilities. Diplomacy of this kind only Jesuitical casuistry can justify: It is beneath the dignity of a ruler, just as acquiescence in such processes of reasoning is beneath the dignity of his minister, if one judges the facts as they really are.

If, however, according to present enlightened ideas of political wisdom, the true glory of a state lies in the uninterrupted development of its power by every possible means, this judgment must certainly strike one as scholastic and pedantic.

(2) No state having an independent existence – whether it be great or small – shall be acquired by another through inheritance, exchange, purchase or donation.

For a state is not a property (*patrimonium*), as may be the ground on which its people are settled. It is a society of human beings over whom no one but itself has the right to rule and to dispose. Like the trunk of a tree, it has its own roots, and to graft it on to another state is to do away with its existence as a moral person, and to make of it a thing. Hence it is in contradiction to the idea of the original contract without which no right over a people is thinkable.[1] Everyone knows to what danger the bias in favour of these modes of acquisition has brought Europe (in other parts of the world it has never been known). The custom of marriage between states, as if they were individuals, has survived even up to the most recent times, and is regarded partly as a new kind of industry by which ascendancy may be acquired through family alliances, without any expenditure of strength – partly as a device for territorial expansion. Moreover, the hiring out of the troops of one state to another to fight against an enemy not at war with their native country is to be reckoned in this connection, for the subjects are in this way used and abused at will as personal property.

*(3) Standing armies (*miles perpetuus*) shall be abolished in course of time.*

For they are always threatening other states with war by appearing to be in constant readiness to fight. They incite the various states to outrival one another in the number of their soldiers, and to this number no limit can be set. Now, since, owing to the sums devoted to this purpose, peace at last becomes even more oppressive than a short war, these standing armies are themselves the cause of wars of aggression, undertaken in order to get rid of this burden. To which we must add that the practice of hiring men to kill or to be killed seems to imply a use of them as mere machines and instruments in the hand of another (namely the state) which cannot easily be reconciled with the right of humanity in our own person.[II] The matter stands quite differently in the case of voluntary periodical military exercise on the part of citizens of the state, who thereby seek to secure themselves and their country against attack from without.

The accumulation of treasure in a state would in the same way be regarded by other states as a menace of war, and might compel them to anticipate this by striking the first blow. For of the three forces (the power of arms, the power of alliance, and the power of money), the last may well become the most reliable instrument of war, did not the difficulty of ascertaining the amount stand in the way.

(4) No national debts shall be contracted in connection with the external affairs of the state.

This source of help is above suspicion, where assistance is sought outside or within the state on behalf of the economic administration of the country (for instance, the improvement of the roads, the settlement and support of new colonies, the establishment of granaries to provide against seasons of scarcity, and so on). But, as a common weapon used by the Powers against one another, a credit system under which debts go on indefinitely increasing and are yet always assured against immediate claims (because all the creditors do not put in their claim at once) is a dangerous money power. This ingenious invention of a commercial people in the present century is, in other words, a treasure for the carrying on of war, which may exceed the treasures of all the other states taken together, and can only be exhausted by a threatening deficiency in the taxes – an event, however, which will long be kept off by the very briskness of commerce resulting from the reaction of this system on industry and trade. The ease, then, with which war may be waged, coupled with the inclination of rulers towards it – an inclination which seems to be implanted in human nature – is a great obstacle in the way of perpetual peace. The prohibition of this system must be laid down as a preliminary article of perpetual peace, all the more necessarily because the final inevitable bankruptcy of the state in question must involve in the loss many who are innocent; and this would be a public injury to these states. Therefore, other nations are at least justified in uniting themselves against such an one and its pretensions.

(5) No state shall violently interfere with the constitution and administration of another.

For what can justify it in so doing? The scandal which is here presented to the subjects of another state? The erring state can much more serve as a warning by exemplifying the great evils which a nation draws down on itself through its own law-lessness. Moreover, the bad example which one free person gives another (as *scandalum acceptum*) does no injury to the latter. In this connection, it is true, we cannot count the case of a state which has become split up through internal corruption into two parts, each of them representing by itself an individual state which lays claim to the whole. Here the yielding of assistance to one faction could not be reckoned as interference on the part of a foreign state with the constitution of another, for here anarchy prevails. So long, however, as the inner strife has not yet reached this stage, the interference of other powers would be a violation of the rights of an independent nation which is only struggling with internal disease. It would therefore itself cause a scandal, and make the autonomy of all states insecure.

*(6) No state at war with another shall countenance such modes of hostility as would make mutual confidence impossible in a subsequent state of peace: such are the employment of assassins (*percussores*) or of poisoners (*venefici*), breaches of capitulation, the instigating and making use of treachery (*perduellio*) in the hostile state.*

These are dishonourable stratagems. For some kind of confidence in the disposition of the enemy must exist even in the midst of war, as otherwise peace could not be concluded, and the hostilities would pass into a war of extermination (*bellum internecinum*). War, however, is only our wretched expedient of asserting a right by force, an expedient adopted in the state of nature, where no court of justice exists which could settle the matter in dispute. In circumstances like these, neither of the two parties can be called an unjust enemy, because this form of speech presupposes a legal decision: the issue of the conflict – just as in the case of the so-called judgments of God – decides on which side right is. Between states, however, no punitive war (*bellum punitivum*) is thinkable, because between them a relation of superior and inferior does not exist. Whence it follows that a war of extermination, where the process of annihilation would strike both parties at once and all right as well, would bring about perpetual peace only in the great graveyard of the human race. Such a war, then, and therefore also the use of all means which lead to it, must be absolutely forbidden. That the methods just mentioned do inevitably lead to this result is obvious from the fact that these infernal arts, already vile in themselves, on coming into use, are not long confined to the sphere of war. Take, for example, the use of spies (*uti exploratoribus*). Here only the dishonesty of others is made use of; but vices such as these, when once encouraged, cannot in the nature of things be stamped out, and would be carried over into the state of peace, where their presence would be utterly destructive to the purpose of that state.

Although the laws stated are, objectively regarded (i.e. in so far as they affect the action of rulers), purely prohibitive laws (*leges prohibitivæ*), some of them (*leges strictæ*) are strictly valid without regard to circumstances, and urgently require to be enforced. Such are Nos. 1, 5, 6. Others, again, (like Nos. 2, 3, 4) although not indeed exceptions to the maxims of law, yet in respect of the practical application of these maxims allow subjectively of a certain latitude to suit particular circumstances. The enforcement of these *leges latæ* may be legitimately put off, so long as we do not lose sight of the ends at which they aim. This purpose of reform does not permit of the deferment of an act of restitution (as, for example, the restoration to certain states of freedom of which they have been deprived in the manner described in Article 2) to an infinitely distant date – as Augustus used to say, to the 'Greek Kalends', a day that will never come. This would be to sanction non-restitution. Delay is permitted only with the intention that restitution should not be made too precipitately and so defeat the purpose we have in view. For the prohibition refers here only to the *mode of acquisition* which is to be no longer valid, and not to the *fact of possession* which, although indeed it has not the necessary title of right, yet at the time of so-called acquisition was held legal by all states, in accordance with the public opinion of the time.[III]

Second Section: Containing the definitive articles of a perpetual peace between states

A state of peace among men who live side by side is not the natural state (*status naturalis*), which is rather to be described as a state of war: that is to say, although there is not perhaps always actual open hostility, yet there is a constant threatening that an outbreak may occur. Thus the state of peace must be *established*. For the mere cessation of hostilities is no guarantee of continued peaceful relations, and unless this guarantee is given by every individual to his neighbour – which can only be done in a state of society regulated by law – one man is at liberty to challenge another and treat him as an enemy.[IV]

(1) The civil constitution of each state shall be republican.

The only constitution which has its origin in the idea of the original contract, upon which the lawful legislation of every nation must be based, is the republican.[V] It is a constitution, in the first place, founded in accordance with the principle of the freedom of the members of society as human beings; secondly, in accordance with the principle of the dependence of all, as subjects, on a common legislation; and thirdly, in accordance with the law of the equality of the members as citizens. It is, then, looking at the question of right, the only constitution whose fundamental principles lie at the basis of every form of civil constitution. And the only question for us now is, whether it is also the one constitution which can lead to perpetual peace.

Now the republican constitution, apart from the soundness of its origin, since it arose from the pure source of the concept of right, has also the prospect of attaining the desired result, namely, perpetual peace. And the reason is this: If, as must be so under this constitution, the consent of the subjects is required to determine whether there shall be war or not, nothing is more natural than that they should weigh the matter well before undertaking such a bad business. For in decreeing war, they would of necessity be resolving to bring down the miseries of war upon their country. This implies: they must fight themselves; they must hand over the costs of the war out of their own property; they must do their poor best to make good the devastation which it leaves behind; and finally, as a crowning ill, they have to accept a burden of debt which will embitter even peace itself, and which they can never pay off on account of the new wars which are always impending. On the other hand, in a government where the subject is not a citizen holding a vote (i.e. in a constitution which is not republican), the plunging into war is the least serious thing in the world. For the ruler is not a citizen but the owner of the state, and does not lose a whit by the war, while he goes on enjoying the delights of his table or sport, or of his pleasure palaces and gala days. He can, therefore, decide on war for the most trifling reasons, as if it were a kind of pleasure party. Any justification of it that is necessary for the sake of decency he can leave without concern to the diplomatic corps who are always only too ready with their services.

The following remarks must be made in order that we may not fall into the common error of confusing the republican with the democratic constitution. The forms of the state (*civitas*) may be classified according to either of two principles of division: the difference of the persons who hold the supreme authority in the state, and the manner in which the people are governed by their ruler whoever he may be. The first is properly called the form of sovereignty (*forma imperii*), and there can be only three constitutions differing in this respect, where, namely, the supreme authority belongs to only one, to several individuals working together, or to the whole people constituting the civil society. Thus we have autocracy or the sovereignty of a monarch, aristocracy or the sovereignty of the nobility, and democracy or the sovereignty of the people. The second principle of division is the form of government (*forma regiminis*), and refers to the way in which the state makes use of its supreme power, for the manner of government is based on the constitution – itself the act of that universal will which transforms a multitude into a nation. In this respect the form of government is either republican or despotic. Republicanism is the political principle of severing the executive power of the government from the legislature. Despotism is that principle in pursuance of which the state arbitrarily puts into effect laws which it has itself made: consequently it is the administration of the public will, but this is identical with the private will of the ruler. Of these three forms of a state, democracy, in the proper sense of the word, is of necessity despotism, because it establishes an executive power, since all decree regarding – and, if need be, against – any individual who dissents from them. Therefore the 'whole people', so-called, who carry their measure are really not all, but only a majority: so that here the universal will is in contradiction with itself and with the principle of freedom.

Every form of government, in fact, which is not representative is really no true constitution at all, because a lawgiver may no more be, in one and the same person, the administrator of his own will than the universal major premise of a syllogism may be, at the same time, the subsumption under itself of the particulars contained in the minor premise. And, although the other two constitutions, autocracy and aristocracy, are always defective in so far as they leave the way open for such a form of government, yet there is at least always a possibility in these cases that they may take the form of a government in accordance with the spirit of a representative system. Thus Frederick the Great used at least to *say* that he was 'merely the highest servant of the state'.[VI] The democratic constitution, on the other hand, makes this impossible, because under such a government every one wishes to be master. We may therefore say that the smaller the staff of the executive – that is to say, the number of rulers – and the more real, on the other hand, their representation of the people, so much the more is the government of the state in accordance with a possible republicanism; and it may hope by gradual reforms to raise itself to that standard. For this reason, it is more difficult under an aristocracy than under a monarchy – while under a democracy it is impossible except by a violent revolution – to attain to this, the one perfectly lawful constitution. The kind of government,[VII] however, is of infinitely more importance to the people than the kind of constitution, although the greater or less aptitude of a people for this ideal greatly depends upon such external form. The form of government, however, if it is to be in accordance with the idea of right, must embody the representative system in which alone a republican form of administration is possible and without which it is despotic and violent, be the constitution what it may. None of the ancient so-called republics were aware of this, and they necessarily slipped into absolute despotism which, of all despotisms, is most endurable under the sovereignty of one individual.

(2) The law of nations shall be founded on a federation of free states.

Nations, as states, may be judged like individuals who, living in the natural state of the society – that is to say, uncontrolled by external law – injure one another through their very proximity. Every state, for the sake of its own security, may – and ought to – demand that its neighbour should submit itself to conditions, similar to those of the civil society where the right of every individual is guaranteed. This would give rise to a federation of nations which, however, would not have to be a state of nations. That would involve a contradiction. For the term 'state' implies the relation of one who rules to those who obey – that is to say, of lawgiver to the subject people; and many nations in one state would constitute only one nation, which contradicts our hypothesis, since here we have to consider the right of one nation against another in so far as they are so many separate states and are not to be fused into one.

The attachment of savages to their lawless liberty, the fact that they would rather be at hopeless variance with one another than submit themselves to a legal authority constituted by themselves, that they therefore prefer their senseless freedom to a reason-governed liberty, is regarded by us with profound contempt as barbarism and uncivilization and the brutal degradation of humanity. So one would think that civilized races, each formed into a state by itself, must come out of such an abandoned condition as soon as they possibly can. On the contrary, however, every state thinks rather that its majesty (the 'majesty' of a people is an absurd expression) lies just in the very fact that it is subject to no external legal authority; and the glory of the ruler consists in this, that, without his requiring to expose himself to danger, thousands stand at his command ready to let themselves be sacrificed for a matter of no concern to them.[VIII] The difference between the savages of Europe and those of America lies chiefly in this, that, while many tribes of the latter have been entirely devoured by their enemies, Europeans know a better way of using the vanquished than by eating them; and they prefer to increase through them the number of their subjects, and so the number of instruments at their command for still more widely spread war.

The depravity of human nature shows itself without disguise in the unrestrained relations of nations to each other, while in the law-governed civil state much of this is hidden by the check of government. This being so, it is astonishing that the word 'right' has not yet been entirely banished from the politics of war as pedantic, and that no state has yet ventured to publicly advocate this point of view. For Hugo Grotius, Puffendorf, Vattel and others – Job's comforters, all of them – are always quoted in good faith to justify an attack, although their codes, whether couched in philosophical or diplomatic terms, have not – nor can have – the slightest legal force, because states, as such, are under no common external authority; and there is no instance of a state having ever been moved by argument to desist from its purpose, even when this was backed up by the testimony of such great men. This homage which every state renders – in words at least – to the idea of right, proves that, although it may be slumbering, there is, notwithstanding, to be found in man a still higher natural moral capacity by the aid of which he will in time gain the mastery over the evil principle in his nature, the existence of which he is unable to deny. And he hopes the same of others, for otherwise the word 'right' would never be uttered by states who wish to wage war, unless to deride it like the Gallic Prince who declared: 'The privilege which nature gives the strong is that the weak must obey them.'

The method by which states prosecute their rights can never be by process of law – as it is where there is an external tribunal – but only by war. Through this means, however, and its favourable issue, victory, the question of right is never decided. A treaty of peace makes, it may be, an end to the war of the moment, but not to the conditions of war which at any time may afford a new pretext for opening hostilities; and this we cannot exactly condemn as unjust, because under these conditions everyone is his own judge. Notwithstanding, not quite the same rule applies to states according to the law of nations as holds good of individuals in a lawless condition according to the law of nature, namely, 'that they ought to advance out of this condition.' This is so, because, as states, they have already within themselves a legal constitution, and have therefore advanced beyond the stage at which others, in accordance with their ideas of right, can force them to come under a wider legal constitution. Meanwhile, however, reason, from her throne of the supreme law-giving moral power, absolutely condemns war as a morally lawful proceeding, and makes a state of peace, on the other hand, an immediate duty.

Without a compact between the nations, however, this state of peace cannot be established or assured. Hence there must be an alliance of a particular kind which we may call a covenant of peace (*fœdus pacificum*), which would differ from a treaty of peace (*pactum pacis*) in this respect, that the latter merely puts an end to one war, while the former would seek to put an end to war forever. This alliance does not aim at the gain of any power whatsoever of the state, but merely at the preservation and security of the freedom of the state for itself, and of other allied states at the same time. The latter do not, however, require, for this reason, to submit themselves like individuals in the state of nature to public laws and coercion. The practicability or objective reality of this idea of federation which is to extend gradually over all states and so lead to perpetual peace can be shown. For, if fortune ordains that a powerful and enlightened people should form a republic – which by its very nature is inclined to perpetual peace – this would serve as a centre of federal union for other states wishing to join, and thus secure conditions of freedom among the states in accordance with the idea of the law of nations. Gradually, through different unions of this kind, the federation would extend further and further.

It is quite comprehensible that a people should say: 'There shall be no war among us, for we shall form ourselves into a state, that is to say, constitute for ourselves a supreme legislative, administrative and judicial power which will settle our disputes peaceably.' But if this state says: 'There shall be no war between me and other states, although I recognize no supreme law-giving power which will secure me my rights and whose rights I will guarantee', then it is not at all clear upon what grounds I could base my confidence in my right, unless it were the substitute for that compact on which civil society is based, namely, free federation which reason must necessarily connect with the idea of the law of nations, if indeed any meaning is to be left in that concept at all.

There is no intelligible meaning in the idea of the law of nations as giving a right to make war; for that must be a right to decide what is just, not in accordance with universal external laws limiting the freedom of each individual, but by means of one-sided maxims applied by force. We must then understand by this that men of such ways of thinking are quite justly served when they destroy one another, and thus find perpetual peace in the wide grave which covers all the abominations of acts of violence as well as the authors of such deeds. For states, in their relation to one another, there can be, according to reason, no other way of advancing from that lawless condition, which unceasing war implies, than by giving up their savage lawless freedom, just as individual men have done, and yielding to the coercion of public laws. Thus they can form a state of nations (*civitas gentium*) – one, too, which will be ever increasing and would finally embrace all the peoples of the earth. States, however, in accordance with their understanding of the law of nations, by no means desire this, and therefore reject *in hypothesi* what is correct *in thesi*. Hence, instead of the positive idea of a world-republic, if all is not to be lost, only the negative substitute for it, [namely] a federation averting war, maintaining its ground, and ever extending over the world, may stop the current of this tendency to war and shrinking from the control of law. But even then there will be a constant danger that this propensity may break out.[IX] *Furor impius intus – fremit horridus ore cruento.* (Virgil)

(3) The rights of men, as citizens of the world, shall be limited to the conditions of universal hospitality.

We are speaking here, as in the previous articles, not of philanthropy, but of right; and in this sphere hospitality signifies the claim of a stranger entering foreign territory to be treated by its owner without hostility. The latter may send him away again, if this can be done without causing his death, but so long as he conducts himself peaceably, he must not be treated as an enemy. It is not a right to be treated as a guest to which the stranger can lay claim – a special friendly compact on his behalf would be required to make him for a given time an actual inmate – but he has a right of visitation. This right to present themselves to society belongs to all mankind in virtue of our common right of possession on the surface of the earth on which, as it is a globe, we cannot be infinitely scattered, and must in the end reconcile ourselves to existence side by side. At the same time, originally no one individual had more right than another to live in any one particular spot. Uninhabitable portions of the surface – ocean and desert – split up the human community, but in such a way that ships and camels ('the ship of the desert') make it possible for men to come into touch with one another across these unappropriated regions and to take advantage of our common claim to the face of the earth with a view to a possible intercommunication. The inhospitality of the inhabitants of certain sea coasts – as, for example, the coast of Barbary – in plundering ships in neighbouring seas or making slaves of shipwrecked mariners, or the behaviour of the Arab Bedouins in the deserts, who think that proximity to nomadic tribes constitutes a right to rob, is thus contrary to the law of nature. This right to hospitality, however – that is to say, the privilege of strangers arriving on foreign soil – does not amount to more than what is implied in a permission to make an attempt at intercourse with the original inhabitants. In this way far distant territories may enter into peaceful relations with one another. These relations may at last come under the public control of law, and thus the human race may be brought nearer the realization of a cosmopolitan constitution.

Let us look now, for the sake of comparison, at the inhospitable behaviour of the civilized nations, especially the commercial states of our continent. The injustice which they exhibit on visiting foreign lands and races – this being equivalent in their eyes to conquest – is such as to fill us with horror. America, the negro countries, the Spice Islands, the Cape etc. were, on being discovered, looked upon as countries which belonged to nobody, for the native inhabitants were reckoned as nothing. In Hindustan, under the pretext of intending to establish merely commercial depots, the Europeans introduced foreign troops; and, as a result, the different states of Hindustan were stirred up to far-spreading wars. Oppression of the natives followed – famine, insurrection, perfidy, and all the rest of the litany of evils which can afflict mankind.

China^X and Japan (Nipon), which had made an attempt at receiving guests of this kind, have now taken a prudent step. Only to a single European people, the Dutch, has China given the right of access to her shores (but not of entrance into the country), while Japan has granted both these concessions, but at the same time they exclude the Dutch who enter, as if they were prisoners, from social intercourse with the inhabitants. The worst, or from the standpoint of ethical judgment the best, of all this is that no satisfaction is derived from all this violence; that all these trading companies stand on the verge of ruin; that the Sugar Islands – that seat of the most horrible and deliberate slavery – yield no real profit, but only have their use indirectly and for no very praiseworthy object, namely, that of furnishing men to be trained as sailors for the men-of-war and thereby contributing to the carrying on of war in Europe. And this has been done by nations who make a great ado about their piety, and who, while they are quite ready to commit injustice, would like, in their orthodoxy, to be considered among the elect.

The intercourse, more or less close, which has been everywhere steadily increasing between the nations of the earth, has now extended so enormously that a violation of right in one part of the world is felt all over it. Hence the idea of a cosmopolitan right is no fantastical, high-flown notion of right, but a complement of the unwritten code of law – constitutional as well as international law – necessary for the public rights of mankind in general and thus for the realization of perpetual peace. For only by endeavouring to fulfil the conditions laid down by this cosmopolitan law can we flatter ourselves that we are gradually approaching that ideal.

First Supplement: Concerning the guarantee of perpetual peace

This guarantee is given by no less a power than the great artist nature (*natura dædala rerum*) in whose mechanical course is clearly exhibited a predetermined design to make harmony spring from human discord, even against the will of man. Now this design, although called fate when looked upon as the compelling force of a cause, the laws of whose operation are unknown to us, is, when considered as the purpose manifested in the course of nature, called providence,[XI] as the deep-lying wisdom of a higher cause, directing itself towards the ultimate practical end of the human race and predetermining the course of things with a view to its realization. This providence we do not, it is true, perceive in the cunning contrivances [*Kunstanstalten*] of nature; nor can we even conclude from the fact of their existence that it is there; but, as in every relation between the form of things and their final cause, we can, and must, supply the thought of a higher wisdom in order that we may be able to form an idea of the possible existence of these products after the analogy of human works of art [*Kunsthandlungen*]. The representation to ourselves of the relation and agreement of these formations of nature to the moral purpose for which they were made and which reason directly prescribes to us, is an idea, it is true, which is in theory superfluous; but in practice it is dogmatic, and its objective reality is well established. Thus we see, for example, with regard to the ideal [*Pflichtbegriff*] of perpetual peace, that it is our duty to make use of the mechanism of nature for the realization of that end. Moreover, in a case like this, where we are interested merely in the theory and not in the religious question, the use of the word 'nature' is more appropriate than that of 'providence' in view of the limitations of human reason, which, in considering the relation of effects to their causes, must keep within the limits of possible experience. And the term 'nature' is also less presumptuous than the other. To speak of a providence knowable by us would be boldly to put on the wings of Icarus in order to draw near to the mystery of its unfathomable purpose.

Before we determine the surety given by nature more exactly, we must first look at what ultimately makes this guarantee of peace necessary – the circumstances in which nature has carefully placed the actors in her great theatre. In the next place, we shall proceed to consider the manner in which she gives this surety.

The provisions she has made are as follows: (1) she has taken care that men *can* live in all parts of the world; (2) she has scattered them by means of war in all directions, even into the most inhospitable regions, so that these too might be populated; (3) by this very means she has forced them to enter into relations more or less controlled by law. It is surely wonderful that on the cold wastes round the Arctic Ocean there is always to be found moss for the reindeer to scrape out from under the snow, the reindeer itself either serving as food or to draw the sledge of the Ostiak or Samoyedes. And salt deserts which would otherwise be left unutilized have the camel, which seems as if created for travelling in such lands. This evidence of design in things, however, is still more clear when we come to know that, besides the fur-clad animals of the shores of the Arctic Ocean, there are seals, walruses and whales whose flesh furnishes food and whose oil fire for the dwellers in these regions. But the providential care of nature excites our wonder above all, when we hear of the driftwood which is carried – whence no one knows – to these treeless shores. For without the aid of this material the natives could neither construct their craft, nor weapons, nor huts for shelter. Here, too, they have so much to do, making war against wild animals, that they live at peace with one another. But what drove them originally into these regions was probably nothing but war.

Of animals, used by us as instruments of war, the horse was the first which man learned to tame and domesticate during the period of peopling of the earth; the elephant belongs to the later period of the luxury of states already established. In the same way, the art of cultivating certain grasses called cereals – no longer known to us in their original form – and also the multiplication and improvement, by transplanting and grafting, of the original kinds of fruit (in Europe, probably only two species: the crab-apple and wild pear) could only originate under the conditions accompanying established states where the rights of property are assured. That is to say, it would be after man, hitherto existing in lawless liberty, had advanced beyond the occupations of a hunter,[XII] a fisherman, or a shepherd, to the life of a tiller of the soil, when salt and iron were discovered (to become, perhaps, the first articles of commerce between different peoples) and were sought far and near. In this way, the peoples would be at first brought into peaceful relation with one another, and so come to an understanding and the enjoyment of friendly intercourse, even with their most distant neighbours.

Now, while nature provided that men could live on all parts of the earth, she also at the same time despotically willed that they *should* live everywhere on it, although against their own inclination and even although this imperative did not presuppose an idea of duty which would compel obedience to nature with the force of a moral law. But, to attain this end, she has chosen war. So we see certain peoples, widely separated, whose common descent is made evident by affinity in their languages. Thus, for instance, we find the Samoyedes on the Arctic Ocean, and again a people speaking a similar language on the Altai Mountains, 200 miles off, between whom has pressed in a mounted tribe, war-like in character and of Mongolian origin, which has driven one branch of the race far from the other into the most inhospitable regions where their own inclination would certainly not have carried them.[XIII] In the same way, through the intrusion of the Gothic and Sarmatian tribes, the Finns in the most northerly regions of Europe, whom we call Laplanders, have been separated by as great a distance from the Hungarians, with whose language their own is allied. And what but war can have brought the Esquimos to the north of America – a race quite distinct from those of that country and probably European adventurers of prehistoric times? And war, too, nature's method of populating the earth, must have driven the Pescherais in South America as far as Patagonia. War itself, however, is in need of no special stimulating cause, but seems engrafted in human nature, and is even regarded as something noble in itself to which man is inspired by the love of glory apart from motives of self-interest. Hence, among the savages of America as well as those of Europe in the age of chivalry, martial courage is looked upon as of great value in itself, not merely when a war is going on, as is reasonable enough, but in order that there should be war; and thus war is often entered upon merely to exhibit this quality. So that an intrinsic dignity is held to attach to war in itself, and even philosophers eulogize it as an ennobling, refining influence on humanity, unmindful of the Greek proverb 'War is evil in so far as it makes more bad people than it takes away.'

So much, then, of what nature does for her own ends with regard to the human race as members of the animal world.

Now comes the question which touches the essential points in this design of a perpetual peace: 'What does nature do in this respect with reference to the end which man's own reason sets before him as a duty? And consequently what does she do to further the realization of his moral purpose? How does she guarantee that what man, by the laws of freedom, ought to do and yet fails to do, he will do, without any infringement of his freedom by the compulsion of nature, and that, moreover, this shall be done in accordance with the three forms of public right – constitutional or political law, international law, and cosmopolitan law?' When I say of nature that she *wills* that this or that should take place, I do not mean that she imposes upon us the duty to do it – for only the free, unrestrained, practical reason can do that – but that she does it herself, whether we will it or not. *Fata volentem ducunt, nolentem trahunt.*

(1) Even if a people were not compelled through internal discord to submit to the restraint of public laws, war would bring this about, working from without. For, according to the contrivance of nature which we have mentioned, every people finds another tribe in its neighbourhood, pressing upon it in such a manner that it is compelled to form itself internally into a state to be able to defend itself as a power should. Now, the republican constitution is the only one which is perfectly adapted to the rights of man, but it is also the most difficult to establish, and still more to maintain. So generally is this recognized that people often say the members of a republican state would require to be angels, because men, with their self-seeking propensities, are not fit for a constitution of so sublime a form. But now nature comes to the aid of the universal, reason-derived will which, much as we honour it, is in practice powerless. And this she does by means of these very self-seeking propensities, so that it only depends – and so much lies within the power of man – on a good organization of the state for their forces to be so pitted against one another, that the one may check the destructive activity of the other, or neutralize its effect. And hence, from the standpoint of reason, the result will be the same as if both forces did not exist, and each individual is compelled to be, if

not a morally good man, yet at least a good citizen. The problem of the formation of the state, hard as it may sound, is not insoluble, even for a race of devils, granted that they have intelligence. It may be put thus: 'Given a multitude of rational beings who, in a body, require general laws for their own preservation, but each of whom, as an individual, is secretly inclined to exempt himself from this restraint, how are we to order their affairs and how establish for them a constitution such that, although their private dispositions may be really antagonistic, they may yet so act as a check upon one another, that, in their public relations, the effect is the same as if they had no such evil sentiments?' Such a problem must be capable of solution. For it deals not with the moral reformation of mankind, but only with the mechanism of nature; and the problem is to learn how this mechanism of nature can be applied to men, in order so to regulate the antagonism of conflicting interests in a people that they may even compel one another to submit to compulsory laws, and thus necessarily bring about the state of peace in which laws have force. We can see in states actually existing, although very imperfectly organized, that in externals they already approximate very nearly to what the idea of right prescribes, although the principle of morality is certainly not the cause. A good political constitution, however, is not to be expected as a result of progress in morality, but rather, conversely, the good moral condition of a nation is to be looked for as one of the first fruits of such a constitution. Hence, the mechanism of nature, working through the self-seeking propensities of man (which, of course, counteract one another in their external effects), may be used by reason as a means of making way for the realization of her own purpose – the empire of right – and, as far as is in the power of the state, to promote and secure in this way internal as well as external peace. We may say, then, that it is the irresistible will of nature that right shall at last get the supremacy. What one here fails to do will be accomplished in the long run, although perhaps with much inconvenience to us. As Bouterwek says, 'If you bend the reed too much, it breaks; he, who would do too much, does nothing.'

(2) The idea of international law presupposes the separate existence of a number of neighbouring and independent states; and, although such a condition of things is in itself already a state of war (if a federative union of these nations does not prevent the outbreak of hostilities), yet, according to the idea of reason, this is better than that all the states should be merged into one under a power which has gained the ascendancy over its neighbours and gradually become a universal monarchy. For the wider the sphere of their jurisdiction, the more laws lose in force; and soulless despotism, when it has choked the seeds of good, at last sinks into anarchy. Nevertheless, it is the desire of every state, or of its ruler, to attain to a permanent condition of peace in this very way; that is to say, by subjecting the whole world as far as possible to its sway. But nature wills it otherwise. She employs two means to separate nations, and prevent them from intermixing: namely, the differences of language and of religion.[XIV] These differences bring with them a tendency to mutual hatred, and furnish pretexts for waging war. But, nonetheless, with the growth of culture and the gradual advance of men to greater unanimity of principle, they lead to concord in a state of peace which, unlike the despotism we have spoken of, (the churchyard of freedom) does not arise from the weakening of all forces, but is brought into being and secured through the equilibrium of these forces in their most active rivalry.

(3) As nature wisely separates nations, which the will of each state, sanctioned even by the principles of international law, would gladly unite under its own sway by stratagem or force, in the same way, on the other hand, she unites nations whom the principle of a cosmopolitan right would not have secured against violence and war. And this union she brings about through an appeal to their mutual interests. The commercial spirit cannot co-exist with war, and sooner or later it takes possession of every nation. For, of all the forces which lie at the command of a state, the power of money is probably the most reliable. Hence states find themselves compelled – not, it is true, exactly from motives of morality – to further the noble end of peace and to avert war, by means of mediation, wherever it threatens to break out, just as if they had made a

permanent league for this purpose. For great alliances with a view to war can, from the nature of things, only very rarely occur, and still more seldom succeed.

In this way nature guarantees the coming of perpetual peace, through the natural course of human propensities; not, indeed, with sufficient certainty to enable us to prophesy the future of this ideal theoretically, but yet clearly enough for practical purposes. And thus this guarantee of nature makes it a duty that we should labour for this end – an end which is no mere chimera.

Second Supplement: A secret article for perpetual peace

A secret article in negotiations concerning public right is, when looked at objectively or with regard to the meaning of the term, a contradiction. When we view it, however, from the subjective standpoint, with regard to the character and condition of the person who dictates it, we see that it might quite well involve some private consideration, so that he would regard it as hazardous to his dignity to acknowledge such an article as originating from him.

The only article of this kind is contained in the following proposition: 'The opinions of philosophers with regard to the conditions of the possibility of a public peace shall be taken into consideration by states armed for war.'

It seems, however, to be derogatory to the dignity of the legislative authority of a state – to which we must, of course, attribute all wisdom – to ask advice from subjects (among whom stand philosophers) about the rules of its behaviour to other states. At the same time, it is very advisable that this should be done. Hence the state will silently invite suggestion for this purpose, while at the same time keeping the fact secret. This amounts to saying that the state will allow philosophers to discuss freely and publicly the universal principles governing the conduct of war and establishment of peace; for they will do this of their own accord, if no prohibition is laid upon them. The arrangement between states on this point does not require that a special agreement should be made merely for this purpose; for it is already involved in the obligation imposed by the universal reason of man which gives the moral law. We would not be understood to say that the state must give a preference to the principles of the philosopher rather than to the opinions of the jurist: the representative of state authority; but only that he should be heard. The latter, who has chosen for a symbol the scales of right and the sword of justice, generally uses that sword not merely to keep off all outside influences from the scales, for, when one pan of the balance will not go down, he throws his sword in it; and then *Væ victis*! The jurist, not being a moral philosopher, is under the greatest temptation to do this, because it is his business only to apply existing laws and not to investigate whether these are not themselves in need of improvement; and this actually lower function of his profession he looks upon as the nobler, because it is linked to power (as is the case also in both the other faculties: theology and medicine). Philosophy occupies a very low position compared with this combined power so that it is said, for example, that she is the handmaid of theology; and the same has been said of her position with regard to law and medicine. It is not quite clear, however, 'whether she bears the torch before these gracious ladies, or carries the train.'

That kings should philosophize, or philosophers become kings, is not to be expected. But neither is it to be desired, for the possession of power is inevitably fatal to the free exercise of reason. But it is absolutely indispensable for their enlightenment as to the full significance of their vocations that both kings and sovereign nations, which rule themselves in accordance with laws of equality, should not allow the class of philosophers to disappear, nor forbid the expression of their opinions, but should allow them to speak openly. And since this class of men, by their very nature, are incapable of instigating rebellion or forming unions for purposes of political agitation, they should not be suspected of propagandism.

Appendix I: On the disagreement between morals and politics with reference to perpetual peace

In an objective sense, morals is a practical science as the sum of laws exacting unconditional obedience, in accordance with which we *ought* to act. Now, once we have admitted the authority of this idea of duty, it is evidently inconsistent that we should think of saying that we *cannot* act thus. For, in this case, the idea of duty falls to the ground of itself; *ultra posse nemo obligatur*. Hence there can be no quarrel between politics, as the practical science of right, and morals, which is also a science of right, but theoretical. That is, theory cannot come into conflict with practice. For, in that case, we would need to understand under the term 'ethics' or 'morals' a universal doctrine of expediency, or, in other words, a theory of precepts which may guide us in choosing the best means for attaining ends calculated for our advantage. This is to deny that a science of morals exists.

Politics says: 'Be wise as serpents'; morals adds the limiting condition: 'and guileless as doves.' If these precepts cannot stand together in one command, then there is a real quarrel between politics and morals. But if they can be completely brought into accord, then the idea of any antagonism between them is absurd, and the question of how best to make a compromise between the two points of view ceases to be even raised. Although the saying 'Honesty is the best policy' expresses a theory which, alas, is often contradicted in practice, yet the likewise theoretical maxim 'Honesty is better than any policy', exalted high above every possible objection, is indeed the necessary condition of all politics.

The terminus of morals does not yield to Jupiter, the terminus of force; for the latter remains beneath the sway of fate. In other words, reason is not sufficiently enlightened to survey the series of predetermining causes which would make it possible for us to predict with certainty the good or bad results of human action, as they follow from the mechanical laws of nature – although we may hope that things will turn out as we should desire. But what we have to do in order to remain in the path of duty guided by the rules of wisdom, reason makes everywhere perfectly clear, and does this for the purpose of furthering her ultimate ends.

The practical man, however, for whom morals is mere theory, even while admitting that what ought to be can be, bases his dreary verdict against our well-meant hopes really on this: He pretends that he can foresee from his observation of human nature that men will never be willing to do what is required in order to bring about the wished-for results leading to perpetual peace. It is true that the will of all individual men to live under a legal constitution according to the principles of liberty – that is to say, the distributive unity of the wills of all – is not sufficient to attain this end. We must have the collective unity of their united will: All as a body must determine these new conditions. The solution of this difficult problem is required in order that civil society should be a whole. To all this diversity of individual wills there must come a uniting cause, in order to produce a common will which no distributive will is able to give. Hence, in the practical realization of that idea, no other beginning of a law-governed society can be counted upon than one that is brought about by force. Upon this force, too, public law afterwards rests. This state of things certainly prepares us to meet considerable deviation in actual experience from the theoretical idea of perpetual peace, since we cannot take into account the moral character and disposition of a law-giver in this connection, or expect that, after he has united a wild multitude into one people, he will leave it to them to bring about a legal constitution by their common will.

It amounts to this: Any ruler who has once got the power in his hands will not let the people dictate laws for him. A state which enjoys an independence of the control of external law will not submit to the judgment of the tribunals of other states, when it has to consider how to obtain its rights against them. And even a continent, when it feels its superiority to another, whether this be in its way or not, will not fail to take advantage of an opportunity offered of strengthening its power by the spoliation or even conquest of this territory. Hence, all theoretical schemes connected with constitutional, international, or cosmopolitan law crumble away into empty impracticable ideals. While, on the other hand, a practical science, based on the empirical principles of human nature, which does not disdain to model its maxims on an observation of actual life, can alone hope to find a sure foundation on which to build up a system of national policy.

Now, certainly, if there is neither freedom nor a moral law founded upon it, and every actual or possible event happens in the mere mechanical course of nature, then politics, as the art of making use of this physical necessity in things for the government of men, is the whole of practical wisdom, and the idea of right is an empty concept. If, on the other hand, we find that this idea of right is necessarily to be conjoined with politics and even to be raised to the position of a limiting condition of that science, then the possibility of reconciling them must be admitted. I can thus imagine a moral politician, that is to say, one who understands the principles of states-manship to be such as do not conflict with morals; but I cannot conceive of a political moralist who fashions for himself such a system of ethics as may serve the interest of statesmen.

The moral politician will always act upon the following principle: 'If certain defects which could not have been avoided are found in the political constitution or foreign relations of a state, it is a duty for all, especially for the rulers of the state, to apply their whole energy to correcting them as soon as possible, and to bringing the constitution and political relations on these points into conformity with the law of nature, as it is held up as a model before us in the idea of reason; and this they should do even at a sacrifice of their own interest.' Now, it is contrary to all politics – which is, in this particular, in agreement with morals – to dissever any of the links binding citizens together in the state, or nations in cosmopolitan union, before a better constitution is there to take the place of what has been thus destroyed. And hence, it would be absurd, indeed, to demand that every imperfection in political matters must be violently altered on the spot. But, at the same time, it may be required of a ruler at least that he should earnestly keep the maxim in mind, which points to the necessity of such a change, so that he may go on constantly approaching the end to be realized, namely, the best possible constitution according to the laws of right. Even although it is still under despotic rule, in accordance with its constitution as then existing, a state may govern itself on republican lines until the people gradually become capable of being influenced by the mere idea of the authority of law, just as if it had physical power. And they become accordingly capable of self-legislation, their faculty for which is founded on original right.

But if, through the violence of revolution, [which is] the product of a bad government, a constitution more in accord with the spirit of law were attained even by unlawful means, it should no longer be held justifiable to bring the people back to the old constitution, although, while the revolution was going on, everyone who took part in it by use of force or stratagem may have been justly punished as a rebel. As regards the external relations of nations, a state cannot be asked to give up its constitution, even although that be a despotism (which is, at the same time, the strongest constitution where foreign enemies are concerned), so long as it runs the risk of being immediately swallowed up by other states. Hence, when such a proposal is made, the state whose constitution is in question must at least be allowed to defer acting upon it until a more convenient time.[XV]

It is always possible that moralists, who rule despotically and are at a loss in practical matters, will come into collision with the rules of political wisdom in many ways, by adopting measures without sufficient deliberation, which show themselves afterwards to have been overestimated. When they thus offend against nature, experience must gradually lead them into a better track. But, instead of this being the case, politicians who are fond of moralizing do all they can to make moral improvement impossible and to perpetuate violations of law, by extenuating political principles which are antagonistic to the idea of right, on the pretext that human nature is not capable of good, in the sense of the ideal which reason prescribes.

These politicians, instead of adopting an open, straight-forward way of doing things (as they boast), mix themselves up in intrigue. They get at the authorities in power, and say what will please them. Their sole bent is to sacrifice the nation, or even, if they can, the whole world, with the one end in view that their own private interest may be forwarded. This is the manner of regular jurists (I mean the journeyman lawyer not the legislator), when they aspire to politics. For, as it is not their business to reason too nicely over legislation, but only to enforce the laws of the country, every legal constitution in its existing form and, when this is changed by the proper authorities, the one which takes its place, will always seem to them the best possible. And the consequence is that everything is purely mechanical. But this adroitness in suiting themselves to any circumstances may lead them to the delusion that they are also capable of giving an opinion about the principles of political constitutions in general, in so far as they conform to ideas of right, and are therefore not empirical, but *a priori*. And they may therefore brag about their knowledge of men – which indeed one expects to find, since they have to deal with so many – without really knowing the nature of man and what can be made of it, to gain which knowledge a higher standpoint of anthropological observation than theirs is required. Filled with ideas of this kind, if they trespass outside their own sphere on the boundaries of political and international law, looked upon as ideals which reason holds before us, they can do so only in the spirit of chicanery. For they will follow their usual method of making everything conform mechanically to compulsory laws despotically made and enforced, even here, where the ideas of reason recognize the validity of a legal compulsory force, only when it is in accordance with the principles of freedom through which a permanently valid constitution becomes first of all possible. The would-be practical man, leaving out of account this idea of reason, thinks that he can solve this problem empirically by looking to the way in which those constitutions which have best survived the test of time were established, even although the spirit of these may have been generally contrary to the idea of right. The principles which he makes use of here, although indeed he does not make them public, amount pretty much to the following sophistical maxims:

(1) *Fac et excusa*. Seize the most favourable opportunity for arbitrary usurpation, either of the authority of the state over its own people or over a neighbouring people. The justification of the act and extenuation of the use of force will come much more easily and gracefully when the deed is done than if one has to think out convincing reasons for taking this step, and first hear through all the objections which can be made against it. This is especially true in the first case mentioned, where the supreme power in the state also controls the legislature which we must

obey without any reasoning about it. Besides, this show of audacity in a statesman even lends him a certain semblance of inward conviction of the justice of his action; and once he has got so far the god of success (*bonus eventus*) is his best advocate.

(2) *Si fecisti, nega.* As for any crime you have committed, such as has, for instance, brought your people to despair and thence to insurrection: deny that it has happened owing to any fault of yours. Say, rather, that it is all caused by the insubordination of your subjects, or, in the case of your having usurped a neighbouring state, that human nature is to blame. For, if a man is not ready to use force and steal a march upon his neighbour, he may certainly count on the latter forestalling him and taking him prisoner.

(3) *Divide et impera.* That is to say, if there are certain privileged persons, holding authority among the people who have merely chosen you for their sovereign as *primus inter pares*, bring about a quarrel among them, and make mischief between them and the people. Now, back up the people with a dazzling promise of greater freedom; everything will now depend unconditionally on your will. Or again, if there is a difficulty with foreign states, then to stir up dissension among them is a pretty sure means of subjecting first one and then the other to your sway under the pretext of aiding the weaker.

It is true that nowadays nobody is taken in by these political maxims, for they are all familiar to everyone. Moreover, there is no need of being ashamed of them, as if their injustice were too patent. For the great powers never feel shame before the judgment of the common herd, but only before one another so that, as far as this matter goes, it is not the revelation of these guiding principles of policy that can make rulers ashamed, but only the unsuccessful use of them. For as to the morality of these maxims, politicians are all agreed. Hence, there is always left political prestige on which they can safely count; and this means the glory of increasing their power by any means that offer.[XVI]

In all these twistings and turnings of an immoral doctrine of expediency, which aims at substituting a state of peace for the warlike conditions in which men are placed by nature, so much at least is clear that men cannot get away from the idea of right in their private any more than in their public relations; and that they do not dare (this is indeed most strikingly seen in the concept of an international law) to base politics merely on the manipulations of expediency, and therefore to refuse all obedience to the idea of a public right. On the contrary, they pay all fitting honour to the idea of right in itself, even although they should, at the same time, devise a hundred subterfuges and excuses to avoid it in practice, and should regard force, backed up by cunning, as having the authority which comes from being the source and unifying principle of all right. It will be well to put an end to this sophistry, if not to the injustice it extenuates, and to bring the false advocates of the mighty of the earth to confess that it is not right but might in whose interest they speak, and that it is the worship of might from which they take their cue, as if in this matter they had a right to command. In order to do this, we must first expose the delusion by which they deceive themselves and others; then discover the ultimate principle from which their plans for a perpetual peace proceed; and thence show that all the evil which stands in the way of the realization of that ideal springs from the fact that the political moralist begins where the moral politician rightly ends, and that, by subordinating principles to an end or putting the cart before the horse, he defeats his intention of bringing politics into harmony with morals.

In order to make practical philosophy consistent with itself, we must first decide the following question: 'In dealing with the problems of practical reason, must we begin from its material principle – the end as the object of free choice – or from its formal principle which is based merely on freedom in its external relation?', from which comes the following law: 'Act so that thou canst will that thy maxim should be a universal law, be the end of thy action what it will.'

Without doubt, the latter determining principle of action must stand first; for, as a principle of right, it carries unconditional necessity with it, whereas the former is obligatory only if we assume the empirical conditions of the end set before us, that is to say, that it is an end capable of

209

being practically realized. And if this end – as, for example, the end of perpetual peace – should be also a duty, this same duty must necessarily have been deduced from the formal principle governing the maxims which guide external action. Now, the first principle is the principle of the political moralist: the problems of constitutional, international, and cosmopolitan law are mere technical problems (*problema technicum*). The second or formal principle, on the other hand, as the principle of the moral politician who regards it as a moral problem (*problema morale*), differs widely from the other principle in its methods of bringing about perpetual peace, which we desire not only as a material good, but also as a state of things resulting from our recognition of the precepts of duty.

To solve the first problem – that, namely, of political expediency – much knowledge of nature is required that her mechanical laws may be employed for the end in view. And yet the result of all knowledge of this kind is uncertain, as far as perpetual peace is concerned. This we find to be so, which-ever of the three departments of public law we take. It is uncertain whether a people could be better kept in obedience, and at the same time prosperity, by severity or by baits held out to their vanity; whether they would be better governed under the sovereignty of a single individual or by the authority of several acting together; whether the combined authority might be better secured merely, say, by an official nobility or by the power of the people within the state; and, finally, whether such conditions could be long maintained. There are examples to the contrary in history in the case of all forms of government, with the exception of the only true republican constitution, the idea of which can occur only to a moral politician. Still more uncertain is a law of nations, ostensibly established upon statutes devised by ministers, for this amounts in fact to mere empty words, and rests on treaties which, in the very act of ratification, contain a secret reservation of the right to violate them. On the other hand, the solution of the second problem – the problem of political wisdom – forces itself, we may say, upon us; it is quite obvious to everyone, and puts all crooked dealings to shame; it leads, too, straight to the desired end, while at the same time, discretion warns us not to drag in the conditions of perpetual peace by force, but to take time and approach this ideal gradually as favourable circumstances permit.

This may be expressed in the following maxim: 'Seek ye first the kingdom of pure practical reason and its righteousness; and the object of your endeavour, the blessing of perpetual peace, will be added unto you.' For the science of morals generally has this peculiarity – and it has it also with regard to the moral principles of public law, and therefore with regard to a science of politics knowable *a priori* – that the less it makes a man's conduct depend on the end he has set before him, his purposed material or moral gain, so much the more, nevertheless, does it conform in general to this end. The reason for this is that it is just the universal will, given *a priori*, which exists in a people or in the relation of different peoples to one another, that alone determines what is lawful among men. This union of individual wills, however, if we proceed consistently in practice in observance of the mechanical laws of nature, may be at the same time the cause of bringing about the result intended, and practically realizing the idea of right. Hence it is, for example, a principle of moral politics that a people should unite into a state according to the only valid concepts of right, [namely] the ideas of freedom and equality; and this principle is not based on expediency, but upon duty. Political moralists, however, do not deserve a hearing, much and sophistically as they may reason about the existence, in a multitude of men forming a society, of certain natural tendencies which would weaken those principles and defeat their intention. They may endeavour to prove their assertion by giving instances of badly organized constitutions, chosen both from ancient and modern times (as, for example, democracies without a representative system), but such arguments are to be treated with contempt, all the more, because a pernicious theory of this kind may perhaps even bring about the evil which it prophesies. For, in accordance with such reasoning, man is thrown into a class with all other living machines which only require the consciousness that they are not free creatures to make them in their own judgment the most miserable of all beings.

Fiat justitia, pereat mundus. This saying has become pro-verbial, and although it savours a little of boastfulness, is also true. We may translate it thus: 'Let justice rule on earth, although all the rogues in the world should go to the bottom.' It is a good, honest principle of right, cutting off all the crooked ways made by knavery or violence. It must not, however, be misunderstood as allowing anyone to exercise his own rights with the utmost severity – a course in contra-diction to our moral duty. But we must take it to signify an obligation, binding upon rulers, to refrain from refusing to yield anyone his rights, or from curtailing them, out of personal feeling or sympathy for others. For this end, in particular, we require, firstly, that a state should have an internal political constitution, established according to the pure principles of right; secondly, that a union should be formed between this state and neighbouring or distant nations for a legal settlement of their differences after the analogy of the universal state. This proposition means nothing more than this: Political maxims must not start from the idea of a prosperity and happiness which are to be expected from observance of such precepts in every state; that is, not from the end which each nation makes the object of its will as the highest empirical principle of political wisdom. But they must set out from the pure concept of the duty of right, [that is] from the *'ought'* whose principle is given *a priori* through pure reason. This is the law, whatever the material consequences may be. The world will certainly not perish by any means, because the number of wicked people in it is becoming fewer. The morally bad has one peculiarity, inseparable from its nature; in its purposes, especially in relation to other evil influences, it is in contradiction with itself, and counteracts its own natural effect, and thus makes room for the moral principle of good, although advance in this direction may be slow.

Hence objectively, in theory, there is no quarrel between morals and politics. But subjectively, in the self-seeking tendencies of men (which we cannot actually call their morality, as we would a course of action based on maxims of reason), this disagreement in principle exists, and may always survive, for it serves as a whetstone to virtue. According to the principle *Tu ne*

cede malis, sed contra audentior ito, the true courage of virtue
in the present case lies not so much in facing the evils and self-
sacrifices which must be met here as in firmly confronting the
evil principle in our own nature and conquering its wiles. For
this is a principle far more dangerous, false, treacherous, and
sophistical, which puts forward the weakness in human nature
as a justification for every transgression.

In fact the political moralist may say that a ruler and people,
or nation and nation, do *one another* no wrong, when they
enter on a war with violence or cunning, although they do
wrong, generally speaking, in refusing to respect the idea of
right which alone could establish peace for all time. For, as
both are equally wrongly disposed to one another, each
transgressing the duty he owes to his neighbour, they are both
quite rightly served, when they are thus destroyed in war. This
mutual destruction stops short at the point of extermination
so that there are always enough of the race left to keep this
game going on through all the ages, and a far-off posterity may
take warning by them. The providence that orders the course
of the world is hereby justified. For the moral principle in
mankind never becomes extinguished, and human reason,
fitted for the practical realization of ideas of right according to
that principle, grows continually in fitness for that purpose
with the ever advancing march of culture, while at the same
time, it must be said, the guilt of transgression increases as
well. But it seems that, by no theodicy or vindication of the
justice of God can we justify creation in putting such a race of
corrupt creatures into the world at all – if, that is, we assume
that the human race neither will nor can ever be in a happier
condition than it is now. This standpoint, however, is too high
a one for us to judge from, or to theorize with the limited
concepts we have at our command, about the wisdom of that
supreme power which is unknowable by us. We are inevitably
driven to such despairing conclusions as these, if we do not
admit that the pure principles of right have objective reality –
that is to say, are capable of being practically realized – and,
consequently, that action must be taken on the part of the
people of a state and, further, by states in relation to one
another, whatever arguments empirical politics may bring
forward against this course. Politics in the real sense cannot

take a step forward without first paying homage to the principles of morals. And, although politics *per se* is a difficult art, in its union with morals no art is required. For in the case of a conflict arising between the two sciences, the moralist can cut asunder the knot which politics is unable to untie. Right must be held sacred by man, however great the cost and sacrifice to the ruling power. Here is no half-and-half course. We cannot devise a happy medium between right and expediency – a right pragmatically conditioned. But all politics must bend the knee to the principle of right, and may, in that way, hope to reach, although slowly perhaps, a level whence it may shine upon men for all time.

Appendix II: Concerning the harmony of politics with morals according to the transcendental idea of public right

If I look at public right from the point of view of most professors of law, and abstract from its *matter* or its empirical elements, varying according to the circumstances given in our experience of individuals in a state, or of states among themselves, then there remains the *form* of publicity. The possibility of this publicity, every legal title implies. For without it there could be no justice, which can only be thought as before the eyes of men; and, without justice, there would be no right, for, from justice only, right can come.

This characteristic of publicity must belong to every legal title. Hence, as, in any particular case that occurs, there is no difficulty in deciding whether this essential attribute is present or not (whether, that is, it is reconcilable with the principles of the agent or not). It furnishes an easily applied criterion which is to be found *a priori* in the reason so that in the particular case we can at once recognize the falsity or illegality of a proposed claim (*praetensio juris*), as it were by an experiment of pure reason.

Having thus, as it were, abstracted from all the empirical elements contained in the concept of a political and international law, such as, for instance, the evil tendency in human nature which makes compulsion necessary, we may give the following proposition as the *transcendental formula* of public right: 'All actions relating to the rights of other men are wrong, if the maxims from which they follow are inconsistent with publicity.'

This principle must be regarded not merely as ethical, as belonging to the doctrine of virtue, but also as juridical, referring to the rights of men. For there is something wrong in a maxim of conduct, which I cannot divulge without at once defeating my purpose – a maxim which must therefore be kept secret, if it is to succeed, and which I could not publicly acknowledge without infallibly stirring up the opposition of everyone. This necessary and universal resistance with which everyone meets me – a resistance therefore evident *a priori* – can be due to no other cause than the injustice with which such a maxim threatens everyone. Further, this testing principle is merely negative; that is, it serves only as a means by which we may know when an action is unjust to others. Like axioms, it has a certainty incapable of demonstration; it is, besides, easy of application as appears from the following examples of public right.

(1) *Constitutional Law.* Let us take in the first place the public law of the state (*jus civitatis*), particularly in its application to matters within the state. Here a question arises which many think difficult to answer, but which the transcendental principle of publicity solves quite readily: 'Is revolution a legitimate means for a people to adopt for the purpose of throwing off the oppressive yoke of a so-called tyrant (*non titulo, sed exercitio talis*)?' The rights of a nation are violated in a government of this kind, and no wrong is done to the tyrant in dethroning him. Of this there is no doubt. Nonetheless, it is in the highest degree wrong of the subjects to prosecute their rights in this way; and they would be just as little justified in complaining, if they happened to be defeated in their attempt, and had to endure the severest punishment in consequence.

A great many reasons for and against both sides of this question may be given, if we seek to settle it by a dogmatic deduction of the principles of right. But the transcendental principle of the publicity of public right can spare itself this diffuse argumentation. For, according to that principle, the people would ask themselves before the civil contract was made, whether they could venture to publish maxims proposing insurrection when a favourable opportunity should present itself. It is quite clear that if, when a constitution is established, it were made a condition that force may be exercised against the sovereign under certain circumstances, the people would be obliged to claim a lawful authority higher than his. But in that case, the so-called sovereign would be no longer sovereign; or, if both powers – that of the sovereign and that of the people – were made a condition of the constitution of the state, then its establishment (which was the aim of the people) would be impossible. The wrongfulness of revolution is quite obvious from the fact that openly to acknowledge maxims which justify this step would make attainment of the end at which they aim impossible. We are obliged to keep them secret. But this secrecy would not be necessary on the part of the head of the state. He may say quite plainly that the ringleaders of every rebellion will be punished by death, even although they may hold that he was he who first transgressed the fundamental law. For, if a ruler is conscious of possessing irresistible sovereign power (and this must be assumed in every civil constitution, because a sovereign who has not power to protect any individual member of the nation against his neighbour has also not the right to exercise authority over him), then he need have no fear that making known the maxims which guide him will cause the defeat of his plans. And it is quite consistent with this view to hold that, if the people are successful in their insurrection, the sovereign must return to the rank of a subject, and refrain from inciting rebellion with a view to regaining his lost sovereignty. At the same time, he need have no fear of being called to account for his former administration.

(2) *International Law.* There can be no question of an international law, except on the assumption of some kind of a law-governed state of things, the external condition under which any right can belong to man. For the very idea of international law, as public right, implies the publication of a universal will, determining the rights and property of each individual nation; and this *status juridicus* must spring out of a contract of some sort, which may not, like the contract to

which the state owes its origin, be founded upon compulsory laws, but may be, at the most, the agreement of a permanent free association, such as the federation, of the different states, to which we have alluded above. For, without the control of law to some extent, to serve as an active bond of union among different merely natural or moral individuals – that is to say, in a state of nature – there can only be private law. And here we find a disagreement between morals, regarded as the science of right, and politics. The criterion, obtained by observing the effect of publicity on maxims, is just as easily applied, but only when we understand that this agreement binds the contracting states solely with the object that peace may be preserved among them, and between them and other states; in no sense with a view to the acquisition of new territory or power. The following instances of antinomy occur between politics and morals, which are given here with the solution in each case.

a) 'When either of these states has promised something to another (as, for instance, assistance, or a relinquishment of certain territory, or subsidies and such like), the question may arise whether, in a case where the safety of the state thus bound depends on its evading the fulfilment of this promise, it can do so by maintaining a right to be regarded as a double person: firstly, as sovereign and accountable to no one in the state of which that sovereign power is head; and, secondly, merely as the highest official in the service of that state, who is obliged to answer to the state for every action. And the result of this is that the state is acquitted in its second capacity of any obligation to which it has committed itself in the first.' But, if a nation or its sovereign proclaimed these maxims, the natural consequence would be that every other would flee from it, or unite with other states to oppose such pretensions. And this is a proof that politics, with all its cunning, defeats its own ends, if the test of making principles of action public, which we have indicated, be applied. Hence the maxim we have quoted must be wrong.

b) 'If a state which has increased its power to a formidable extent (*potentia tremenda*) excites anxiety in its neighbours, is it right to assume that, since it has the means, it will also have the will to oppress others; and does that give less powerful states a right to unite and attack the greater nation without any definite cause of offence?' A state which would here answer openly in the affirmative would only bring the evil about more surely and speedily. For the greater power would forestall those smaller nations, and their union would be but a weak reed of defence against a state which knew how to apply the maxim *divide et impera*. This maxim of political expediency then, when openly acknowledged, necessarily defeats the end at which it aims, and is therefore wrong.

c) 'If a smaller state by its geographical position breaks up the territory of a greater, so as to prevent a unity necessary to the preservation of that state, is the latter not justified in subjugating its less powerful neighbour, and uniting the territory in question with its own?' We can easily see that the greater state dare not publish such a maxim beforehand, for, either all smaller states would without loss of time unite against it, or other powers would contend for this booty. Hence the impracticability of such a maxim becomes evident under the light of publicity. And this is a sign that it is wrong, and that in a very great degree; for, although the victim of an act of injustice may be of small account, that does not prevent the injustice done from being very great.

(3) *Cosmopolitan Law*. We may pass over this department of right in silence, for, owing to its analogy with international law, its maxims are easily specified and estimated.

In this principle of the incompatibility of the maxims of international law with their publicity, we have a good indication of the non-agreement between politics and morals, regarded as a science of right. Now we require to know under what conditions these maxims do agree with the law of nations. For we cannot conclude that the converse holds, and that all maxims which can bear publicity are therefore just. For anyone who has a decided supremacy has no need to make any secret about his maxims. The condition of a law of nations being possible at all is that, in the first place, there should be a law-governed state of things. If this is not so, there can be no public right, and all right which we can think of outside the law-governed state – that is to say, in the state of nature – is mere private right. Now, we have seen above that something of the nature of a federation between nations, for the sole purpose of doing away with war, is the only rightful condition of things reconcilable with their individual freedom. Hence, the agreement of politics and morals is only possible in a federative union – a union which is necessarily given *a priori* – according to the principles of right. And the lawful basis of all politics can only be the establishment of this union in its widest possible extent. Apart from this end, all political sophistry is folly and veiled injustice. Now, this sham politics has a casuistry, not to be excelled in the best Jesuit school. It has its mental reservation (*reservatio mentalis*): as, in the drawing up of a public treaty in such terms as we can, if we will interpret when occasion serves to our advantage; for example, the distinction between the *status quo* in fact (*de fait*) and in right (*de droit*). Secondly, it has its probabilism, when it pretends to discover evil intentions in another, or makes the probability of their possible future ascendancy a lawful reason for bringing about the destruction of other peaceful states. Finally, it has its philosophical sin (*peccatum philosophicum, peccatillum, baggatelle*) which is that of holding it a trifle easily pardoned that a smaller state should be swallowed up, if this be to the gain of a nation much more powerful; for such an increase in power is supposed to tend to the greater prosperity of the whole world.[XVII]

Duplicity gives politics the advantage of using one branch or the other of morals, just as suits its own ends. The love of our fellowmen is a duty; so, too, is respect for their rights. But the former is only conditional; the latter, on the other hand, an unconditional, absolutely imperative duty; and anyone who would give himself up to the sweet consciousness of well-doing must be first perfectly assured that he has not transgressed its commands. Politics has no difficulty in agreeing with morals in the first sense of the term, as ethics, to secure that men should give to superiors their rights. But when it comes to morals in its second aspect, as the science of right before which politics must bow the knee, the politician finds it prudent to have nothing to do with compacts, and rather to deny all reality to morals in this sense, and reduce all duty to mere benevolence. Philosophy could easily frustrate the artifices of a politics like this, which shuns the light of criticism, by publishing its maxims, if only statesmen would have the courage to grant philosophers the right to ventilate their opinions.

With this end in view, I propose another principle of public right, which is at once transcendental and affirmative. Its formula would be as follows: 'All maxims which require publicity, in order that they may not fail to attain their end, are in agreement both with right and politics.'

For, if these maxims can only attain the end at which they aim by being published, they must be in harmony with the universal end of mankind, which is happiness; and to be in sympathy with this (to make the people contented with their lot) is the real business of politics. Now, if this end should be attainable only by publicity, or in other words, through the removal of all distrust of the maxims of politics, these must be in harmony with the right of the people, for a union of the ends of all is only possible in a harmony with this right.

I must postpone the further development and discussion of this principle till another opportunity. That it is a transcendental formula is quite evident from the fact that all the empirical conditions of a doctrine of happiness, or the *matter* of law, are absent, and that it has regard only to the *form* of universal conformity to law.

If it is our duty to realize a state of public right, if at the same time there are good grounds for hope that this ideal may be realized, although only by an approximation advancing *ad infinitum*, then perpetual peace, following hitherto falsely so-called conclusions of peace, which have been in reality mere cessations of hostilities, is no mere empty idea. But, rather, we have here a problem which gradually works out its own solution and, as the periods in which a given advance takes place towards the realization of the ideal of perpetual peace will, we hope, become with the passing of time shorter and shorter, we must approach ever nearer to this goal.

Notes

I   An hereditary kingdom is not a state which can be inherited by another state, but one whose sovereign power can be inherited by another physical person. The state then acquires a ruler, not the ruler as such (that is, as one already possessing another realm) the state.

II   A Bulgarian Prince thus answered the Greek Emperor who magnanimously offered to settle a quarrel with him not by shedding the blood of his subjects, but by a duel: 'A smith who has tongs will not take the red-hot iron from the fire with his hands.'

III   It has been hitherto doubted, not without reason, whether there can be laws of permission (*leges permissivæ*) of pure reason as well as commands (*leges præceptivæ*) and prohibitions (*leges prohibitivæ*). For law in general has a basis of objective practical necessity. Permission, on the other hand, is based upon the contingency of certain actions in practice. It follows that a law of permission would enforce what cannot be enforced; and this would involve a contradiction, if the object of the law should be the same in both cases. Here, however, in the present case of a law of permission, the presupposed prohibition is aimed merely at the future manner of acquisition of a right – for example, acquisition through inheritance; the exemption from this prohibition (i.e. the permission) refers to the present state of possession. In the transition from a state of nature to the civil state, this holding of property can continue as a *bona fide*, if usurpatory, ownership under the new social conditions, in accordance with a permission of the law of nature. Ownership of this kind, as soon as its true nature becomes known, is seen to be mere nominal possession (*possessio putativa*) sanctioned by opinion and customs in a natural state of society. After the transition stage is passed, such modes of acquisition are likewise forbidden in the subsequently evolved civil state; and this power to remain in possession would not be admitted, if the supposed acquisition had taken place in the civilized community. It would be bound to come to an end as an injury to the right of others, the moment its illegality became patent.

    I have wished here only by the way to draw the attention of teachers of the law of nature to the idea of a *lex permissiva* which presents itself spontaneously in any system of rational classification. I do so chiefly because use is often made of this concept in civil law with reference to statutes; with this difference that the law of prohibition stands alone by itself, while permission is not, as it ought to be, introduced into that law as a limiting clause, but is thrown among the exceptions. Thus 'this or that is forbidden' – say, Nos.1, 2, 3 and so on in an infinite progression – while permissions are only added to the law incidentally: they are not reached by the application of some principle, but only by groping about among cases which have actually occurred. Were this not so, qualifications would have had to be brought into the formula of laws of prohibition, which would have immediately transformed them into laws of permission. Count von

Windischgrätz, a man whose wisdom was equal to his discrimination, urged this very point in the form of a question propounded by him for a prize essay. One must therefore regret that this ingenious problem has been so soon neglected and left unsolved. For the possibility of a formula similar to those of mathematics is the sole real test of a legislation that would be consistent. Without this, the so-called *jus certum* will remain forever a mere pious wish: we can have only general laws valid on the whole; no general laws possessing the universal validity which the concept law seems to demand.

IV   It is usually accepted that a man may not take hostile steps against anyone, unless the latter has already injured him by act. This is quite accurate, if both are citizens of a law-governed state. For, in becoming a member of this community, each gives the other the security he demands against injury, by means of the supreme authority exercising control over them both. The individual, however, (or nation) who remains in a mere state of nature deprives me of this security, and does me injury by mere proximity. There is perhaps no active (*facto*) molestation, but there is a state of lawlessness (*status injustus*) which, by its very existence, offers a continual menace to me. I can therefore compel him either to enter into relations with me under which we are both subject to law, or to withdraw from my neighbourhood so that the postulate upon which the following articles are based is: 'All men who have the power to exert a mutual influence upon one another must be under a civil government of some kind.'

A legal constitution is, according to the nature of the individuals who compose the state:

1. A constitution formed in accordance with the right of citizenship of the individuals who constitute a nation (*jus civitatis*).
2. A constitution whose principle is international law which determines the relations of states (*jus gentium*).
3. A constitution formed in accordance with cosmopolitan law in so far as individuals and states, standing in an external relation of mutual reaction, may be regarded as citizens of one world-state (*jus cosmopoliticum*).

This classification is not an arbitrary one, but is necessary with reference to the idea of perpetual peace. For, if even one of these units of society were in a position physically to influence another, while yet remaining a member of a primitive order of society, then a state of war would be joined with these primitive conditions; and from this it is our present purpose to free ourselves.

V   Lawful, that is to say, external freedom cannot be defined, as it so often is, as the right [*Befügniss*] 'to do whatever one likes so long as this does not wrong anyone else.' For what is this right? It is the possibility of actions which do not lead to the injury of others. So the explanation of a 'right' would be something like this: 'Freedom is the possibility of actions which do not injure anyone. A man does not wrong another – whatever his action – if he does not wrong another':

which is empty tautology. My external (lawful) freedom is rather to be explained in this way: it is the right through which I require not to obey any external laws except those to which I could have given my consent. In exactly the same way, external (legal) equality in a state is that relation of the subjects in consequence of which no individual can legally bind or oblige another to anything, without at the same time submitting himself to the law which ensures that he can, in his turn, be bound and obliged in like manner by this other.

The principle of lawful independence requires no explanation, as it is involved in the general concept of a constitution. The validity of this hereditary and inalienable right, which belongs of necessity to mankind, is affirmed and ennobled by the principle of a lawful relation between man himself and higher beings, if indeed he believes in such beings. This is so, because he thinks of himself, in accordance with these very principles, as a citizen of a transcendental world as well as of the world of sense. For, as far as my freedom goes, I am bound by no obligation even with regard to divine laws, which are apprehended by me only through my reason, except in so far as I could have given my assent to them, for it is through the law of freedom of my own reason that I first form for myself a concept of a divine will. As for the principle of equality, in so far as it applies to the most sublime being in the universe next to God – a being I might perhaps figure to myself as a mighty emanation of the divine spirit – there is no reason why, if I perform my duty in the sphere in which I am placed, as that aeon does in his, the duty of obedience alone should fall to my share, the right to command to him. That this principle of equality (unlike the principle of freedom) does not apply to our relation to God is due to the fact that to this being alone the idea of duty does not belong.

As for the right to equality which belongs to all citizens as subjects, the solution of the problem of the admissibility of an hereditary nobility hinges on the following question: 'Does social rank – acknowledged by the state to be higher in the case of one subject than another – stand above desert, or does merit take precedence of social standing?' Now it is obvious that, if high position is combined with good family, it is quite uncertain whether merit, that is to say, skill and fidelity in office, will follow as well. This amounts to granting the favoured individual a commanding position without any question of desert; and to that, the universal will of the people – expressed in an original contract which is the fundamental principle of all right – would never consent, for it does not follow that a nobleman is a man of noble character. In the case of the official nobility, as one might term the rank of higher magistracy – which one must acquire by merit – the social position is not attached like property to the person, but to his office, and equality is not thereby disturbed; for, if a man gives up office, he lays down with it his official rank, and falls back into the rank of his fellows.

VI The lofty appellations which are often given to a ruler – such as the Lord's Anointed, the Administrator of the Divine Will upon Earth and Vicar of God – have been many times censured as flattery gross enough to make one giddy. But it seems to me without cause. Far from making a prince arrogant, names like these must rather make him humble at heart, if he has any intelligence – which we take for granted he has – and reflects that he has undertaken an office which is too great for any human being. For, indeed, it is the holiest which God has on earth – namely, the right of ruling mankind; and he must ever live in fear of injuring this treasure of God in some respect or other.

VII Mallet du Pan boasts in his seemingly brilliant but shallow and superficial language that, after many years experience, he has come at last to be convinced of the truth of the well known saying of Pope: 'For forms of government let fools contest; whate'er is best administered is best.' If this means that the best administered government is best administered, then, in Swift's phrase, he has cracked a nut to find a worm in it. If it means, however, that the best conducted government is also the best kind of government – that is, the best form of political constitution – then it is utterly false, for examples of wise administration are no proof of the kind of government. Who ever ruled better than Titus and Marcus Aurelius? And yet the one left Domitian, the other Commodus, as his successor. This could not have happened where the constitution was a good one, for their absolute unfitness for the position was early enough known, and the power of the emperor was sufficiently great to exclude them.

VIII A Greek Emperor, who magnanimously volunteered to settle by a duel his quarrel with a Bulgarian Prince, got the following answer: 'A smith who has tongs will not pluck the glowing iron from the fire with his hands.'

IX On the conclusion of peace at the end of a war, it might not be unseemly for a nation to appoint a day of humiliation after the festival of thanksgiving, on which to invoke the mercy of Heaven for the terrible sin which the human race are guilty of in their continued unwillingness to submit (in their relations with other states) to a law-governed constitution, preferring rather in the pride of their independence to use the barbarous method of war, which after all does not really settle what is wanted, namely, the right of each state in a quarrel. The feasts of thanksgiving during a war for a victorious battle, the hymns which are sung – to use the Jewish expression – 'to the Lord of Hosts' are not in less strong contrast to the ethical idea of a father of mankind; for, apart from the indifference these customs show to the way in which nations seek to establish their rights – sad enough as it is – these rejoicings bring in an element of exultation that a great number of lives, or at least the happiness of many, has been destroyed.

X In order to call this great empire by the name which it gives itself – namely, China, not Sina or a word of similar sound – we have only to look at Georgii: *Alphab. Tibet.*, pp. 651–4, particularly *note* b. below. According to the observation of Professor Fischer of St Petersburg, there is really no particular name which it always goes by: the most usual is the word *Kin*, i.e. gold, which the inhabitants of Tibet call *Ser*. Hence the emperor is called the king of gold, i.e. the king of the most splendid country in the world. This word *Kin* may probably be *Chin* in the empire itself, but be pronounced *Kin* by the Italian missionaries on account of the gutturals. Thus we see that the country of the Seres, so often mentioned by the Romans, was China. The silk, however, was dispatched to Europe across Greater Tibet, probably through Smaller Tibet and Bucharia, through Persia, and then on. This leads to many reflections as to the antiquity of this wonderful state, as compared with Hindustan, at the time of its union with Tibet and thence with Japan. On the other hand, the name Sina or Tschina which is said to be given to this land by neighbouring peoples leads to nothing.

Perhaps we can explain the ancient intercourse of Europe with Tibet – a fact at no time widely known – by looking at what Hesychius has preserved on the matter. I refer to the shout, $Kον\xi$ $Oμπα\xi$ (*Konx Ompax*), the cry of the Hierophants in the Eleusinian mysteries (cf. *Travels of Anacharsis the Younger*, Part V., p. 447, *seq*.). For, according to Georgii *Alph. Tibet*., the word *Concioa* which bears a striking resemblance to *Konx* means God. *Pah-cio* (*ib*. p. 520) which might easily be pronounced by the Greeks like *pax* means *promulgator legis*, the divine principle permeating nature (called also, on p. 177, *Cencresi*). *Om*, however, which La Croze translates by *benedictus*, i.e. blessed, can, when applied to the deity, mean nothing but beatified (p. 507). Now, P. Franz. Horatius, when he asked the lamas of Tibet, as he often did, what they understood by God (*Concioa*) always got the answer: 'It is the assembly of all the saints', i.e. the assembly of those blessed ones who have been born again according to the faith of the lama and, after many wanderings in changing forms, have at last returned to God, to Burchane. That is to say, they are beings to be worshipped; souls which have undergone transmigration (p. 223). So the mysterious expression *Konx Ompax* ought probably to mean the holy (*Knox*), blessed (*Om*), and wise (*Pax*) supreme being pervading the universe – the personification of nature. Its use in the Greek mysteries probably signified monotheism for the Epoptes, in distinction from the polytheism of the people, although elsewhere P. Horatius scented atheism here. How that mysterious word came by way of Tibet to the Greeks may be explained as above; and, on the other hand, in this way is made probable an early intercourse of Europe with China across Tibet – earlier perhaps than the communication with Hindustan.

XI In the mechanical system of nature to which man belongs as a sentient being, there appears, as the underlying ground of its existence, a certain *form* which we cannot make intelligible to ourselves except by thinking into the physical world the idea of an end preconceived by the Author of the universe. This predetermination of nature on the part of God we generally call Divine Providence. In so far as this providence appears in the origin of the universe, we speak of providence as founder of the world (*providentia conditrix*; *semel jussit*, *semper parent.* Augustine). As it maintains the course of nature, however, according to universal laws of adaptation to preconceived ends, we call it a ruling providence (*providentia gubernatrix*). Further, we name it the guiding providence (*providentia directrix*), as it appears in the world for special ends, which we could not foresee, but suspect only from the result. Finally, regarding particular events as divine purposes, we speak no longer of providence, but of dispensation (*directio extraordinaria*). As this term, however, really suggests the idea of miracles, although the events are not spoken of by this name, the desire of fathom dispensation as such, is a foolish presumption in men. For, from one single occurrence, to jump at the conclusion that there is a particular principle of efficient causes, and that this event is an end and not merely the natural [*naturmechanische*] sequence of a design quite unknown to us is absurd and presumptuous, in however pious and humble spirit we may speak of it. In the same way, to distinguish between a universal and a particular providence when regarding it *materialiter*, in its relation to actual objects in the world (to say, for instance, that there may be, indeed, a providence for the preservation of the different species of creation, but that individuals are left to chance) is false and contradictory. For providence is called universal for the very reason that no single thing may be thought of as shut out from its care. Probably the distinction of two kinds of providence, *formaliter* or subjectively considered, had reference to the manner in which its purposes are fulfilled. So that we have ordinary providence (e.g. the yearly decay and awakening to new life in nature with change of season) and what we may call unusual or special providence (e.g. the bringing of timber by ocean currents to Arctic shores where it does not grow, and where without this aid the inhabitants could not live). Here, although we can quite well explain the psycho-mechanical cause of these phenomena – in this case, for example, the banks of the rivers in temperate countries are overgrown with trees, some of which fall into the water and are carried along, probably by the Gulf Stream – we must not overlook the teleological cause which points to the providential care of a ruling wisdom above nature. But the concept, commonly used in the schools of philosophy, of a co-operation on the part of the deity or a concurrence (*concursus*) in the operations going on in the world of sense, must be dropped. For it is, firstly, self-contradictory to couple the like and the unlike together (*gryphes jungere equis*) and to let Him, who is Himself the entire cause of the changes in the universe, make good any shortcomings in His own predetermining providence (which to require this must be defective) during the course of the world. For example, to say that the physician has restored the sick with the help of God: that is to say that He has been present as a support. For *causa solitaria non juvat*. God created the physician as well as his means of healing; and we must ascribe the result wholly to Him, if we will go back to the supreme first cause which, theoretically, is beyond our comprehension. Or we can ascribe the result entirely to the physician in so far as we follow up this event as explicable in the chain of physical causes according to the order of nature. Secondly, moreover, such a way of looking at this question destroys all the fixed principles by which we judge an effect. But, from the ethico-practical point of view which looks entirely to the transcendental side of things, the idea of a divine concurrence is quite proper and even necessary; for example, in the faith that God will make good the imperfection of our human justice, if only our feelings and intentions are sincere; and that He will do this by means beyond our comprehension, and therefore we should not slacken our efforts after what is good. Whence it follows, as a matter of course, that no one must attempt to explain a good action as a mere event in time by this *concursus*, for that would be to pretend a theoretical knowledge of the supersensible, and hence be absurd.

XII Of all modes of livelihood, the life of the hunter is undoubtedly most incompatible with a civilized condition of society, because, to live by hunting, families must isolate themselves from their neighbours, soon becoming estranged and spread over widely scattered forests, to be before long on terms of hostility, since each requires a great deal of space to obtain food and raiment.

God's command to Noah not to shed blood (I. *Genesis*, IX. 4–6) is frequently quoted, and was afterwards – in another connection it is true – made by the baptized Jews a condition to which Christians, newly converted from heathendom, had to conform. Cf. *Acts* XV. 20; XXI. 25. This command seems originally to have been nothing else than a prohibition of the life of the hunter; for here the possibility of eating raw flesh must often occur, and, in forbidding the one custom, we condemn the other.

XIII The question might be put: 'If it is nature's will that these Arctic shores should not remain unpopulated, what will become of their inhabitants, if, as is to be expected, at some time or other no more driftwood should be brought to them? For we may believe that, with the advance of civilization, the inhabitants of temperate zones will utilize better the wood which grows on the banks of their rivers, and not let it fall into the stream and so be swept away.' I answer: the inhabitants of the shores of the River Obi, the Yenisei, the Lena will supply them with it through trade, and take in exchange the animal produce in which the seas of Arctic shores are so rich – that is, if nature has first of all brought about peace among them.

XIV Difference of religion! A strange expression, as if one were to speak of different kinds of morality. There may indeed be different historical forms of belief – that is to say, the various means which have been used in the course of time to promote religion – but they are mere subjects of learned investigation, and do not really lie within the sphere of religion. In the same way, there are many religious works – the *Zendavesta*, *Veda*, *Koran* etc. – but there is only one religion, binding for all men and for all times. These books are each no more than the accidental mouthpiece of religion, and may be different according to differences in time and place.

XV   These are *permissive* laws of reason which allow us to leave a system of public law, when it is tainted by injustice, to remain just as it is until everything is entirely revolutionized through an internal development, either spontaneous, or fostered and matured by peaceful influences. For any legal constitution whatsoever, even although it conforms only slightly with the spirit of law, is better than none at all – that is to say, anarchy, which is the fate of a precipitate reform. Hence, as things now are, the wise politician will look upon it as his duty to make reforms on the lines marked out by the ideal of public law. He will not use revolutions, when these have been brought about by natural causes, to extenuate still greater oppression than caused them, but will regard them as the voice of nature, calling upon him to make such thorough reforms as will bring about the only lasting constitution – a lawful constitution based on the principles of freedom.

XVI It is still sometimes denied that we find in members of a civilized community a certain depravity rooted in the nature of man; and it might, indeed, be alleged with some show of truth that not an innate corruptness in human nature, but the barbarism of men, the defect of a not yet sufficiently developed culture, is the cause of the evident antipathy to law which their attitude indicates. In the external relations of states, however, human wickedness shows itself incontestably, without any attempt at concealment. Within the state, it is covered over by the compelling authority of civil laws. For, working against the tendency every citizen has to commit acts of violence against his neighbour, there is the much stronger force of the government which not only gives an appearance of morality to the whole state (*causae non causae*), but, by checking the outbreak of lawless propensities, actually aids the moral qualities of men considerably in their development of a direct respect for the law. For every individual thinks that he himself would hold the idea of right sacred, and follow faithfully what it prescribes, if only he could expect that everyone else would do the same. This guarantee is in part given to him by the government; and a great advance is made by this step, which is not deliberately moral, towards the idea of fidelity to the concept of duty for its own sake, without thought of return. As, however, every man's good opinion of himself presupposes an evil disposition in everyone else, we have an expression of their mutual judgment of one another, namely, that when it comes to hard facts, none of them are worth much; but whence this judgment comes remains unexplained, as we cannot lay the blame on the nature of man, since he is a being in the possession of freedom. The respect for the idea of right, of which it is absolutely impossible for man to divest himself, sanctions in the most solemn manner the theory of our power to conform to its dictates. And hence, every man sees himself obliged to act in accordance with what the idea of right prescribes, whether his neighbours fulfil their obligation or not.

XVII We can find the voucher for maxims such as these in Herr Hofrichter Garve's essay, *On the Connection of Morals with Politics*, 1788. This worthy scholar confesses at the very beginning that he is unable to give a satisfactory answer to this question. But his sanction of such maxims, even when coupled with the admission that he cannot altogether clear away the arguments raised against them, seems to be a greater concession in favour of those who show considerable inclination to abuse them than it might perhaps be wise to admit.

Select Bibliography

Alberoni, Giulio, *Cardinal Alberoni's Scheme for Reducing the Turkish Empire to the Obedience of Christian Princes: And for A Partition of the Conquests, Together with A Scheme of A Perpetual Diet for Establishing the Publick Tranquillity*, 2nd edn, (tr.) Prince de la Torella (London: Printed for J. Torbuck, 1736).

—— 'Cardinal Alberoni's Scheme for Reducing the Turkish Empire to the Obedience of Christian Princes: And for A Partition of the Conquests, Together with A Scheme of A Perpetual Diet for Establishing the Publick Tranquillity', *The American Journal of International Law*, 7:1 (January 1913), 83–107.

Anchor, Robert, *The Enlightenment Tradition* (Berkeley, CA: University of California Press, 1967).

Anderson-Gold, Sharon, *Cosmopolitanism and Human Rights* (Cardiff: University of Wales Press, 2001).

Archibugi, Daniele and David Held (eds), *Cosmopolitan Democracy: An Agenda for a New World Order* (Cambridge: Polity, 1995).

——, David Held and Martin Köhler (eds), *Re-imagining Political Community: Studies in Cosmopolitan Democracy* (London: Polity, 1998).

Ba, Alice D. and Matthew J. Hoffmann (eds), *Contending Perspectives on Global Governance: Coherence, Contestation and World Order* (London: Routledge, 2005).

Bellers, John, *Some Reasons for an European State, Proposed to the Powers of Europe by An Universal Guarantee and An Annual Congress, Senate, Diet, or Parliament, to Settle Any Disputes about the Bounds and Rights of Princes and States Hereafter* (London: 1710).

Bentham, Jeremy, *The Works of Jeremy Bentham*, vol. 2, (ed.) John Bowring (Edinburgh: William Tait; London: Simpkin, Marshall & Co., 1843).

Bernstein, Eduard, *Cromwell and Communism* [1895], (tr.) H. J. Stenning (London: George Allen & Unwin, 1930 and 1963).

Bodeker, Hans Erich, '"Europe" in the discourse of the sciences of state in 18th century Germany', *Cromohs*, 8 (2003), 1–14, available online at *http://www.cromohs.unifi.it/8_2003/bodeker.html* (October 2006).

Bohman, James and Matthias Lutz-Bachmann (eds), *Perpetual Peace: Essays on Kant's Cosmopolitan Ideal* (Cambridge, MA: The MIT Press, 1997).

Bok, Sissela, 'Early advocates of lasting world peace: Utopians or realists?', *Ethics and International Affairs*, 4 (1990), 145–62.

Boucher, David and Paul Kelly (eds), *The Social Contract from Hobbes to Rawls* (London: Routledge, 1994).

Bradford Jr., Colin I. and Johannes F. Linn (eds), *Global Governance Reform: Breaking the Stalemate* (Washington, D.C.: Brookings Institution Press, 2007).

Breckenridge, Carol A., Sheldon Pollock, Homi K. Bhabha and Dipesh Chakrabarty (eds), *Cosmopolitanism* (Durham, NC: Duke University Press, 2002).

Buchan, Bruce, 'Explaining war and peace: Kant and liberal IR theory', *Alternatives*, 27 (2002), 407–28.

Calonne, Charles Alexandre de, *The Political State of Europe at the Beginning of 1796, or Considerations on the Most Effectual Means of Procuring A Solid and Permanent Peace*, (tr.) D. St. Quentin (Dublin: Printed by P. Byrne, 1796).

Cavallar, Georg, *Pax Kantiana: Systematisch-historische Untersuchung des Entwurfs "Zum Ewigen Frieden" (1795) von Immanuel Kant* (Wien: Böhlau, 1992).

——— 'Kantian perspectives on democratic peace: Alternatives to Doyle', *Review of International Studies*, 27 (2001), 229–48.

Cederman, Lars-Erik, 'Back to Kant: Reinterpreting the democratic peace as a macrohistorical learning process', *American Political Science Review*, 95 (2001), 15–31.

Collinson, Diané and Kathryn Plant, *Fifty Major Philosophers*, 2nd edn (London and New York: Routledge, 2006).

Commission on Global Governance, *Our Global Neighbourhood: The Report of the Commission on Global Governance* (Oxford: Oxford University Press, 1995).

Cranston, Maurice, *The Noble Savage: Jean-Jacques Rousseau, 1754–1762* (London: Allen Lane, The Penguin Press, 1991).

Crimmins, James E., 'Bentham and Hobbes: An issue of influence', *Journal of the History of Ideas*, 63 (2002), 677–95.

Damrosch, Leo, *Jean-Jacques Rousseau: Restless Genius* (Boston, MA: Houghton Mifflin Company, 2005).

Dingwerth, Klaus and Philipp Pattberg, 'Global governance as a perspective on world politics', *Global Governance*, 12 (2006), 185–203.

Djelic, Marie-Laure and Kerstin Sahlin-Andersson (eds), *Transnational Governance: Institutional Dynamics of Regulation* (Cambridge: Cambridge University Press, 2006).

Doyle, Michael, 'Kant, liberal legacies, and foreign affairs', Parts 1 and 2, *Philosophy and Public Affairs*, 12 (1983), 205–35; 325–53.

Easley, Eric S., *The War over* Perpetual Peace: *An Exploration into the History of a Foundational International Relations Text* (Houndmills: Palgrave Macmillan, 2004).

Forsyth, M. G., H. M. A. Keens-Soper and P. Savigear (eds), *The Theory of International Relations: Selected Texts from Gentili to Treitschke* (London: George Allen and Unwin Ltd, 1970).

Gargaz, Pierre-André, *A Project of Universal and Perpetual Peace*, (tr. and ed.) George Simpson Eddy (New York: 1922).

Grotius Society [The], *Jeremy Bentham's Plan for An Universal and Perpetual Peace* (London: Sweet & Maxwell Ltd, 1927).

Held, David, *Democracy and the Global Order: From the Modern State to Cosmopolitan Governance* (Stanford, CA: Stanford University Press, 1996).

—— and Mathias Koenig-Archibugi (eds), *Global Governance and Public Accountability* (Malden, MA: Blackwell, 2005).

Henderson, Gordon P., 'The public and peace: the consequences for citizenship of the democratic peace literature', *International Studies Review*, 8 (2006), 199–224.

Hewson, Martin and Timothy J. Sinclair (eds), *Approaches to Global Governance Theory* (Albany, NY: State University of New York Press, 1999).

Hinsley, F. H., *Power and the Pursuit of Peace: Theory and Practice in the History of Relations between States* (Cambridge: Cambridge University Press, 1963).

Hoogensen, Gunhild, 'Bentham's international manuscripts versus the published "Works"', *Journal of Bentham Studies*, 4 (2001).

—— *International Relations, Security and Jeremy Bentham* (London: Routledge, 2005).

Huntington, Samuel P., *The Clash of Civilizations and the Remaking of World Order* (New York: Simon and Schuster, 1996).

Janis, M. W., 'Jeremy Bentham and the fashioning of "international law"', *The American Journal of International Law*, 78 (1984), 405–18.

Johnson, James Turner, *The Quest for Peace: Three Moral Traditions in Western Cultural History* (Princeton, NJ: Princeton University Press, 1987).

Kant, Immanuel, *Perpetual Peace: A Philosophical Essay*, (tr.) Mary Campbell Smith (London: Swan Sonnenschein, 1903).

—— *Werke in Zwölf Bänden*, Vol. XI, (Frankfurt: Suhrkamp Verlag, 1964).

—— *Kant's Political Writings*, (ed.) Hans Siegbert Reiss, (tr.) H. B. Nisbet (Cambridge: Cambridge University Press, 1970).

Kennedy, Paul, Dirk Messner and Franz Nuscheler (eds), *Global Trends and Global Governance* (London: Pluto Press, 2002).

Krahmann, Elke, 'National, regional, and global governance: one phenomenon or many?', *Global Governance*, 9 (2003), 323–46.

Larner, Wendy and William Walters (eds), *Global Governmentality: Governing International Spaces* (London: Routledge, 2004).

Lederer, Markus and Philipp S. Müller (eds), *Criticizing Global Governance* (New York, NY: Palgrave Macmillan, 2005).

Lieberman, David, 'Jeremy Bentham: Biography and intellectual biography', *History of Political Thought*, 20:1 (1999), 187–204.

Morrow, John, *The History of Political Thought: A Thematic Introduction* (Houndmills: Macmillan, 1998).

Nussbaum, Martha C., 'Kant and Stoic cosmopolitanism', *The Journal of Political Philosophy* 5 (1997), 1–25.

Orwin, Clifford and Nathan Tarcov (eds), *The Legacy of Rousseau* (Chicago and London: The University of Chicago Press, 1997).

Parekh, Bhikhu (ed.), *Jeremy Bentham: Ten Critical Essays* (London: Frank Cass, 1974).

Patomäki, Heikki, 'Problems of democratizing global governance: time, space and the emancipatory process', *European Journal of International Relations*, 9 (2003), 347–76.

Penn, William, *A Collection of the Works of William Penn*, vol. 2, (London: Printed for J. Sowle, 1726).

Riley, Patrick, *Will and Political Legitimacy: A Critical Exposition of Social Contract Theory in Hobbes, Locke, Rousseau, Kant, and Hegel* (Cambridge, MA: Harvard University Press, 1982).

Roosevelt, Grace, *Reading Rousseau in the Nuclear Age* (Philadelphia, PA: Temple University Press, 1990).

—— 'Rousseau versus Rawls on international relations', *European Journal of Political Theory*, 5:3 (2006), 301–20.

Rosato, Sebastian, 'The flawed logic of the democratic peace', *American Political Science Review*, 97 (2003), 585–602.

Rosenau, James N. and Ernst-Otto Czempiel (eds), *Governance without Government: Order and Change in World Politics* (Cambridge: Cambridge University Press, 1992).

Rousseau, Jean-Jacques, *A Lasting Peace through the Federation of Europe and The State of War*, (tr.) C. E. Vaughan (London: Constable and Company Limited, 1917).

—— *A Project of Perpetual Peace: Rousseau's Essay*, (tr. and ed.) Edith M. Nuttall (London: Richard Cobden-Sanderson, 1927).

—— *The Social Contract and Other Later Political Writings*, (ed.) Victor Gourevitch (Cambridge: Cambridge University Press, 1997).

Saint-Pierre, Charles Irénée Castel de, *A Project for Settling An Everlasting Peace in Europe, First Proposed by Henry IV of France, and Approved of by Queen Elizabeth and Most of the Then Princes of Europe, and Now Discussed at Large and Made Practicable by the Abbot St. Pierre of the French Academy* (London: Printed for J. Watts, 1714).

—— *Selections from the Second Edition of the Abrégé du Projet de Paix Perpétuelle*, (tr.) H. Hale Bellot (London: Sweet & Maxwell Limited, 1927).

Schofield, Philip, *Utility and Democracy: The Political Thought of Jeremy Bentham* (Oxford: Oxford University Press, 2006).

Schwartz, Thomas and Kiron K. Skinner, 'The myth of the democratic peace', *Orbis*, 46 (2002), 159–72.

Sidgwick, Henry, 'Bentham and Benthamism in Politics and Ethics', *The Fortnightly Review*, 21 (January–June 1877), 627–52.

Souleyman, Elizabeth V., *The Vision of World Peace in Seventeenth and Eighteenth-Century France* (Port Washington, NY: Kennikat Press, 1941).

Steintrager, James, *Bentham* (London: George Allen & Unwin Ltd, 1977).

Stuart, James Francis Edward, *Declaration of James the Third, King of England, Scotland and Ireland etc. to All His Subjects to Serve as a Foundation for a Lasting Peace* (1722); also available online at *http://www.jacobite.ca/documents/17221010.htm* (October 2006).

van den Dungen, Peter, 'The Abbé de Saint-Pierre and the English "Irenists" of the 18th century (Penn, Bellers, and Bentham)', *International Journal on World Peace*, 17:2 (June 2000), 5–31.

Vertovec, Steven and Robin Cohen (eds), *Conceiving Cosmopolitanism: Theory, Context, and Practice* (Oxford: Oxford University Press, 2002).

Vesnitch, Mil. R., 'Cardinal Alberoni: An Italian precursor of pacifism and international arbitration', *The American Journal of International Law*, 7:1 (1913), 51–82.

Weiss, Thomas G., 'Governance, good governance and global governance: conceptual and actual challenges', *Third World Quarterly*, 21 (2000), 795–814.

Wilkinson, Rorden (ed.), *The Global Governance Reader* (London: Routledge, 2005).

William Penn Tercentenary Committee [The], *Remember William Penn, 1644–1944 – A Tercentenary Memorial*, 2nd edn (Harrisburg, PA: Commonwealth of Pennsylvania, 1945).

Williams, Alfred Tuttle, *The Concept of Equality in the Writings of Rousseau, Bentham and Kant* (New York: Teachers College, Columbia University, 1907).

Williams, David Lay, 'Justice and the general will: Affirming Rousseau's ancient orientation', *Journal of the History of Ideas*, 66 (2005), 383–411.

Williams, Howard, *Kant's Critique of Hobbes: Sovereignty and Cosmopolitanism* (Cardiff: University of Wales Press, 2003).

Williams, Michael, 'The discipline of the democratic peace: Kant, liberalism, and the social construction of security communities', *European Journal of International Relations*, 7 (2001), 525–53.

York, Elizabeth, *Leagues of Nations: Ancient, Mediaeval, and Modern* (London: The Swarthmore Press, 1919).

Index